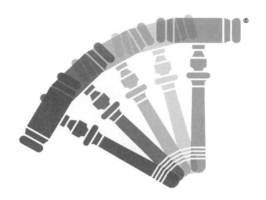

Casenote™ Legal Briefs

CRIMINAL PROCEDURE

Keyed to Courses Using

Allen, Hoffmann, Livingston, and Stuntz's
Comprehensive Criminal Procedure

Second Edition

ASPEN

PUBLISHERS

111 Eighth Avenue, New York, NY 10011

www.aspenpublishers.com

© 2005 Aspen Publishers, Inc.
A Wolters Kluwer Company
www.aspenpublishers.com

Printed in the United States of America.

ISBN 0-7355-5220-7

1 2 3 4 5 6 7 8 9 0

About Aspen Publishers

Aspen Publishers, headquartered in New York City, is a leading information provider for attorneys, business professionals, and law students. Written by preeminent authorities, our products consist of analytical and practical information covering both U.S. and international topics. We publish in the full range of formats, including updated manuals, books, periodicals, CDs, and online products.

Our proprietary content is complemented by 2,500 legal databases, containing over 11 million documents, available through our Loislaw division. Aspen Publishers also offers a wide range of topical legal and business databases linked to Loislaw's primary material. Our mission is to provide accurate, timely, and authoritative content in easily accessible formats, supported by unmatched customer care.

To order any Aspen Publishers title, go to *www.aspenpublishers.com* or call 1-800-638-8437.

For more information on Loislaw products, go to *www.loislaw.com* or call 1-800-364-2512.

For Customer Care issues, e-mail *CustomerCare@aspenpublishers.com*; call 1-800-234-1660; or fax 1-800-901-9075.

Aspen Publishers
A Wolters Kluwer Company

Format for the Casenote Legal Brief

Nature of Case: This section identifies the form of action (e.g., breach of contract, negligence, battery), the type of proceeding (e.g., demurrer, appeal from trial court's jury instructions) or the relief sought (e.g., damages, injunction, criminal sanctions).

Palsgraf v. Long Island R.R. Co.

Injured bystander (P) v. Railroad company (D)

N.Y. Ct. App., 248 N.Y. 339, 162 N.E. 99 (1928).

Party ID: Quick identification of the relationship between the parties.

Fact Summary: This is included to refresh your memory and can be used as a quick reminder of the facts.

NATURE OF CASE: Appeal from judgment affirming verdict for plaintiff seeking damages for personal injury.

FACT SUMMARY: Helen Palsgraf (P) was injured on R.R.'s (D) train platform when R.R.'s (D) guard helped a passenger aboard a moving train, causing his package to fall on the tracks. The package contained fireworks which exploded, creating a shock that tipped a scale onto Palsgraf (P).

Rule of Law: Summarizes the general principle of law that the case illustrates. It may be used for instant recall of the court's holding and for classroom discussion or home review.

RULE OF LAW
The risk reasonably to be perceived defines the duty to be obeyed.

FACTS: Helen Palsgraf (P) purchased a ticket to Rockaway Beach from R.R. (D) and was waiting on the train platform. As she waited, two men ran to catch a train that was pulling out from the platform. The first man jumped aboard, but the second man, who appeared as if he might fall, was helped aboard by the guard on the train who had kept the door open so they could jump aboard. A guard on the platform also helped by pushing him onto the train. The man was carrying a package wrapped in newspaper. In the process, the man dropped his package, which fell on the tracks. The package contained fireworks and exploded. The shock of the explosion was apparently of great enough strength to tip over some scales at the other end of the platform, which fell on Palsgraf (P) and injured her. A jury awarded her damages, and R.R. (D) appealed.

Facts: This section contains all relevant facts of the case, including the contentions of the parties and the lower court holdings. It is written in a logical order to give the student a clear understanding of the case. The plaintiff and defendant are identified by their proper names throughout and are always labeled with a (P) or (D).

ISSUE: Does the risk reasonably to be perceived define the duty to be obeyed?

HOLDING AND DECISION: (Cardozo, C.J.) Yes. The risk reasonably to be perceived defines the duty to be obeyed. If there is no foreseeable hazard to the injured party as the result of a seemingly innocent act, the act does not become a tort because it happened to be a wrong as to another. If the wrong was not willful, the plaintiff must show that the act as to her had such great and apparent possibilities of danger as to entitle her to protection. Negligence in the abstract is not enough upon which to base liability. Negligence is a relative concept, evolving out of the common law doctrine of trespass on the case. To establish liability, the defendant must owe a legal duty of reasonable care to the injured party. A cause of action in tort will lie where harm, though unintended, could

have been averted or avoided by observance of such a duty. The scope of the duty is limited by the range of danger that a reasonable person could foresee. In this case, there was nothing to suggest from the appearance of the parcel or otherwise that the parcel contained fireworks. The guard could not reasonably have had any warning of a threat to Palsgraf (P), and R.R. (D) therefore cannot be held liable. Judgment is reversed in favor of R.R. (D).

DISSENT: (Andrews, J.) The concept that there is no negligence unless R.R. (D) owes a legal duty to take care as to Palsgraf (P) herself is too narrow. Everyone owes to the world at large the duty of refraining from those acts that may unreasonably threaten the safety of others. If the guard's action was negligent as to those nearby, it was also negligent as to those outside what might be termed the "danger zone." For Palsgraf (P) to recover, R.R.'s (D) negligence must have been the proximate cause of her injury, a question of fact for the jury.

Concurrence/Dissent: All concurrences and dissents are briefed whenever they are included by the casebook editor.

▶ ANALYSIS

The majority defined the limit of the defendant's liability in terms of the danger that a reasonable person in defendant's situation would have perceived. The dissent argued that the limitation should not be placed on liability, but rather on damages. Judge Andrews suggested that only injuries that would not have happened but for R.R.'s (D) negligence should be compensable. Both the majority and dissent recognized the policy-driven need to limit liability for negligent acts, seeking, in the words of Judge Andrews, to define a framework "that will be practical and in keeping with the general understanding of mankind." The Restatement (Second) of Torts has accepted Judge Cardozo's view.

Analysis: This last paragraph gives you a broad understanding of where the case "fits in" with other cases in the section of the book and with the entire course. It is a hornbook-style discussion indicating whether the case is a majority or minority opinion and comparing the principal case with other cases in the casebook. It may also provide analysis from restatements, uniform codes, and law review articles. The analysis will prove to be invaluable to classroom discussion.

Quicknotes

FORESEEABILITY A reasonable expectation that change is the probable result of certain acts or omissions.

NEGLIGENCE Conduct falling below the standard of care that a reasonable person would demonstrate under similar conditions.

PROXIMATE CAUSE The natural sequence of events without which an injury would not have been sustained.

Issue: The issue is a concise question that brings out the essence of the opinion as it relates to the section of the casebook in which the case appears. Both substantive and procedural issues are included if relevant to the decision.

Holding and Decision: This section offers a clear and in-depth discussion of the rule of the case and the court's rationale. It is written in easy-to-understand language and answers the issues(s) presented by applying the law to the facts of the case. When relevant, it includes a thorough discussion of the exceptions to the case as listed by the court, any major cites to the other cases on point, and the names of the judges who wrote the decisions.

Quicknotes: Conveniently defines legal terms found in the case and summarizes the nature of any statutes, codes, or rules referred to in the text.

Aspen Publishers is proud to offer *Casenote Legal Briefs*—continuing thirty years of publishing America's best-selling legal briefs.

Casenote Legal Briefs are designed to help you save time when briefing assigned cases. Organized under convenient headings, they show you how to abstract the basic facts and holdings from the text of the actual opinions handed down by the courts. Used as part of a rigorous study regime, they can help you spend more time analyzing and critiquing points of law than on copying out bits and pieces of judicial opinions into your notebook or outline.

Casenote Legal Briefs should never be used as a substitute for assigned casebook readings. They work best when read as a follow-up to reviewing the underlying opinions themselves. Students who try to avoid reading and digesting the judicial opinions in their casebooks or on-line sources will end up shortchanging themselves in the long run. The ability to absorb, critique, and restate the dynamic and complex elements of case law decisions is crucial to your success in law school and beyond. It cannot be developed vicariously.

Casenote Legal Briefs represent but one of the many offerings in Aspen's Study Aid Timeline, which includes:

- Casenote *Legal Briefs*
- Emanuel *Law Outlines*
- *Examples & Explanations* Series
- *Introduction to Law* Series
- Emanuel *Law in a Flash* Flashcards
- Emanuel *CrunchTime* Series

Each of these series is designed to provide you with easy-to-understand explanations of complex points of law. Each volume offers guidance on the principles of legal analysis and, consulted regularly, will hone your ability to spot relevant issues. We have titles that will help you prepare for class, prepare for your exams, and enhance your general comprehension of the law along the way.

To find out more about Aspen Study Aid publications, visit us on-line at *www.aspenpublishers.com* or e-mail us at *legaledu@aspenpubl.com*. We'll be happy to assist you.

Free access to Briefs on-line!

Download the cases you want in your notes or outlines using the full cut-and-paste feature accompanying our on-line briefs. Please fill out this form for full access to this useful feature. No photocopies of this form will be accepted.

Name	Phone ( )
Address	Apt. No.
City	State	ZIP Code
Law School	Year (check one) ☐ 1st ☐ 2nd ☐ 3rd

Cut out the UPC found on the lower left-hand corner of the back cover of this book. Staple the UPC inside this box. Only the original UPC from the book cover will be accepted. No photocopies or store stickers are allowed.

Attach UPC inside this box.

E-mail (Print LEGIBLY or you may not get access!)
Title of this book (course subject)
Used with which casebook (provide author's name)

Mail the completed form to:
Aspen Publishers, Inc.
Legal Education Division
Casenote On-line Access
675 Massachusetts Ave., 11th floor
Cambridge, MA 02139

I understand that on-line access is granted solely to the purchaser of this book for the academic year in which it was purchased. Any other usage is not authorized and will result in immediate termination of access. Sharing of codes is strictly prohibited.

Signature _____

Upon receipt of this completed form, you will be e-mailed codes so that you may access the Briefs for this Casenote Legal Brief. On-line Briefs may not be available for all titles. For a full list of available titles, please check *www.aspenpublishers.com/casenotes*.

A. Decide on a Format and Stick to It

Structure is essential to a good brief. It enables you to arrange systematically the related parts that are scattered throughout most cases, thus making manageable and understandable what might otherwise seem to be an endless and unfathomable sea of information. There are, of course, an unlimited number of formats that can be utilized. However, it is best to find one that suits your needs and stick to it. Consistency breeds both efficiency and the security that when called upon you will know where to look in your brief for the information you are asked to give.

Any format, as long as it presents the essential elements of a case in an organized fashion, can be used. Experience, however, has led *Casenotes* to develop and utilize the following format because of its logical flow and universal applicability.

NATURE OF CASE: This is a brief statement of the legal character and procedural status of the case (e.g., "Appeal of a burglary conviction").

There are many different alternatives open to a litigant dissatisfied with a court ruling. The key to determining which one has been used is to discover *who is asking this court for what.*

This first entry in the brief should be kept *as short as possible.* Use the court's terminology if you understand it. But since jurisdictions vary as to the titles of pleadings, the best entry is the one that addresses who wants what in this proceeding, not the one that sounds most like the court's language.

RULE OF LAW: A statement of the general principle of law that the case illustrates (e.g., "An acceptance that varies any term of the offer is considered a rejection and counter-offer").

Determining the rule of law of a case is a procedure similar to determining the issue of the case. Avoid being fooled by red herrings; there may be a few rules of law mentioned in the case excerpt, but usually only one is *the* rule with which the casebook editor is concerned. The techniques used to locate the issue, described below, may also be utilized to find the rule of law. Generally, your best guide is simply the chapter heading. It is a clue to the point the casebook editor seeks to make and should be kept in mind when reading every case in the respective section.

FACTS: A synopsis of only the essential facts of the case, i.e., those bearing upon or leading up to the issue.

The facts entry should be a short statement of the events and transactions that led one party to initiate legal proceedings against another in the first place. While some cases conveniently state the salient facts at the beginning of the decision, in other instances they will have to be culled from hiding places throughout the text, even from concurring and dissenting opinions. Some of the "facts" will often be in dispute and should be so noted. Conflicting evidence may be briefly pointed up. "Hard" facts must be included. Both must be *relevant* in order to be listed in the facts entry. It is impossible to tell what is relevant until the entire case is read, as the ultimate determination of the rights and liabilities of the parties may turn on something buried deep in the opinion.

Generally, the facts entry should not be longer than three to five *short* sentences.

It is often helpful to identify the role played by a party in a given context. For example, in a construction contract case the identification of a party as the "contractor" or "builder" alleviates the need to tell that that party was the one who was supposed to have built the house.

It is always helpful, and a good general practice, to identify the "plaintiff" and the "defendant." This may seem elementary and uncomplicated, but, especially in view of the creative editing practiced by some casebook editors, it is sometimes a difficult or even impossible task. Bear in mind that the *party presently* seeking something from this court may not be the plaintiff, and that sometimes only the cross-claim of a defendant is treated in the excerpt. Confusing or misaligning the parties can ruin your analysis and understanding of the case.

ISSUE: A statement of the general legal question answered by or illustrated in the case. For clarity, the issue is best put in the form of a question capable of a "yes" or "no" answer. In reality, the issue is simply the Rule of Law put in the form of a question (e.g., "May an offer be accepted by performance?").

The major problem presented in discerning what is *the* issue in the case is that an opinion usually purports to raise and answer several questions. However, except for rare cases, only one such question is really the issue in the case. Collateral issues not necessary to the resolution of the matter in controversy are handled by the court by language known as *"obiter dictum"* or merely *"dictum."* While dicta may be included later in the brief, they have no place under the issue heading.

To find the issue, ask *who wants what* and then go on to ask *why did that party succeed or fail in getting it.* Once this is determined, the "why" should be turned into a question.

The complexity of the issues in the cases will vary, but in all cases a single-sentence question should sum up the issue.

In a few cases, there will be two, or even more rarely, three issues of equal importance to the resolution of the case. Each should be expressed in a single-sentence question.

Since many issues are resolved by a court in coming to a final disposition of a case, the casebook editor will reproduce the portion of the opinion containing the issue or issues most relevant to the area of law under scrutiny. A noted law professor gave this advice: "Close the book; look at the title on the cover." Chances are, if it is Property, you need not concern yourself with whether, for example, the federal government's treatment of the plaintiff's land really raises a federal question sufficient to support jurisdiction on this ground in federal court.

The same rule applies to chapter headings designating sub-areas within the subjects. They tip you off as to what the text is designed to teach. The cases are arranged in a casebook to show a progression or development of the law, so that the preceding cases may also help.

It is also most important to remember to *read the notes and questions* at the end of a case to determine what the editors wanted you to have gleaned from it.

HOLDING AND DECISION: This section should succinctly explain the rationale of the court in arriving at its decision. In capsulizing the "reasoning" of the court, it should always include an application of the general rule or rules of law to the specific facts of the case. Hidden justifications come to light in this entry; the reasons for the state of the law, the public policies, the biases and prejudices, those considerations that influence the justices' thinking and, ultimately, the outcome of the case. At the end, there should be a short indication of the disposition or procedural resolution of the case (e.g., "Decision of the trial court for Mr. Smith (P) reversed").

The foregoing format is designed to help you "digest" the reams of case material with which you will be faced in your law school career. Once mastered by practice, it will place at your fingertips the information the authors of your casebooks have sought to impart to you in case-by-case illustration and analysis.

B. Be as Economical as Possible in Briefing Cases

Once armed with a format that encourages succinctness, it is as important to be economical with regard to the time spent on the actual reading of the case as it is to be economical in the writing of the brief itself. This does not mean "skimming" a case. Rather, it means reading the case with an "eye" trained to recognize into which "section" of your brief a particular passage or line fits and having a system for quickly and precisely marking the case so that the passages fitting any one particular part of the brief can be easily identified and brought together in a concise and accurate manner when the brief is actually written.

It is of no use to simply repeat everything in the opinion of the court; record only enough information to trigger your recollection of what the court said. Nevertheless, an accurate statement of the "law of the case," i.e., the legal principle applied to the facts, is absolutely essential to class preparation and to learning the law under the case method.

To that end, it is important to develop a "shorthand" that you can use to make margin notations. These notations will tell you at a glance in which section of the brief you will be placing that particular passage or portion of the opinion.

Some students prefer to underline all the salient portions of the opinion (with a pencil or colored underliner marker), making marginal notations as they go along. Others prefer the color-coded method of underlining, utilizing different colors of markers to underline the salient portions of the case, each separate color being used to represent a different section of the brief. For example, blue underlining could be used for passages relating to the rule of law, yellow for those relating to the issue, and green for those relating to the holding and decision, etc. While it has its advocates, the color-coded method can be confusing and time-consuming (all that time spent on changing colored markers). Furthermore, it can interfere with the continuity and concentration many students deem essential to the reading of a case for maximum comprehension. In the end, however, it is a matter of personal preference and style. Just remember, whatever method you use, underlining must be used sparingly or its value is lost.

If you take the marginal notation route, an efficient and easy method is to go along underlining the key portions of the case and placing in the margin alongside them the following "markers" to indicate where a particular passage or line "belongs" in the brief you will write:

N (NATURE OF CASE)
RL (RULE OF LAW)
I (ISSUE)
HL (HOLDING AND DECISION, relates to the RULE OF LAW behind the decision)
HR (HOLDING AND DECISION, gives the RATIONALE or reasoning behind the decision)
HA (HOLDING AND DECISION, APPLIES the general principle(s) of law to the facts of the case to arrive at the decision)

Remember that a particular passage may well contain information necessary to more than one part of your brief, in which case you simply note that in the margin. If you are using the color-coded underlining method instead of margin notation, simply make asterisks or checks in the margin next to the passage in question in the colors that indicate the additional sections of the brief where it might be utilized.

The economy of utilizing "shorthand" in marking cases for briefing can be maintained in the actual brief writing process itself by utilizing "law student shorthand" within the brief. There are many commonly used words and phrases for which abbreviations can be substituted in your briefs (and in your class notes also). You can develop abbreviations that are personal to you and which will save you a lot of time. A reference list of briefing abbreviations can be found on page xii of this book.

C. Use Both the Briefing Process and the Brief as a Learning Tool

Now that you have a format and the tools for briefing cases efficiently, the most important thing is to make the time spent in briefing profitable to you and to make the most advantageous use of the briefs you create. Of course, the briefs are invaluable for classroom reference when you are called upon to explain or analyze a particular case. However, they are also useful in reviewing for exams. A quick glance at the fact summary should bring the case to mind, and a rereading of the rule of law should enable you to go over the underlying legal concept in your mind, how it was applied in that particular case, and how it might apply in other factual settings.

As to the value to be derived from engaging in the briefing process itself, there is an immediate benefit that arises from being forced to sift through the essential facts and reasoning from the court's opinion and to succinctly express them in your own words in your brief. The process ensures that you understand the case and the point that it illustrates, and that means you will be ready to absorb further analysis and information brought forth in class. It also ensures you will have something to say when called upon in class. The briefing process helps develop a mental agility for getting to the *gist* of a case and for identifying, expounding on, and applying the legal concepts and issues found there. The briefing process is the mental process on which you must rely in taking law school examinations; it is also the mental process upon which a lawyer relies in serving his clients and in making his living.

acceptance	acp	offer	O
affirmed	aff	offeree	OE
answer	ans	offeror	OR
assumption of risk	a/r	ordinance	ord
attorney	atty	pain and suffering	p/s
beyond a reasonable doubt	b/r/d	parol evidence	p/e
bona fide purchaser	BFP	plaintiff	P
breach of contract	br/k	prima facie	p/f
cause of action	c/a	probable cause	p/c
common law	c/l	proximate cause	px/c
Constitution	Con	real property	r/p
constitutional	con	reasonable doubt	r/d
contract	K	reasonable man	r/m
contributory negligence	c/n	rebuttable presumption	rb/p
cross	x	remanded	rem
cross-complaint	x/c	res ipsa loquitur	RIL
cross-examination	x/ex	respondeat superior	r/s
cruel and unusual punishment	c/u/p	Restatement	RS
defendant	D	reversed	rev
dismissed	dis	Rule Against Perpetuities	RAP
double jeopardy	d/j	search and seizure	s/s
due process	d/p	search warrant	s/w
equal protection	e/p	self-defense	s/d
equity	eq	specific performance	s/p
evidence	ev	statute of limitations	S/L
exclude	exc	statute of frauds	S/F
exclusionary rule	exc/r	statute	S
felony	f/n	summary judgment	s/j
freedom of speech	f/s	tenancy in common	t/c
good faith	g/f	tenancy at will	t/w
habeas corpus	h/c	tenant	t
hearsay	hr	third party	TP
husband	H	third party beneficiary	TPB
in loco parentis	ILP	transferred intent	TI
injunction	inj	unconscionable	uncon
inter vivos	I/v	unconstitutional	unconst
joint tenancy	j/t	undue influence	u/e
judgment	judgt	Uniform Commercial Code	UCC
jurisdiction	jur	unilateral	uni
last clear chance	LCC	vendee	VE
long-arm statute	LAS	vendor	VR
majority view	maj	versus	v
meeting of minds	MOM	void for vagueness	VFV
minority view	min	weight of the evidence	w/e
Miranda warnings	Mir/w	weight of authority	w/a
Miranda rule	Mir/r	wife	W
negligence	neg	with	w/
notice	ntc	within	w/i
nuisance	nus	without prejudice	w/o/p
obligation	ob	without	w/o
obscene	obs	wrongful death	wr/d

Table of Cases

CHAPTER 2

The Idea of Due Process

Quick Reference Rules of Law

PAGE

Hurtado v. California

Criminal defendant (D) v. State (P)

110 U.S. 516 (1884).

NATURE OF CASE: Appeal of murder conviction.

FACT SUMMARY: Hurtado (D) was charged with first-degree murder by information, rather than by grand jury indictment.

🏛 RULE OF LAW
The Due Process Clause of the Fourteenth Amendment does not require a state to obtain a grand jury indictment before prosecuting an individual for a capital offense.

FACTS: As provided by California law, Hurtado (D) was charged with first-degree murder by information, rather than by grand jury indictment. He was convicted. Hurtado (D) appealed to the California Supreme Court, claiming the Due Process Clause of the Fourteenth Amendment to the U.S. Constitution required a state to obtain a grand jury indictment before prosecuting an individual for a capital offense. The California Supreme Court upheld the conviction, and Hurtado (D) appealed to the U.S. Supreme Court.

ISSUE: Does the Due Process Clause of the Fourteenth Amendment require a state to obtain a grand jury indictment before prosecuting an individual for a capital offense?

HOLDING AND DECISION: (Matthews, J.) No. The Due Process Clause of the Fourteenth Amendment does not require a state to obtain a grand jury indictment before prosecuting an individual for a capital offense. First, under English law, principles like due process applied only against the executive, but under the U.S. Constitution they also apply against legislative authority. Detailed application of these restraints may be appropriate against executive power but might obstruct the necessary discretion of legislative power. Thus, application of a Bill of Rights provision to void legislative acts (such as the California statute allowing charge by information) must be limited to cases clearly within the scope of the provision. Under the Due Process Clause, any legal proceeding enforced by public authority, sanctioned by custom, or newly devised in the discretion of legislative power, in furtherance of the general public good, which preserves liberty and justice, must be held to be due process. Under these principles, the California law provides due process. Indictment is but a preliminary proceeding, and the information may be issued only after a magistrate's finding of probable guilt. A suspect's rights are guarded carefully. Second, the Fourteenth Amend-

ment must be construed with regard to the same words which appear in the Fifth Amendment. The Fifth Amendment expressly provides for grand jury indictment in addition to providing for due process, so if this Court were to hold that a grand jury indictment was fundamental to due process, the Grand Jury Clause would be redundant. Affirmed.

DISSENT: (Harlan, J.) Due process of law does not mean one thing with reference to the states and another with reference to the federal government. There are fundamental principles of liberty and justice which no state may violate consistent with due process under the Fourteenth Amendment. The right to a grand jury indictment for a capital offense was settled law in England at the time the United States was founded, was put in the Bill of Rights by the people of the original states, and was required by all 37 states at the time the Fourteenth Amendment was ratified. Clearly, the right was considered a fundamental principle of liberty and justice. The majority's argument concerning separate enumeration of the right to a grand jury leads to the untenable conclusion that all rights separately enumerated in the Bill of Rights are not necessary to due process. Under the California statute, nothing stands between a citizen and prosecution for a capital offense except a judgment of a justice of the peace. This is not due process of law.

▶ ANALYSIS

The Supreme Court has expressly incorporated every criminal procedure provision of the Bill of Rights into the Due Process Clause of the Fourteenth Amendment (thus, applying them to the states), except for the Fifth Amendment right to a grand jury indictment and the Eighth Amendment right against excessive bail.

■■■■

Quicknotes

GRAND JURY A group summoned to investigate, inform, and accuse persons of crimes when sufficient evidence exists to do so.

INDICTMENT A formal written accusation made by the prosecution to the grand jury under oath, charging an individual with a criminal offense.

CAPITAL CASE An action involving an offense that is punishable by death.

■■■■

Duncan v. Louisiana

Criminal defendant (D) v. State (P)

391 U.S. 145 (1968).

NATURE OF CASE: Review of conviction of battery.

FACT SUMMARY: Duncan (D), convicted of battery after a court trial, contended that he was constitutionally entitled to a jury trial.

🏛 RULE OF LAW
States must provide a defendant in a non-petty criminal proceeding the right to trial by jury.

FACTS: Duncan (D) was charged with simple battery, an offense with a maximum penalty of two years in state penitentiary. He requested a jury trial but was denied. Convicted by a court, he was sentenced to 60 days in a parish (county) jail. The Louisiana Supreme Court upheld the conviction, and the U.S. Supreme Court granted review.

ISSUE: Must states provide a defendant in a nonpetty criminal proceeding the right to trial by jury?

HOLDING AND DECISION: (White, J.) Yes. States must provide a defendant in a nonpetty criminal proceeding the right to trial by jury. The Fourteenth Amendment imposes upon states the obligation not to deny due process of law to their citizens. Increasingly, the rights enumerated in the first eight amendments have been incorporated into the Fourteenth Amendment's Due Process Clause. Whether such incorporation is appropriate depends upon whether the right at issue is fundamental to liberty and basic to our system of jurisprudence. The Sixth Amendment's right to trial by jury is such a right. Jury trials exist in criminal cases to protect citizens from corrupt or incompetent prosecutors and biased or unfair judges. Despite its flaws, the jury system has become so central to the American notion of liberty that it cannot be said that due process can exist without it. Consequently, the Fourteenth Amendment requires that any nonpetty offense prosecution afford the right to trial by jury. Here, the charged offense carried a penalty of up to two years' imprisonment and, hence, cannot be called petty. Therefore, Duncan (D) was entitled to a jury trial. Reversed.

▌ ANALYSIS

The extent to which the Fourteenth Amendment's Due Process Clause incorporates the Bill of Rights is an old one. Some Supreme Court jurists, most notably Justice Black, called for 100 percent incorporation. This has never been fully done, although most of the Bill of Rights have in fact been incorporated. On the other hand, the Court has read into the Clause rights not found in the Bill of Rights, most notably privacy.

■═■

Quicknotes

BATTERY Unlawful contact with the body of another person.

FOURTEENTH AMENDMENT DUE PROCESS CLAUSE Provides that protections mandated by the U.S. Constitution and observed by the federal government are equally applicable, and therefore must be observed by the States.

■═■

Medina v. California

Criminal defendant (D) v. State (P)

505 U.S. 437 (1992).

NATURE OF CASE: Review of criminal conviction.

FACT SUMMARY: Medina (D), a criminal defendant, contended that a California law that required him to prove his incompetency to stand trial violated due process.

RULE OF LAW

A state may constitutionally place the burden of proof on a criminal defendant raising incompetency as an issue.

FACTS: Medina (D) was criminally charged. He raised the issue of competence to stand trial. A hearing was held on the matter. California law placed the burden of proof on the defendant to prove incompetency by a preponderance of evidence. Medina (D) failed to carry that burden and was held to be competent to stand trial. He was convicted and appealed, contending that placing the burden of proving incompetency upon him violated due process. He argued that, to determine the allocation of the burden of proof, the court should have applied the test enunciated in *Mathews v. Eldridge*, 424 U.S. 319 (1976), whereby the deprivation of an individual's private interest is weighed against administrative efficiency.

ISSUE: May a state constitutionally place the burden of proof on a defendant raising incompetency as an issue?

HOLDING AND DECISION: (Kennedy, J.) Yes. A state may constitutionally place the burden of proof on a defendant raising incompetency as an issue. In the realm of criminal procedure, the states have, in most cases, more experience and expertise than the federal government. For that reason, only those state procedures that violate a narrowly defined concept of fundamental fairness will be held to violate due process. The Bill of Rights, as incorporated into the Fourteenth Amendment, largely sets the limits on state procedural powers. A state procedure not prohibited by the Bill of Rights will be held to violate due process only if it offends some principle of justice so rooted in the traditions and conscience of our people as to be ranked as fundamental. In the context of this case, there is no settled tradition on the proper allocation of burden of proof in a competency hearing. Consequently, California's burden of proof does not offend due process. Affirmed.

CONCURRENCE: (O'Connor, J.) The balancing of equities test of *Mathews v. Eldridge* may be appropriate in a due process evaluation of a state criminal procedure.

ANALYSIS

The Court has created very different tests for evaluating due process in the civil and criminal arenas. The test for the criminal context is described in the above case. The civil framework fashioned in *Mathews v. Eldridge*, which is considerably less deferential, involves a three-part test: the court must consider (1) the private interest that will be affected by the official action; (2) the risk of an erroneous deprivation of such interest and the value of additional procedural safeguards; and (3) the government's interest, including the fiscal burdens that additional procedural safeguards would entail.

Quicknotes

BURDEN OF PROOF The duty of a party to introduce evidence to support a fact that is in dispute in an action.

FOURTEENTH AMENDMENT Declares that no state shall make or enforce any law that shall abridge the privileges and immunities of citizens of the United States. No state shall deny to any person within its jurisdiction the equal protection of the laws.

CHAPTER 3

The Right to Counsel and Other Assistance

Quick Reference Rules of Law

Gideon v. Wainwright

Indigent defendant (D) v. Warden (P)

372 U.S. 335 (1963).

NATURE OF CASE: Proceeding on request for writ of habeas corpus.

FACT SUMMARY: Gideon (D) was charged with a felony in a state prosecution. He requested court-appointed counsel, but was refused on the basis state law only required appointment of counsel in capital cases.

🏛 RULE OF LAW
The right of an indigent to appointed counsel is a right fundamental and essential to a fair trial.

FACTS: Gideon (D) was charged with felony breaking and entering, a violation of state law. He was without funds and requested the court to appoint an attorney for him at trial. The request was refused since the state law did not require appointment of counsel for indigents except in capital offense cases. Gideon (D) then conducted his own defense and was convicted and sentenced to five years. He filed for a writ of habeas corpus based on the denial of counsel at trial.

ISSUE: Is the right to the assistance of counsel at trial a fundamental and essential right required to ensure a fair trial?

HOLDING AND DECISION: (Black, J.) Yes. This Court first expressed the view that the right to counsel at trial was a fundamental right essential to a fair trial in *Powell v. Alabama*, 287 U.S. 45 (1932). That decision was limited to its facts, however. In *Betts v. Brady*, 316 U.S. 455 (1942), the right to counsel was predicated on a case-by-case examination of special circumstances to determine if denial of counsel was a denial of a fair trial. But it is evident that every defendant who can afford a lawyer will have one at his criminal trial. It does not appear to be a luxury but is viewed as a necessity. This Court is of the opinion, now, that *Powell* was right in holding that the right to counsel is fundamental to a fair trial and that *Betts* was wrong in limiting that right to special circumstances. The Court holds that the right to counsel is a fundamental right for all criminal defendants at trial.

CONCURRENCE: (Douglas, J.) First, the Fourteenth Amendment should be understood as incorporating the entire Bill of Rights. Second, as the Court has held, rights protected against state invasion by the Due Process Clause of the Fourteenth Amendment are equal versions of what the Bill of Rights protects against federal invasion.

CONCURRENCE: (Clark, J.) The Sixth Amendment guarantees a right to counsel in all federal criminal cases, and prior Court decisions have recognized a Fourteenth Amend-

ment right to counsel in state capital cases. This case extends the right to counsel to all state criminal cases, erasing a distinction between capital and noncapital cases having no basis in the Constitution. The Constitution requires due process of law for deprivations of "life" and "liberty," and constitutionally, there cannot be a difference in the quality of the process.

CONCURRENCE: (Harlan, J.) Under the "special circumstances" rule, the Fourteenth Amendment has not been considered to guarantee a right to counsel in all state criminal cases but only where presence of counsel is a necessary requisite of due process. The special circumstances rule has been eliminated in state capital cases and has been steadily eroded in noncapital cases. The Court has recognized that the mere existence of a serious criminal charge carrying the possibility of a substantial prison sentence constitutes special circumstances requiring presence of counsel. However, this decision should not be read to "incorporate" the Sixth Amendment into the Fourteenth. A Sixth Amendment right to counsel and a Fourteenth Amendment right to counsel may mean different things, considering the different legitimate interests of federal and state governments.

▶ ANALYSIS

Upon retrial, with the assistance of appointed counsel, *Gideon* was acquitted. The *Gideon* decision was read to require counsel in only non-petty (i.e., six months or more imprisonment) cases. However, in a subsequent case, *Argersinger v. Hamlin*, the right to appointed counsel was extended to any case where the possibility of imprisonment existed. There was no minimum time specified and so if the judge wishes to imprison the defendant, if convicted, he must have appointed counsel, if indigent. The denial of counsel at trial where imprisonment results is error per se not subject to the harmless error rule.

■══■

Quicknotes

FOURTEENTH AMENDMENT DUE PROCESS CLAUSE Provides that protections mandated by the U.S. Constitution and observed by the federal government are equally applicable, and therefore must be observed by the States.

SIXTH AMENDMENT Provides the right to a speedy and public trial by impartial jury, the right to be informed of the accusation, the right to confront witnesses, and the right to have the assistance of counsel in all criminal prosecutions.

■══■

Alabama v. Shelton

State (P) v. Misdemeanor convict (D)

535 U.S. 654 (2002).

NATURE OF CASE: Appeal from reversal of a misdemeanor assault conviction.

FACT SUMMARY: When LeReed Shelton (D) represented himself and was convicted of a third-degree assault misdemeanor, being given no jail time but an automatic two year probation, he argued that he was deprived of the Sixth Amendment right to counsel since he was never offered a court appointed attorney.

🏛 RULE OF LAW
A suspended sentence which could result in actual deprivation of liberty may not be imposed in the absence of the Sixth Amendment right to appointed counsel.

FACTS: LeReed Shelton (D), convicted of third-degree assault, a misdemeanor, was sentenced to a 30 day jail term, which the trial court immediately suspended, placing him on probation for two years. Shelton (D), who represented himself, was at no time offered appointed counsel. Shelton (D) appealed on Sixth Amendment grounds, the Alabama Court of Criminal Appeals holding that a suspended sentence does not trigger the right to appointed counsel unless there is evidence in the record that the defendant has actually been deprived of liberty. The Supreme Court of Alabama reversed, holding that a suspended sentence constitutes a "term of imprisonment" even though incarceration is not immediate or inevitable. Alabama (P) petitioned to the U.S. Supreme Court.

ISSUE: May a suspended sentence which could result in actual deprivation of liberty be imposed in the absence of the Sixth Amendment right to appointed counsel?

HOLDING AND DECISION: (Ginsburg, J.) No. A suspended sentence which could result in actual deprivation of liberty may not be imposed in the absence of the Sixth Amendment right to appointed counsel. A suspended sentence, as here, is a prison term imposed for the offense of conviction. Once the prison term is triggered, the defendant is incarcerated not for the probation violation, but for the underlying offense. The uncounseled conviction at that point "results in imprisonment," hence ends up in the actual deprivation of a person's liberty, precisely what the Sixth Amendment does not allow. This Court rejects the argument that a rule requiring appointed counsel in every case involving a suspended sentence would unduly hamper the states' attempts to impose effective probationary punishment. The sole issue at the

probation revocation hearing is whether defendant breached the terms of probation; the validity or reliability of the underlying conviction is beyond attack. A hearing so timed and structured cannot compensate for the absence of trial counsel since it does not even address the key Sixth Amendment inquiry: whether the adjudication of guilt corresponding to the prison sentence is sufficiently reliable to permit incarceration in the first place. Deprived of counsel when tried, convicted, and sentenced, and unable to challenge the original judgment at a subsequent probation revocation hearing, a defendant in Shelton's (D) circumstances faces incarceration on a conviction that has never been subjected to "the crucible of meaningful adversarial testing." Affirmed.

DISSENT: (Scalia, J.) This Court is here asked to decide only one question as set forth in the certiorari petition: whether imposition of a suspended sentence or conditional sentence in a misdemeanor case invokes a defendant's Sixth Amendment right to counsel. Since *imposition* of a suspended sentence does not deprive a defendant of his personal liberty, the answer to that question is plainly no. Prior opinions of this Court place considerable weight on the practical consequences of expanding the right to appointed counsel beyond cases of actual imprisonment. The Court's decision today imposes a large, new burden on the majority of the states, including some of the poorest.

▶ ANALYSIS

As the *Shelton* decision notes, most jurisdictions already provide a state-law right to appointed counsel more generous than that afforded by the Federal Constitution. All but 16 states, for example, provide counsel to a defendant in Shelton's circumstances, either because the defendant received a substantial fine or because state law authorized incarceration for the charged offense or provided for a maximum prison term of one year.

■■■

Quicknotes

SIXTH AMENDMENT Provides the right to a speedy and public trial by impartial jury, the right to be informed of the accusation, the right to confront witnesses, and the right to have the assistance of counsel in all criminal prosecutions.

■■■

Ross v. Moffitt

Warden (P) v. Indigent defendant (D)

417 U.S. 600 (1974).

NATURE OF CASE: Review of order granting writ of habeas corpus.

FACT SUMMARY: Moffitt (D) contended that he was entitled, due to his indigence, to court-appointed counsel to handle his petition for discretionary review of his criminal conviction.

🏛 RULE OF LAW
An indigent defendant is not entitled to court-appointed counsel to handle a discretionary appeal.

FACTS: Moffitt (D) was convicted of a crime [not specified in the casebook opinion] in North Carolina state court. As an indigent, he was afforded court-appointed counsel, as he was on his appeal as of right to the state court of appeals, which affirmed his conviction. For his petition for review in the North Carolina Supreme Court, he was not afforded counsel, and his petition was denied. He then petitioned for a writ of habeas corpus, contending that the failure to provide him with counsel in his petition for discretionary review violated his Sixth and Fourteenth Amendment rights to counsel. The Fourth Circuit agreed and issued the writ. The Supreme Court granted review.

ISSUE: Is an indigent defendant entitled to court-appointed counsel to handle a discretionary appeal?

HOLDING AND DECISION: (Rehnquist, J.) No. An indigent defendant is not entitled to court-appointed counsel to handle a discretionary appeal. This Court has held that due process and/or equal protection entitles an indigent defendant to appointed counsel at trial and at appeals as of right. However, the right to counsel is not unlimited. With respect to due process, it has already been held that a state is not obligated to provide appellate review at all, so due process does not require counsel on appeal in any form. This Court has held that equal protection requires that an indigent defendant be given court-appointed counsel in an appeal as of right. However, a discretionary appeal is different. This type of appeal, generally made to a state supreme court or to this Court, does not involve issues of the petitioner's own guilt so much as broader issues of social policy. Since the petitioner's guilt is less directly implicated, equal protection issues fade in significance, so much so that court-appointed counsel is no longer required. The Fourth Circuit was therefore in error. Reversed.

DISSENT: (Douglas, J.) Permissive review is often the most meaningful review a convicted defendant will get, and the right to counsel is as powerful there as in a review as of right.

▶ ANALYSIS

The Supreme Court first took up the issue of an indigent's right to counsel in *Griffin v. Illinois*, 351 U.S. 12 (1956), in which it held that an indigent had a right to a free transcript in his appeal. Since then, the issue has been revisited in a number of contexts. The Court's most well-known foray into this issue was *Gideon v. Wainwright*, 372 U.S. 335 (1963), in which it held that an indigent was entitled to trial counsel.

Quicknotes

HABEAS CORPUS A proceeding in which a defendant brings a writ to compel a judicial determination of whether he is lawfully being held in custody.

INDIGENT A person who is poor and thus is unable to obtain counsel to defend himself in a criminal proceeding and for whom counsel must be appointed.

Strickland v. Washington

Warden (P) v. Criminal defendant (D)

466 U.S. 668 (1984).

NATURE OF CASE: Review of grant of writ of habeas corpus.

FACT SUMMARY: Washington (D), in a federal habeas proceeding, contended that, in a capital sentence hearing, he had been denied effective assistance of counsel.

🏛 RULE OF LAW
At a capital sentence hearing, a Sixth Amendment violation occurs only if counsel's performance was deficient and such deficiency resulted in actual prejudice.

FACTS: Washington (D) went on a crime spree that resulted in three deaths. He was charged with numerous offenses, including burglary, kidnapping, and murder. Against his attorney's wishes, he confessed. Also against his attorney's advice, he waived a jury. Finally, he pleaded guilty on all counts, again against his attorney's advice. At the sentence hearing, his attorney stressed Washington's (D) absence of a prior criminal record, his generally good character, and alleged mental disturbance due to poor economic circumstances. He did not introduce character witnesses. He neither introduced psychiatric testimony, as he had not been able to find a mental health professional who would testify that Washington (D) was mentally disturbed. The judge, citing numerous aggravating circumstances due to the gruesome nature of the murders, imposed the death sentence. The Florida Supreme Court affirmed. Washington (D) petitioned for a writ of habeas corpus. The district court denied relief, but the Eleventh Circuit reversed. The Supreme Court granted review.

ISSUE: At a capital sentence hearing, will a Sixth Amendment violation occur only if counsel's performance was deficient and such deficiency resulted in actual prejudice?

HOLDING AND DECISION: (O'Connor, J.) Yes. At a capital sentence hearing, a Sixth Amendment violation occurs only if counsel's performance was deficient and such deficiency resulted in actual prejudice. The Sixth Amendment's right to counsel envisions effective assistance of counsel; ineffective assistance is tantamount to no assistance. The purpose of assistance of counsel is to ensure a fair trial. Consequently, ineffectiveness of counsel is that type of ineffectiveness that renders a trial unfair. The proper standard for evaluating effectiveness is that counsel will be considered ineffective if counsel's performance is so deficient that it fell below an objective standard of reasonableness. Further, such deficiency must result in prejudice, as an absence of prejudice removes

concerns of trial fairness. Exactly what constitutes a deficient performance by counsel cannot be set out in specific guidelines; rather, counsel's performance must be viewed against professional standards, taking into account the facts reasonably available to counsel at the time of his tactical decisions. It must be emphasized that counsel's competence is to be presumed, and counsel's performance should not be second-guessed with the benefit of hindsight not available to counsel at the time of his decisions. With respect to prejudice, prejudice will not be presumed in other than a narrow set of circumstances, such as corruption or conflict of interest. Applying the foregoing standards to the present case, it is clear that Washington's (D) counsel's performance was far from ineffective. Operating under severe disadvantages, not the least being Washington's (D) habitual rejection of his advice, counsel made certain tactical decisions with respect to evidence and argument that were quite reasonable. Beyond this, the circumstances were so aggravating that it is unlikely that prejudice could have resulted from ineffectiveness even had it occurred. Therefore, no Sixth Amendment violation occurred in this case. Reversed.

DISSENT: (Marshall, J.) The majority opinion is excessively deferential to counsel in several respects. The standard for competency is too lenient and the level of prejudice that needs to be shown for a Sixth Amendment violation to occur is excessive. Finally, the Court errs in applying the same standard to capital cases as less crucial cases.

▶ ANALYSIS

Prior to the present opinion, lower courts had grappled with the same issue, reaching widely varied results. Both objective and subjective standards of competence had been applied. With respect to prejudice, some courts had employed the "outcome-determinative" test the Court used. Others had held prejudice to be presumed.

■═■

Quicknotes

SIXTH AMENDMENT Provides the right to a speedy and public trial by impartial jury, the right to be informed of the accusation, the right to confront witnesses, and the right to have the assistance of counsel in all criminal prosecutions.

WRIT OF HABEAS CORPUS A proceeding in which a defendant brings a writ to compel a judicial determination of whether he is lawfully being held in custody.

■═■

Cuyler v. Sullivan

Warden (P) v. Convicted murderer (D)

446 U.S. 335 (1980).

NATURE OF CASE: Review of order granting federal habeas corpus relief.

FACT SUMMARY: Sullivan (D) contended that the trial court erred in not undertaking its own inquiry as to whether his attorney's multiple representation created a possibility of conflict.

RULE OF LAW
(1) A state trial judge is under no duty to inquire into the propriety of multiple representation, absent objection.
(2) The mere possibility of a conflict of interest does not create a Sixth Amendment violation.

FACTS: Sullivan (D) was indicted with two others for first-degree murder. Two private attorneys represented all three defendants, each tried separately. At no time during this trial did Sullivan (D) object that his counsel had a conflict of interest. After the trial, which resulted in a conviction, Sullivan (D) appealed, both directly and in a state collateral proceeding. The Pennsylvania Supreme Court upheld the conviction. Sullivan (D) then filed a federal habeas action. The district court denied the petition. The Third Circuit reversed, holding that the trial court should have inquired as to the possibility of a conflict. The Supreme Court granted review.

ISSUE:
(1) Is a state trial judge under a duty to inquire into the propriety of multiple representation?
(2) Does the possibility of a conflict of interest create a Sixth Amendment violation?

HOLDING AND DECISION: (Powell, J.)
(1) A state trial judge is under no duty to inquire into the propriety of multiple representation, absent objection.
(2) No. The mere possibility of a conflict of interest does not create a Sixth Amendment violation. Defense counsel has an ethical obligation to advise the court of conflicts, and such counsel is usually in a better position than the courts to see the conflict arise. Courts rely on counsel in this area, and nothing in this Court's precedent mandates anything to the contrary. With respect to whether the possibility of conflict gives rise to a Sixth Amendment violation, a Sixth Amendment violation occurs only when counsel is actually ineffective. The possibility of conflict, which exists in almost all cases of multiple representation, is not sufficient to give rise to a violation. The cause is reversed

and remanded for a determination of whether an actual conflict of interest adversely affected the performance of Sullivan's counsel, which would constitute a violation of his Sixth Amendment rights.

CONCURRENCE: (Brennan, J.) When it is clear, as here, that a defendant agreed to joint representation, it is fair to require an actual conflict for a Sixth Amendment violation to be shown.

CONCURRENCE AND DISSENT IN PART: (Marshall, J.) The potential for conflict in multiple representation is so grave that a court should make its own inquiry as to possible conflicts. Furthermore, if an actual conflict of interest existed, that alone is sufficient evidence of a Sixth Amendment violation.

ANALYSIS

The level of the Court's analysis was that of the Constitution. It should be remembered that constitutional law only provides a minimum level of rights; statutes can go beyond this level. In the context of this case, Fed. R. Crim. P. 44(c) provides for judicial inquiry as to conflicts in some limited instances.

■━■

Quicknotes

HABEAS CORPUS A proceeding in which a defendant brings a writ to compel a judicial determination of whether he is lawfully being held in custody.

SIXTH AMENDMENT Provides the right to a speedy and public trial by impartial jury, the right to be informed of the accusation, the right to confront witnesses, and the right to have the assistance of counsel in all criminal prosecutions.

■━■

Faretta v. California

Criminal defendant (D) v. State (P)

422 U.S. 806 (1975).

NATURE OF CASE: Appeal of a conviction for grand theft.

FACT SUMMARY: Faretta (D) was charged with grand theft. Before and during trial, he moved to represent himself. The trial judge refused, and he was convicted.

🏛 RULE OF LAW
A state may not constitutionally impose a lawyer on a defendant who wishes to represent himself, so long as the defendant has made a knowing and intelligent waiver of his right to a lawyer.

FACTS: Faretta (D) was charged with grand theft. Several weeks before the date of his trial, Faretta (D) requested that he be permitted to defend himself. The trial judge, in a preliminary ruling, accepted Faretta's (D) waiver of counsel. Several weeks later, but still before trial, the judge held a sua sponte hearing to determine Faretta's (D) ability to conduct his own defense, and decided on the basis of Faretta's (D) answers to questions on state law that Faretta (D) had not made a knowing and intelligent waiver of his right to assistance of counsel. The trial judge ruled that Faretta (D) had no constitutional right to conduct his own defense and appointed a public defender to represent him. Faretta (D) was convicted and sentenced to prison. This decision was affirmed by the court of appeals, and the state supreme court refused to hear the case. The U.S. Supreme Court granted certiorari.

ISSUE: Can a state constitutionally impose a lawyer on a defendant who wishes to represent himself, if the defendant has made a knowing and intelligent waiver of his right to a lawyer?

HOLDING AND DECISION: (Stewart, J.) No. A state may not constitutionally impose a lawyer on a defendant who wishes to represent himself so long as the defendant has made a knowing and intelligent waiver of his right to a lawyer. The rationale for this rule lies within the structure of the Sixth Amendment in that it is consistent with the Sixth Amendment's right to make a personal defense. Here, Faretta (D) was literate and competent, and knowingly exercised his free will to make a choice to represent himself. His level of legal knowledge was not relevant to an assessment of his knowing exercise of the right to defend himself. Vacated and remanded.

DISSENT: (Burger, C.J.) Society has an interest in ensuring that trials are fair, and permitting an ill-advised defendant to represent himself undercuts that interest. Moreover, the "right" recognized here is found nowhere in the Constitution.

DISSENT: (Blackmun, J.) The rule announced here creates a great capacity for procedural confusion.

▶ ANALYSIS

The right of an accused to proceed pro se is a constitutional right. Moreover, on the federal level, it is a statutory right as well. However, this right is qualified by the requirement that a waiver of counsel is, taking into account all of the circumstances, knowingly and intelligently made. The trial judge should himself ask the accused about the circumstances of the waiver. If a defendant has successfully waived his right to counsel, a written memorial of this should be made. (Wright, Fed. Prac. & Proc., Vol. 3, at 213-216.)

Quicknotes

SIXTH AMENDMENT Provides the right to a speedy and public trial by impartial jury, the right to be informed of the accusation, the right to confront witnesses, and the right to have the assistance of counsel in all criminal prosecutions.

McKaskle v. Wiggins

State prosecutor (P) v. Convicted robber (D)

465 U.S. 168 (1984).

NATURE OF CASE: Review of grant of federal writ of habeas corpus.

FACT SUMMARY: Wiggins (D), a pro se defendant, contended that court-appointed standby counsel's failure to remain silent constituted a Sixth Amendment violation.

🏛 RULE OF LAW
Standby counsel to a pro se criminal defendant does not commit a Sixth Amendment violation by failing to remain silent.

FACTS: Wiggins (D) was charged with burglary. Prior to trial, he insisted on representing himself. Over his objection, the trial court appointed a public defender as standby counsel. During the course of the trial, Wiggins's (D) attitude toward standby counsel fluctuated: he first wished to proceed entirely without assistance, but later requested that standby counsel conduct voir dire. He later again objected to counsel's presence, but then had counsel make closing argument. During the course of the trial, counsel, out of the jury's presence, disagreed with some of Wiggins's (D) tactical decisions. However, Wiggins (D) always had the final say. Wiggins (D) was convicted and sentenced to life imprisonment as a recidivist. This was affirmed on appeal. Wiggins (D) petitioned for a federal writ of habeas corpus. The Fifth Circuit granted the writ, ruling that counsel had overstepped his bounds by not always being silent when so instructed by Wiggins (D). The Supreme Court granted review.

ISSUE: Does standby counsel to a pro se criminal defendant commit a Sixth Amendment violation by failing to remain silent?

HOLDING AND DECISION: (O'Connor, J.) No. Standby counsel to a pro se criminal defendant does not commit a Sixth Amendment violation by failing to remain silent. A criminal defendant has an absolute right to present his own defense. However, respect for these rights does not require that standby counsel, if any, be "seen and not heard." The question is whether the defendant had a fair chance to present his case his own way. He must have control over how the case is presented, and standby counsel cannot be allowed to destroy the jury's perception that the defendant is presenting his own defense. As long as standby counsel does not interfere with these conditions, the defendant has no cause to complain. Here, standby counsel's disagreements with Wiggins (D) were out of the jury's presence, and all the decisions regarding tactics were Wiggins's (D). Moreover, Wiggins's (D) conduct was inconsistent, to say the least, which further mitigates any claim to a Sixth Amendment violation he might have. Reversed.

DISSENT: (White, J.) The majority's two-part test provides no guidance for counsel and judges, imposes burdens on appellate courts, and erodes a defendant's right to proceed pro se. The majority's ruling has the effect of leaving courts incapable of assessing the subtle and not-so-subtle effects of counsel's participation on the defense. Furthermore, the majority's test will prove incapable of safeguarding the interest in individual autonomy because many disagreements between the pro se defendant and standby counsel will not be resolved by the trial court. In addition, the majority's opinion ignores the emphasis on the defendant's own perception of the criminal justice system set forth in *Faretta*, and implies that the Court actually adheres to the result-oriented harmless error standard it purports to reject.

▶ ANALYSIS

This case was a corollary to *Faretta v. California*, 422 U.S. 806 (1975). That case established the right of a criminal defendant to represent himself. The present decision was the first Supreme Court decision defining how far that right extends.

■▬■

Quicknotes

PRO SE An individual appearing on his own behalf.

SIXTH AMENDMENT Provides the right to a speedy and public trial by impartial jury, the right to be informed of the accusation, the right to confront witnesses, and the right to have the assistance of counsel in all criminal prosecutions.

■▬■

Caplin & Drysdale, Chartered v. United States

Law firm (P) v. Federal government (D)

491 U.S. 617 (1989).

NATURE OF CASE: Review of order refusing to release funds forfeited pursuant to statute.

FACT SUMMARY: Caplin & Drysdale (P) contended that a federal law allowing forfeiture of moneys obtained through drug trafficking was unconstitutional so far as the funds would be used to pay defense costs.

🏛 RULE OF LAW
A forfeiture statute is not unconstitutional because it prevents a defendant from obtaining private counsel.

FACTS: Reckmeyer was indicted for violations of federal drug trafficking laws. Pursuant to 21 U.S.C. § 853, the Government obtained an order freezing all of Reckmeyer's assets to the extent they were obtained through such trafficking. Reckmeyer eventually pleaded guilty, and the assets were forfeited. Caplin & Drysdale (P), the law firm that had represented Reckmeyer (D), filed a claim against the funds. The petition was granted by the district court. The Fourth Circuit held en banc that the forfeiture of funds to be used to pay for counsel violated the Sixth Amendment. The court of appeals reversed. The Supreme Court granted review.

ISSUE: Is a forfeiture statute unconstitutional because it may prevent a defendant from obtaining private counsel?

HOLDING AND DECISION: (White, J.) No. A forfeiture statute is not unconstitutional because it may prevent a defendant from obtaining private counsel. The Sixth Amendment gives an accused the right to effective assistance of counsel; it gives no right to counsel of choice if such counsel is beyond the defendant's means. A defendant has no Sixth Amendment right to spend money on defense that is not lawfully his own. Caplin & Drysdale (P) argued that the interests of the defendant and the government should be "balanced" to decide who has the greater interest in the funds. This is not so because a defendant has no interest in his ill-gotten gains. Even under such an analysis, governmental interest is high. The forfeiture law provides funds to pay for law enforcement and serves to break the power of organized crime. The judgment of the court of appeals is affirmed.

DISSENT: (Blackmun, J.) The statute represents a grave danger to the administration of justice. It constitutes a powerful tool for the government to decimate the effectiveness of the criminal defense bar and upsets the balance of power between the government and criminal defendants. This is completely antithetical to the Sixth Amendment.

▶ ANALYSIS

Under 21 U.S.C. § 853(n), a party with an interest in sequestered property is permitted to file a claim against it. To qualify under this section, a claimant has to have entered into a bona fide transaction with a defendant and with no reason to believe that the funds were tainted. An attorney representing a defendant would be very unlikely to meet the latter part of the test.

Quicknotes

FORFEITURE The loss of a right or interest as a penalty for failing to fulfill an obligation.

SIXTH AMENDMENT Provides the right to a speedy and public trial by impartial jury, the right to be informed of the accusation, the right to confront witnesses, and the right to have the assistance of counsel in all criminal prosecutions.

CHAPTER 4

The Rise and Fall of *Boyd v. United States*

Quick Reference Rules of Law

Boyd v. United States

Forfeiture defendant (D) v. Federal government (P)

116 U.S. 616 (1886).

NATURE OF CASE: Review of order compelling forfeiture of property.

FACT SUMMARY: Boyd (D) contended that the federal law mandating production of personal papers in a forfeiture proceeding was unconstitutional.

🏛 RULE OF LAW
It is unconstitutional for the government to mandate production of personal papers in a forfeiture proceeding.

FACTS: The Government (P) instituted a forfeiture proceeding against certain cases of glass belonging to Boyd (D), contending that appropriate customs duties had not been paid. Prior to trial, the Government (P) demanded, pursuant to statute, that Boyd (D) produce certain documentation in his possession. Boyd (D) complied, under objection that it was unconstitutional for the court to compel him to produce personal papers. The trial court ordered the glass forfeited. The Supreme Court granted review.

ISSUE: Is it unconstitutional for the government to mandate production of personal papers in a forfeiture proceeding?

HOLDING AND DECISION: (Bradley, J.) Yes. It is unconstitutional for the government to mandate production of personal papers in a forfeiture proceeding. The Fourth Amendment's guarantee against unreasonable searches and seizures and the Fifth Amendment's protection against self-incrimination technically apply to criminal proceedings. However, a forfeiture proceeding is sufficiently quasi-criminal that the amendments apply. The law in question, which compels production of personal papers and records, is functionally similar to the odious general warrants and writs of assistance against which the Fourth and Fifth Amendments were a reaction. To compel production is the equivalent of a search; the contents of such documents may constitute self-incrimination. Consequently, the forced production of personal documents in a forfeiture proceeding constitutes a violation of the Fourth and Fifth Amendments. Reversed.

CONCURRENCE: (Miller, J.) The law at question does compel self-incrimination, but production itself does not constitute search and seizure.

▶ ANALYSIS

This case is useful as a history lesson in Fourth and Fifth Amendment law but is no longer vital, its major elements all having been abandoned. A forfeiture proceeding without the prospect of a jail sentence would today be seen purely as civil. Also, production of papers is seen neither as a search and seizure nor as self-incrimination.

◼═◼

Quicknotes

FIFTH AMENDMENT Provides that no person shall be compelled to serve as a witness against himself, or be subject to trial for the same offense twice, or be deprived of life, liberty, or property without due process of law.

FORFEITURE The loss of a right or interest as a penalty for failing to fulfill an obligation.

FOURTH AMENDMENT Provides that persons be secure as to their person and private belongings against unreasonable searches and seizures.

◼═◼

Schmerber v. California

Criminal defendant (D) v. State (P)

384 U.S. 757 (1966).

NATURE OF CASE: Appeal from conviction of driving under the influence of alcohol.

FACT SUMMARY: Results of blood sample tests of blood taken from Schmerber (D) against his will were used to convict him of drunk driving.

🏛 RULE OF LAW
The use of body tissue evidence against an accused does not violate the Fifth Amendment.

FACTS: Schmerber (D) was hospitalized after a traffic accident. At the hospital, at the direction of a police officer and over Schmerber's (D) objections, a doctor drew a blood sample. The blood tested at over the legal limit of intoxication for driving. Based on this evidence, Schmerber (D) was convicted of drunk driving. The Supreme Court granted review.

ISSUE: Does the use of body tissue evidence against an accused violated the Fifth Amendment?

HOLDING AND DECISION: (Brennan, J.) No. The use of body tissue evidence against an accused does not violate the Fifth Amendment. The purpose of the Fifth Amendment is to prohibit the practice of the prosecution establishing its case against an accused through the use of the accused's own (and often coerced) testimony. Consequently, an item of evidence falls within the ambit of the Fifth Amendment only if it is testimonial in nature. The privilege does not extend to using non-testimonial aspects of a defendant to incriminate him. Physical evidence regarding an accused, even if it consists of his own tissue, is not testimonial and, therefore, raises no Fifth Amendment implications. Because no privilege applied, compelling him to submit to the test did not violate his Sixth Amendment right to counsel. The Fourth Amendment was implicated, however, the seizure of Schmerber's (D) blood having been reasonable under the circumstances. Affirmed.

DISSENT: (Warren, C.J.) I believe it is sufficient for me to reiterate my dissenting opinion in *Breithaupt v. Abram*, 352 U.S. 432 (1957), which upheld a conviction based in part on an analysis of blood extracted from an unconscious suspect as the basis on which to reverse this conviction.

DISSENT: (Black, J.) The use of forcibly extracted tissue has both a testimonial and communicative character to it. Further, neither of these requirements for self-incrimination is found in the Fifth Amendment.

DISSENT: (Douglas, J.) This case implicates the Fifth and Fourteenth Amendments' due process–based right to privacy and the Fourth Amendment right to be secure in one's person.

DISSENT: (Fortas, J.) The Due Process Clause prohibits the forcible extraction of blood from a suspect.

▶ ANALYSIS

The Fifth Amendment, on its face, does not limit itself to testimonial self-incrimination. However, it is clear that this was the concern of the drafters of the Amendment. Its framers were concerned with preventing the introduction of Star Chamber-type inquisitorial prosecution systems.

■═■

Quicknotes

DUE PROCESS CLAUSE Clauses found in the Fifth and Fourteenth Amendments to the United States Constitution providing that no person shall be deprived of "life, liberty, or property, without due process of law."

FIFTH AMENDMENT Provides that no person shall be compelled to serve as a witness against himself, or be subject to trial for the same offense twice, or be deprived of life, liberty, or property without due process of law.

■═■

Warden, Maryland Penitentiary v. Hayden

Warden (P) v. Convicted robber (D)

387 U.S. 294 (1967).

NATURE OF CASE: Review of order granting federal writ of habeas corpus.

FACT SUMMARY: Seizure of property belonging to Hayden (P), which aided in his conviction, was challenged as unconstitutional because such property had solely evidentiary value.

🏛 RULE OF LAW
That an object has evidentiary value only does not render its seizure unconstitutional.

FACTS: Authorities conducted a search of Hayden's (D) home and seized certain items of clothing. These items aided in identification and, thus, helped secure a conviction of armed robbery. The conviction was affirmed. Hayden (D) petitioned for a federal writ of habeas corpus. The district court denied the petition, but the Fourth Circuit reversed, holding the items to have had evidentiary value only and, therefore, not to be subject to search and seizure. The Supreme Court granted review.

ISSUE: Does the fact that an object has evidentiary value only render its seizure unconstitutional?

HOLDING AND DECISION: (Brennan, J.) No. That an object has evidentiary value only does not render its seizure unconstitutional. Traditionally, a distinction has been made between the fruits or instrumentalities of a crime and items having value only as evidence of guilt. The traditional rule is that since the government has no interest in such objects apart from securing a conviction, the introduction of such objects constitutes compelled self-incrimination, and, therefore, their original seizure was unreasonable and, consequently, unconstitutional. This is a flawed analysis. First, since such objects are not testimonial in nature, no Fifth Amendment concerns are raised. Second, since the Fourth Amendment protects privacy, not property, the traditional rule improperly injects proprietary requirements into Fourth Amendment analysis. Finally, the privacy interests of a citizen in his possessions do not turn on whether they can be characterized as evidence or instrumentality. Therefore, this traditional distinction is improper and is hereby abolished. Reversed.

CONCURRENCE: (Fortas, J.) The ruling here, while correct in this case, improperly dispenses with the "mere evidence" rule in all cases. There are still instances when its application would be proper.

DISSENT: (Douglas, J.) The foundation of the opinion in this case is that evidence such as that at issue here is not testimonial. As this premise is incorrect, the entire opinion founders.

▶ ANALYSIS

In the case *Boyd v. United States*, 116 U.S. 616 (1886), the Court held compelled production of documents to violate the Fifth Amendment. *Boyd* is still technically good law but has been held to, more or less, its own facts. The physical evidence here was clearly not the type of documentary evidence at issue in *Boyd*.

Quicknotes

FIFTH AMENDMENT Provides that no person shall be compelled to serve as a witness against himself, or be subject to trial for the same offense twice, or be deprived of life, liberty, or property without due process of law.

FOURTH AMENDMENT Provides that persons be secure as to their person and private belongings against unreasonable searches and seizures.

United States v. Hubbell

Federal government (P) v. Convicted informant (D)

530 U.S. 27 (2000).

NATURE OF CASE: Grant of writ of certiorari to review conditional plea agreement and Court of Appeals decision.

FACT SUMMARY: Pursuant to a subpoena and a grant of immunity from prosecution, Hubbell (D) produced documents to the Independent Counsel (P). A grand jury later returned an indictment against Hubbell (D) after the Government (P) presented evidence based on the same documents Hubbell (D) produced.

🏛 RULE OF LAW
The Fifth Amendment prevents the government from compelling a suspect to produce incrim-inating documents under a grant of immunity and then prosecuting that suspect using information gained from those incriminating documents.

FACTS: Hubbell (D) pled guilty and was sentenced to prison. In the plea agreement, Hubbell (D) agreed to provide information about matters related to the Whitewater investigation. While Hubbell (D) was serving his sentence, the Independent Counsel (P) served him with a subpoena requesting the production of certain documents. Hubbell (D) refused, invoking his Fifth Amendment right against self-incrimination. The Government (P) obtained a court order directing Hubbell (D) to produce the documents under a grant of immunity. The documents were then produced. A second prosecution arose out of information gained from these documents. The district court dismissed the indictment, holding that the evidence was derived from the testimonial aspects of the immunized act of producing documents. The court of appeals vacated that judgment and remanded for the lower court to hold a hearing to establish the extent of the Government's (P) independent knowledge of the documents. On remand, the Government (P) entered into a conditional plea bargain with Hubbell (D), and the U.S. Supreme Court granted the Government's (P) request for a writ of certiorari.

ISSUES:
(1) Does the Fifth Amendment privilege against compelled self-incrimination protect a witness from being compelled to disclose the existence of incriminating documents that the government is unable to describe with reasonable particularity?
(2) If the witness produces such documents pursuant to a grant of immunity, does such immunity prevent the gov-

ernment from using them to prepare criminal charges against him?

HOLDING AND DECISION: (Stevens, J.)
(1) Yes. The Fifth Amendment privilige against self-incrimination protects a witness from being compelled to disclose the existence of incriminating documents that the government is unable to describe with reasonable particularity.
(2) Yes. If the witness produces such documents pursuant to a grant of immunity, such immunity prevents the government from using them to prepare criminal charges against him. Thus, although a person may be compelled to provide documents, even though they may contain incriminating evidence, the Fifth Amendment protects a witness from the prosecution using this incriminating information, whether it was derived directly or indirectly from the compelled production of documents. Hubbell's (D) action of producing hundreds of documents was the first step in a chain of evidence that led to his own prosecution. The documents were produced only under a grant of immunity and a district court order. Compliance under these circumstances cannot then be turned against him. The indictment against Hubbell (D) must be dismissed. Affirmed.

CONCURRENCE: (Thomas, J.) This decision involves the act-of-production doctrine that provides that those who are compelled to produce incriminating physical evidence pursuant to a subpoena may invoke the Fifth Amendment privilege as a bar to production when the act of producing the evidence would contain testimonial features. The Fifth Amendment may be broader than this doctrine, however, and protect against compelled production of any incriminating evidence. The Fifth Amendment provides that no person shall be compelled in any criminal case to be a witness against himself. *Witness* has been defined as "a person who provides testimony." This definition restricts the Fifth Amendment. *Witness* also means a person who gives or furnishes evidence. Therefore, a person who responds to a subpoena by producing documentation is also a witness.

DISSENT: (Rehnquist, C.J.) I would reverse the judgment of the court of appeals in part, for the reasons given by Judge Williams in his dissenting opinion in that court, 167 F.3d 552 (C.A.D.C. 1999).

Continued on next page.

▶ *ANALYSIS*

In its holding, the court of appeals likened the use of the contents of the produced documents to the use of data drawn from a forced blood draw or compelled handwriting exemplar. The difference, however, may be that the forced blood draws or the giving of handwriting samples are usually not done under grants of immunity.

■≡■

Quicknotes

FIFTH AMENDMENT Provides that no person shall be compelled to serve as a witness against himself, or be subject to trial for the same offense twice, or be deprived of life, liberty, or property without due process of law.

■≡■

The Fourth Amendment

Quick Reference Rules of Law

Mapp v. Ohio

Criminal defendant (D) v. State (P)

367 U.S. 643 (1961).

NATURE OF CASE: Review of conviction for possession of obscene materials.

FACT SUMMARY: Mapp (D), having been subjected to a warrantless search of her premises by city police, contended that contraband found therein should be suppressed.

🏛 RULE OF LAW
The exclusionary rule is applicable to searches and seizures by state officials.

FACTS: Police entered Mapp's (D) premises without a warrant. Inside, they found pornographic photos and literature. She was charged with possession of obscene material. At trial, she contended that the materials seized should have been suppressed. The motion was denied, and she was convicted. The Ohio Supreme Court affirmed. An appeal to the U.S. Supreme Court was taken.

ISSUE: Is the exclusionary rule applicable to searches and seizures by state officials?

HOLDING AND DECISION: (Clark, J.) Yes. The exclusionary rule is applicable to searches and seizures by state officials. This Court has held that the Due Process Clause of the Fourteenth Amendment incorporates the Fourth Amendment. However, the Court previously declined to extend the exclusionary rule, created to enforce the rule, to state prosecutions. This approach has now been shown to be erroneous. Time has demonstrated that other approaches to combat illegal searches and seizures at the state level have proved fruitless. Also, various procedural problems with enforcing the rule have been corrected through judicial decision. Most important, it is necessary that government at all levels be compelled to obey its own laws as a failure to do so destroys its legitimacy and breeds contempt for law and order. The exclusionary rule has been shown to be the best vehicle to compel such obedience and for that reason should be as applicable to the states as it is to the federal government. Reversed.

CONCURRENCE: (Black, J.) The Fourth Amendment does not in itself justify the exclusionary rule, but when combined with the Fifth Amendment, such justification exists.

CONCURRENCE: (Douglas, J.) The asymmetry in this area of law has properly been ended.

MEMORANDUM: (Stewart, J.) While expressing no view as to the merits of the constitutional issue today decided by this Court, I would reverse the judgment because § 2905.34 of the Ohio Revised Code, upon which the conviction was based, is not consistent with the rights of free thought and expression assured against state action by the Fourteenth Amendment.

DISSENT: (Harlan, J.) The exclusionary rule is a rule of procedure which should not be imposed by this Court upon the court systems of sovereign states.

▶ ANALYSIS

With the possible exception of the Miranda rule, no Supreme Court action in criminal procedure has been as criticized as the exclusionary rule. It has been attacked as failing to achieve its deterrence goal despite a high social cost. The opposition to the rule was perhaps best stated by Judge (later Justice) Cardozo, who described it thusly: "the criminal is to go free because the constable has blundered." Later cases have narrowed the exclusionary rule to limit suppression to knowing violations of search and seizure rules by police where deterrence should have its greatest effect.

Quicknotes

DUE PROCESS CLAUSE Clauses found in the Fifth and Fourteenth Amendments to the United States Constitution providing that no person shall be deprived of "life, liberty, or property, without due process of law."

EXCLUSIONARY RULE A rule precluding the introduction at trial of evidence unlawfully obtained in violation of the federal constitutional safeguards against unreasonable searches and seizures.

FOURTEENTH AMENDMENT Declares that no state shall make or enforce any law that shall abridge the privileges and immunities of citizens of the United States. No state shall deny to any person within its jurisdiction the equal protection of the laws.

Katz v. United States

Convicted gambler (D) v. Federal government (P)

389 U.S. 347 (1967).

NATURE OF CASE: Appeal from criminal conviction for transmitting betting information over the phone.

FACT SUMMARY: At Katz's (D) trial for transmitting wagering information by telephone to another state, the Government (P) introduced recordings of his conversation made by attaching a listening and recording device to the outside of a phone booth.

🏛 **RULE OF LAW**
The Fourth Amendment protects a person from search and seizure if, under the circumstances, he has a justifiable expectation of privacy, regardless of whether an actual physical trespass occurred.

FACTS: Katz (D) was arrested and convicted for transmitting betting information by telephone to another state in violation of a federal statute. At his trial, the prosecution introduced recordings of phone conversations Katz (D) had made. These recordings were made by attaching a recording and listening device to the outside of a phone booth that Katz (D) used to make his calls. There was no search warrant. The government used this device only after it had made an investigation indicating that the phone booth was being used to transmit such information, and agents only recorded conversations that Katz (D) personally had.

ISSUE: Is the attachment of a listening device to the outside of a public telephone booth a search and seizure within the meaning of the Fourth Amendment?

HOLDING AND DECISION: (Stewart, J.) Yes. The Fourth Amendment protects a person's justifiable expectations of privacy, and protects people and not places. Whatever a person knowingly exposes to the public, even in his own home, is therefore not protected by the Fourth Amendment, but what a person keeps private, even in a public place, may be protected. Earlier cases stated that a surveillance without a trespass or seizure of a material object is outside of the Fourth Amendment, and now these cases must be overturned. Even though the phone booth was a public place, and there was no physical trespass (the device was on the outside of the booth), there was a search because the government violated the privacy upon which Katz (D) justifiably relied. There also is a seizure even though no tangible property was taken because the recording of a statement overheard, even if there is no trespass, is a seizure. The remaining question, then, is wheth-

er the government complied with the constitutional standards of the Fourth Amendment. Although the government reasonably believed that the phone booth was being illegally used, and the search and seizure was carefully limited both in scope and duration, the action cannot be upheld because no search warrant was issued. A search warrant is a safeguard in several ways: a neutral magistrate on the basis of information presented to him determines whether a warrant should issue; the search warrant carefully limits the scope of the search; and the government must report back on the evidence it finds. Without such safeguards, even if the search is in fact reasonable, it cannot be upheld.

CONCURRENCE: (Harlan, J.) The key to this decision is that one has a reasonable expectation of privacy when he shuts the doors of a telephone booth behind him and pays the fee for use of the telephone.

DISSENT: (Black, J.) The words of the Fourth Amendment do not bear the meaning that the Court gives them in this decision, nor is it the role of the Court to rewrite them to bring them into harmony with the times, as it has done. When the Fourth Amendment was adopted, eavesdropping was a common practice, and if the framers of the Constitution wished to limit that procedure they would have used appropriate language. This case, then, goes against the plain meaning of the Fourth Amendment, which was solely aimed at limiting the practice of breaking into buildings and seizing tangible property. Therefore, wiretapping, which is a form of eavesdropping, is not subject to the Fourth Amendment.

▶ *ANALYSIS*

Katz rejects the old rule which held that there was no search unless there was a physical trespass and substitutes a new rule based on the defendant's expectation of privacy. One facet of this privacy concept is the place involved—for example, if, unlike *Katz*, the defendant had engaged in conversation in a public place that was audible to others, there would be no search within the meaning of the Fourth Amendment. Also, the privacy concept turns on action of the defendant. If he had engaged in a loud conversation even in his own home which was audible to a person standing outside of his door, there would be no search since the conversation was exposed by the defendant to the public.

Continued on next page.

Quicknotes

FOURTH AMENDMENT Provides that persons be secure as to their person and private belongings against unreasonable searches and seizures.

■━■

Florida v. Riley

State (P) v. Marijuana grower (D)

488 U.S. 445 (1989).

NATURE OF CASE: Review of a finding requiring a search warrant.

FACT SUMMARY: When the police, without a search warrant, conducted a 400-foot helicopter surveillance of the interior of his partially covered greenhouse in his backyard, Riley (D) argued that such surveillance constituted a "search" for which a warrant is required under the Fourth Amendment.

🏛 RULE OF LAW
Surveillance of the interior of a partially covered greenhouse in a residential backyard from a helicopter at 400 feet does not constitute a "search" for which a warrant is required under the Fourth Amendment.

FACTS: Based on a tip that Riley (D) was growing marijuana in his residential backyard and greenhouse, law enforcement officials, without a search warrant, circled Riley's (D) backyard from a police helicopter at a height of 400 feet. With naked eye, the police could see through openings in the greenhouse roof's partially open sides, and believed they observed marijuana. A warrant was obtained based on these observations. The ensuing search revealed marijuana. Riley (D) was charged with marijuana possession. The Florida Supreme Court held that the helicopter surveillance constituted a "search" for which a warrant is required under the Fourth Amendment. Florida (P) petitioned to the U.S. Supreme Court.

ISSUE: Does surveillance of the interior of a partially covered greenhouse in a residential backyard from a helicopter at 400 feet constitute a "search" for which a warrant is required under the Fourth Amendment?

HOLDING AND DECISION: (White, J.) No. Surveillance of the interior of a partially covered greenhouse in a residential backyard from a helicopter at 400 feet does not constitute a "search" for which a warrant is required under the Fourth Amendment. In an age where private and commercial flight in the public airways is routine, it is unreasonable for an individual to expect that his marijuana plants will be constitutionally protected from being observed with the naked eye from a helicopter. The Fourth Amendment simply does not require the police traveling in the public airways at 400 feet to obtain a warrant to observe what is visible to the naked eye. Here, although Riley (D) no doubt intended and

expected this his greenhouse would not be open to public inspection, because the sides and roof were left partially open, what was growing in the greenhouse was in fact subject to viewing from the air. Any member of the public, as well as the police, could legally have been flying over Riley's (D) property at 400 feet and have observed the greenhouse. The police did no more. Reversed.

CONCURRENCE: (O'Connor, J.) A defendant must bear the burden of proving that his expectation of privacy was a reasonable one and thus that a Fourth Amendment "search" even took place. Here, Riley (D) introduced no evidence of expectation that his curtilage was protected from naked-eye aerial observation from an altitude of 400 feet. However, public use of lower altitudes may be sufficiently rare that police surveillance from such altitudes would violate reasonable expectations of privacy, despite compliance with FAA air safety regulations.

DISSENT: (Brennan, J.) It is a curious notion that the reach of the Fourth Amendment can be so largely defined by administrative regulations issued for purposes of flight safety. The police officer positioned 400 feet above Riley's (D) backyard was not standing on a public road; such vantage point was not one any citizen could readily share. The issue is not the legality of the officer's viewing position, but whether the public observation of Riley's (D) curtilage was so commonplace that Riley's (D) expectation of privacy in his backyard could not be considered reasonable.

DISSENT: (Blackmun, J.) Because private helicopters rarely fly over curtilages at 400 feet, the prosecution should bear the burden of proving that Riley (D) lacked a reasonable expectation of privacy. Here, the prosecution did not meet this burden of proof.

▶ ANALYSIS

In *Riley*, the Court, stating that the inspection of the curtilage of a house from an aircraft may not always pass muster under the Fourth Amendment simply because the aircraft is within navigable airspace specified by law, stressed that it was "of obvious importance" that the helicopter here was not violating the law. Nor, noted the Court, was there any evidence that the police helicopter had interfered with Riley's (D) normal use of his greenhouse or of other parts of the curtilage.

Continued on next page.

Quicknotes

FOURTH AMENDMENT Provides that persons be secure as to their person and private belongings against unreasonable searches and seizures.

■▬■

United States v. White

Federal government (P) v. Convicted narcotics dealer (D)

401 U.S. 745 (1971).

NATURE OF CASE: Review of reversal of narcotics convictions.

FACT SUMMARY: White (D) was convicted of illegal narcotics transactions following introduction of an audiotape made on the person of a Government (P) informant.

> 🏛 **RULE OF LAW**
> An audiotape made by being placed on the person of a defendant's accomplice/informant is admissible over a Fourth Amendment objection.

FACTS: White (D) and accomplice Jackson effected certain illegal narcotics transactions. Unbeknownst to White (D), Jackson was a Government (P) informant who was "wired" with audiotape equipment. White (D) was indicted. At trial, because Jackson could not be located by the Government (P), it introduced, over White's (D) Fourth Amendment objection, incriminating tapes made on Jackson's person. White (D) was convicted, but the Seventh Circuit reversed. The Supreme Court granted review.

ISSUE: Is an audiotape made by being placed on the person of a defendant's accomplice/informant admissible over a Fourth Amendment objection?

HOLDING AND DECISION: (White, J.) Yes. An audiotape made by being placed on the person of a defendant's accomplice/informant is admissible over a Fourth Amendment objection. Whether the Fourth Amendment is implicated by a search depends upon whether the party invoking the amendment had a reasonable expectation of privacy. In the context of this case, one venturing on a criminal enterprise must be presumed to be aware of the occupational hazard of an accomplice being or becoming an informant. This being established, it is of no moment as to how the informant provides incriminating evidence—live testimony or electronic recording. Consequently, White (D) had no reasonable expectation of privacy here. Reversed.

CONCURRENCE: (Black, J.) I concur in the judgment of the Court for the reasons set forth in my dissent in *Katz v. United States*, 389 U.S. 347 (1967). See Black's dissent in *Katz* on page 25 of this Casenote Legal Briefs book.

DISSENT: (Douglas, J.) The Court equates electronic surveillance with eavesdropping, but the former has a far greater capacity to invade one's privacy.

DISSENT: (Harlan, J.) The proper analysis here is to assess the nature of a practice and the likely extent of its impact upon the individual's sense of security balanced against the utility of the conduct as a means of law enforcement. Here, electronic recording poses a far greater potential to curb individual liberty than standard informing.

▶ *ANALYSIS*

The present case was a plurality opinion—only three other justices joined Justice White's opinion. In such cases, one must look to the concurrences to assess the case's precedential value. Here, Justice Black concurred for reasons basically unrelated to the Court's reasoning, thus diminishing the value of this case as sound precedent.

◼═◼

Quicknotes

FOURTH AMENDMENT Provides that persons be secure as to their person and private belongings against unreasonable searches and seizures.

◼═◼

California v. Greenwood

State (P) v. Garbage owner (D)

486 U.S. 35 (1988).

NATURE OF CASE: Review of dismissal of charges of narcotics possession.

FACT SUMMARY: Greenwood (D) was caught in possession of narcotics when police searched his house on the authority of a warrant issued based on evidence obtained through a search of Greenwood's (D) garbage.

RULE OF LAW
Garbage left in a public space for collection may be searched without a warrant.

FACTS: Suspecting that Greenwood (D) was involved with narcotics, a police officer searched Greenwood's (D) garbage, which had been placed on the street for collection. Evidence of narcotics was found. Based on this evidence, a warrant was issued. Police searched Greenwood's (D) home, and narcotics were found. Greenwood (D) was arrested and charged. The Superior Court dismissed the charges; the court of appeal affirmed; and the California Supreme Court denied the State's (P) petition for review.

ISSUE: May garbage left in a public space for collection be searched without a warrant?

HOLDING AND DECISION: (White, J.) Yes. Garbage left in a public space for collection may be searched without a warrant. The necessity for a warrant in any given situation is based on whether an individual has a reasonable expectation of privacy. In the case of garbage left in a public space for collection, it is well known that animals, children, and scavengers can and do rummage through garbage. Therefore, it is not reasonable to expect the contents of a garbage bag to remain private. This being so, no reasonable expectation of privacy existed here, and no warrant was needed. The judgment of the court of appeal is reversed.

DISSENT: (Brennan, J.) Scrutiny of another's trash is contrary to commonly accepted notions of civilized behavior. A single bag of trash testifies eloquently to the social status and personal habits of the person who produced it and can relate intimate details about the person's sexual and health practices, professional status, political associations and inclinations, private thoughts, and personal relationships. It is just this intimate activity associated with the sanctities of home and the privacies of life that the Fourth Amendment is designed to protect from warrantless scrutiny. The bags used by Greenwood (D) should not be deprived of Fourth Amendment protections merely because they were used to discard rather than transport his personal effects. This is particularly true since Greenwood (D) was required by a municipal ordinance to leave trash on his curb for pickup and prohibited from disposing of it any other way.

▶ ANALYSIS

It appears that a rule that can be gleaned from this case, and others, such as *California v. Ciraolo*, 476 U.S. 207 (1986), is as follows: police are not to be expected to be less inquisitive than the most inquisitive members of the general public. Most individuals do not go through others' trash. Some, however, do. This being so, the police may reasonably be expected to do so as well.

Quicknotes

FOURTH AMENDMENT Provides that persons be secure as to their person and private belongings against unreasonable searches and seizures.

United States v. Karo

Federal government (P) v. Accused cocaine trafficker (D)

468 U.S. 705 (1984).

NATURE OF CASE: Appeal from court of appeals judgment overturning conviction.

FACT SUMMARY: Drug Enforcement Administration (DEA) agents arranged to have a beeper placed in cans of ether that were allegedly to be used to extract cocaine from clothing.

🏛 RULE OF LAW
The delivery of an electronic tracking device in a container of chemicals to a buyer without knowledge of the device does not violate the Fourth Amendment.

FACTS: Through a government informant, the DEA learned that Karo (D) and his confederates were planning to extract cocaine from clothing impregnated with the drug and imported into the United States. A DEA agent arranged with the informant, who was supplying Karo (D) with the ether, to substitute a can containing a beeper for one of the cans of ether. The agent had a court order for the installation and monitoring of the device. A court of appeals overturned Karo's (D) conviction, holding that his Fourth Amendment rights were violated when the can containing the beeper was given to him. The Supreme Court granted the Government's (P) petition for certiorari.

ISSUE: Does the delivery of an electronic tracking device in a container of chemicals to a buyer without knowledge of the device violate the Fourth Amendment?

HOLDING AND DECISION: (White, J.) No. The delivery of an electronic tracking device in a container of chemicals to a buyer without knowledge of the device does not violate the Fourth Amendment. The Fourth Amendment protects against unreasonable searches and seizures. Although the monitoring of the device may have constituted a search, the mere transfer of the can to Karo (D) did not. Likewise, Karo's (D) possessory interests were not meaningfully interfered with by the transfer, so no seizure occurred. At most, there was a technical trespass. The judgment of the court of appeals is reversed.

CONCURRENCE AND DISSENT: (Stevens, J.) The majority correctly concludes that a search occurs when the beeper surveillance reveals the locale of property concealed from public view, but it overlooks the necessary conclusion that the attachment of the beeper was a seizure. Karo (D) had the right to exclude the world from his property; by attaching the bug, the Government (P) infringed upon that exclusionary right.

▶ ANALYSIS

The Court examined the actual monitoring of the beeper as well. It held that the use of the beeper to track Karo (D) in his private residence, an area not open to visual surveillance in which he had a legitimate expectation of privacy, violated his Fourth Amendment rights.

Quicknotes

POSSESSORY INTEREST The right to possess particular real property to the exclusion of others.

Kyllo v. United States

Resident (D) v. Federal government (P)

533 U.S. 27 (2001).

NATURE OF CASE: Appeal from indictment of manufacturing marijuana.

FACT SUMMARY: Federal agents suspected Kyllo (D) of growing marijuana in his residence and used a thermal scanner to prove he was doing so.

🏛 RULE OF LAW
Where the government uses a device that is not in general public use to explore details of the home that would previously have been unknowable without physical intrusion, the surveillance is a "search" and is presumptively unreasonable without a warrant.

FACTS: Federal agents suspected Kyllo (D) was growing marijuana in his home and used a thermal imager to scan the residence. The agents concluded that Kyllo (D) was using halide lights to grow marijuana in his house and a magistrate issued a search warrant on the basis of the thermal scan, tips from informants, and Kyllo's (D) heating bills. Kyllo (D) was indicted and unsuccessfully moved to suppress the evidence. The court of appeals remanded the case for an evidentiary hearing regarding the intrusiveness of the thermal imaging. The district court upheld the warrant and affirmed denial of the motion. The court of appeals affirmed.

ISSUE: Does the use of a thermal-imaging device aimed at a private home from the street to detect relative amounts of heat within the home constitute a "search" within the meaning of the Fourth Amendment?

HOLDING AND DECISION: (Scalia, J.) Yes. Where the government uses a device that is not in general public use to explore details of the home that would previously have been unknowable without physical intrusion, the surveillance is a "search" and is presumptively unreasonable without a warrant. The Fourth Amendment draws "a fine line at the entrance of the house." We believe the line must be not only fine, but also bright. The methods of surveillance that require a warrant must be clearly specified. The rule we must adopt must take account of sophisticated systems already in use or development. [Remanded to the district court to determine whether probable cause existed independent of the evidence from the thermal visioning. Reversed and remanded.]

DISSENT: (Stevens, J.) There is a distinction between "through-the-wall surveillance" that gives the observer direct access to information in a private area and the thought pro-cesses used to draw inferences from information in the public domain. The Court has crafted a rule that purports to deal with direct observation of the inside of the home. This case, however, involves indirect deductions from observations of the exterior of the home.

▶ ANALYSIS

The Court upholds the test of "reasonableness" set forth in *Katz v. United States*, 389 U.S. 347 (1967), that whether the individual has an expectation of privacy depends on whether society is prepared to recognize such expectation as reasonable. The Court rejects the erosion of Fourth Amendment protection by technological advances, concluding that any such technological "intrusion into a constitutionally protected area" constitutes a search, especially if the product of the use of a device not available to the general public.

Quicknotes

SEARCH An inspection conducted in order to obtain evidence to be utilized for the prosecution of a crime.

FOURTH AMENDMENT Provides that persons be secure as to their person and private belongings against unreasonable searches and seizures.

WARRANT An order issued by a court directing an officer to undertake a certain act (e.g., arrest or search).

PROBABLE CAUSE A reasonable basis for believing that a crime has been committed.

Florida v. Bostick

State (P) v. Bus passenger (D)

501 U.S. 429 (1991).

NATURE OF CASE: Review of reversal of conviction for narcotics possession.

FACT SUMMARY: Police officers displaying badges and a gun boarded a bus in interstate transit and questioned Bostick (D), a passenger, without reasonable suspicion.

🏛 RULE OF LAW
When police officers board a bus and question a passenger without reasonable suspicion, a seizure occurs only if a reasonable passenger would not feel free to terminate the questioning.

FACTS: Two police officers displaying badges and insignia boarded a bus en route to Atlanta from Miami during a brief stop to take on passengers in Fort Lauderdale. One officer also carried a "recognizable zipper bag, containing a pistol." The officers singled out Bostick (D) without reasonable suspicion and asked to see his ticket and identification, which Bostick (D) provided without incident. One officer stood in front of Bostick's (D) seat, blocking his access to the aisle. The officers then requested Bostick's (D) permission to search his luggage and identified themselves as narcotics agents looking for drugs. They informed Bostick (D) of his right to refuse consent to the search, to which Bostick (D) consented. Cocaine was found in Bostick's (D) suitcase. The Florida Supreme Court held that because the police conduct occurred on a bus, it constituted a seizure in violation of the Fourth Amendment. Florida (P) appealed.

ISSUE: When police officers board a bus and question a passenger without reasonable suspicion, does a seizure occur only if a reasonable passenger would not feel free to terminate the questioning?

HOLDING AND DECISION: (O'Connor, J.) Yes. When police officers board a bus and question a passenger without reasonable suspicion, a seizure occurs only if a reasonable passenger would not feel free to terminate the questioning. Bostick's (D) freedom of movement was restricted by a factor independent of police conduct, i.e., his being a passenger on a bus scheduled to depart. The appropriate inquiry therefore is whether, based on the totality of the circumstances, a reasonable person would feel free to terminate the encounter. No determination of this issue was made in the courts below. Remanded to allow the Florida (P) courts to evaluate the seizure issue under the correct legal standard.

DISSENT: (Marshall, J.) The boarding by police officers of a bus in transit in a suspicionless dragnet-style sweep, with badges and a gun displayed, is itself an intimidating show of authority. The officers blocked Bostick's (D) path to the aisle and failed to advise him of his right to terminate the questioning. From the manner in which the officers boarded the bus, Bostick (D) reasonably could have believed that refusing to answer questions would have intensified, rather than terminated the interrogation. The imminent departure of the bus prevented Bostick (D) from leaving the bus, even if Bostick (D) believed the officers would let him leave. These circumstances constitute a seizure within the meaning of the Fourth Amendement.

▌ *ANALYSIS*

According to *Florida v. Royer*, 460 U.S. 491 (1983), confrontations between police and citizens fall generally into three categories: (1) an encounter not involving a seizure, requiring no justification under the Fourth Amendment; (2) a stop as defined in Terry, in which reasonable suspicion for the stop must be shown; and (3) an arrest, which must be justified by probable cause. As the plurality in *Royer* pointed out, a single incident can run the gamut of these categories, depending on the amount of constraint applied to the citizen's freedom of movement at a particular time during the encounter. This definition of seizure was accepted by the Court in *Delgado*, which Justice O'Connor relied on as the basis for the majority opinion in *Bostick*.

■═■

Quicknotes

FOURTH AMENDMENT Provides that persons be secure as to their person and private belongings against unreasonable searches and seizures.

■═■

United States v. Drayton

Federal government (P) v. Drug possessor (D)

536 U.S. 194 (2002).

NATURE OF CASE: Appeal by government from suppression of drug evidence.

FACT SUMMARY: When a police officer conducted a pat-down search of his person during a "bus sweep," Christopher Drayton (D) argued that any purported consent he may have given was vitiated in the absence of some positive indication that consent could have been refused.

RULE OF LAW
Law enforcement officers do not violate the Fourth Amendment prohibition of unreasonable searches merely by approaching individuals on the street or in other public places and putting questions to them if they are willing to listen.

FACTS: Christopher Drayton (D) was traveling on a Greyhound bus. As part of a routine drug and weapons interdiction effort, police officers, dressed in plain clothes and with concealed weapons but visible badges, entered the bus, and randomly asked passengers, "Do you mind if I check your bags?" and "Do you mind if I check your person?" When Officer Lang asked Drayton (D) if he minded to a search of his baggy pants, Drayton (D) responded by lifting his hands about eight inches from his legs, and Lang conducted a pat-down search, found bundles of cocaine, and arrested Drayton (D). Drayton (D) was charged with drug crimes, and the federal district court denied his motion to suppress the drugs on the ground that the entire procedure was a consensual encounter. The court of appeals reversed, and the Government (P) appealed.

ISSUE: Do law enforcement officers violate the Fourth Amendment prohibition of unreasonable searches merely by approaching individuals on the street or in other public places and putting questions to them if they are willing to listen?

HOLDING AND DECISION: (Kennedy, J.) No. Law enforcement officers do not violate the Fourth Amendment prohibition of unreasonable searches merely by approaching individuals on the street or in other public places and putting questions to them if they are willing to listen. Even when law enforcement officers have no basis for suspecting a particular individual, they may pose questions, ask for identification, and request consent to search luggage provided they do not induce cooperation by coercive means. If a reasonable person would feel free to terminate the encounter, as here, then he or she has not been seized. Here, the officers gave the passengers no reason to believe that they were required to answer the officers' questions. When Officer Lang approached Drayton (D), he did not brandish a weapon or make any intimidating movements. He left the aisle free so that Drayton (D) could exit. He spoke to passengers one by one and in a polite, quiet voice. Nothing he said would suggest to a reasonable person that he or she was barred from leaving the bus or otherwise terminating the encounter. There was no application of force, no intimidating movement, no overwhelming show of force, no blocking of exits, no command, not even an authoritative tone of voice. It is beyond question that had this encounter occurred on the street, it would be constitutional. The fact that an encounter takes place on a bus does not on its own transform standard police questioning of citizens into an illegal seizure. Furthermore, even the presence of a holstered firearm is unlikely to contribute to the coerciveness of the encounter absent active brandishing of the weapon. Reversed and remanded.

DISSENT: (Souter, J.) Although anyone who travels by air today clearly submits to searches of the person and luggage as a condition of boarding the aircraft, the commonplace precautions of air travel have not, thus far, been justified for ground transportation. There is therefore "an air of unreality" about the majority's explanation that bus passengers consent to searches of their luggage to enhance their own safety and the safety of those around them. Furthermore, a police officer who is certain to get his way has no need to shout.

ANALYSIS

In Drayton, the Supreme Court notes that although Officer Lang did not inform Drayton (D) of his right to refuse the search, he did request permission to search and that the totality of the circumstances indicated that the consent was voluntary, hence the search was admissible. In a society based on law, said the court, the concept of agreement and consent should be given "a weight and dignity of its own."

Quicknotes

FOURTH AMENDMENT Provides that persons be secure as to their person and private belongings against unreasonable searches and seizures.

United States v. Verdugo-Urquidez

Federal government (P) v. Alleged drug smuggler (D)

494 U.S. 259 (1990).

NATURE OF CASE: Appeal from the granting of a motion to suppress evidence.

FACT SUMMARY: When documents were seized without a search warrant from his residence in Mexico by U.S. agents, Rene Martin Verdugo-Urquidez (D), a citizen and resident of Mexico, moved to suppress the documents on the grounds that the Fourth Amendment applied to the searches.

RULE OF LAW
The Fourth Amendment does not apply to the search and seizure by U.S. agents of property owned by a nonresident alien and located in a foreign country.

FACTS: Rene Martin Verdugo-Urquidez (D), a citizen and resident of Mexico, was apprehended by Mexican authorities in Mexico for drug smuggling and transported to the United States. Following the arrest, a Federal DEA agent searched Verdugo-Urquidez's (D) residence in Mexico, with no search warrant, but with authorization for the search from the Director General of the Mexican Federal Judicial Police, and seized certain documents. The federal district court granted Verdugo-Urquidez's (D) motion to suppress the evidence, concluding that the Fourth Amendment applied to the searches. The federal court of appeals affirmed, and the Government (P) appealed.

ISSUE: Does the Fourth Amendment apply to the search and seizure by U.S. agents of property owned by a nonresident alien and located in a foreign country?

HOLDING AND DECISION: (Rehnquist, C.J.) No. The Fourth Amendment does not apply to the search and seizure by U.S. agents of property owned by a nonresident alien and located in a foreign country. The text of the Fourth Amendment, by contrast with the Fifth and Sixth Amendments, extends its reach only to "the people." Close examination of the precise wording of the Constitution and the Fourth Amendment suggests that "the people" refers to a class of persons who are a part of a national community or who have otherwise developed sufficient connection with this country to be considered part of that community. The language of the Fourth Amendment contrasts with the words "person" and "accused" used in the Fifth and Sixth Amendments regulating procedure in criminal cases. What we know of the history of the drafting of the Fourth Amendment also suggests that its purpose was to restrict searches and seizures which might be conducted by the United States in domestic matters. The purpose of the Fourth Amendment was to protect the people of the United States against arbitrary action "by their own Government;" it was never suggested that the provision was intended to restrain the actions of the federal government against aliens outside the United States territory. There is likewise no indication that the Fourth Amendment was intended to apply to activities of the United States directed against aliens in foreign territory or in international waters. Reversed.

CONCURRENCE: (Kennedy, J.) The words "the people" in the Fourth Amendment do not detract from its force or its reach. The language of the Fourth Amendment may be interpreted to underscore the importance of the right, rather than to restrict the category of persons who may assert it.

CONCURRENCE: (Stevens, J.) The Government (P) argues correctly that the search conducted by the federal agents was not "unreasonable."

DISSENT: (Brennan, J.) The fact that Verdugo-Urquidez (D) is being prosecuted for violation of U.S. law and may well spend the rest of his life in a U.S. prison, supplies a "sufficient connection" between him and the U.S. to provide him with Fourth Amendment search and seizure protection. The need to protect those suspected of criminal activity from the unbridled discretion of investigating officers is no less important abroad than at home.

DISSENT: (Blackmun, J.) When the purpose of a search is the procurement of evidence for a criminal prosecution, such search, to be reasonable, must be based upon probable cause. Here, the issue of probable cause has never been reached.

ANALYSIS

In *Verdugo-Urquidez*, the nonresident alien defendant relied on a series of Supreme Court decisions in which the Court held that aliens did in fact enjoy particular constitutional rights, such as, for example, certain First and Fifth Amendment rights. Those cases, however, said the Supreme Court, establish only that aliens receive constitutional protections when they have come within the territory of the United States and developed substantial connections with this country. The Court further noted that not only were history and case law against Verdugo-Urquidez, but the result of

Continued on next page.

accepting his claim would have "deleterious consequences" for the United States in conducting investigative activities beyond its boundaries.

━■━

Quicknotes

FIFTH AMENDMENT Provides that no person shall be compelled to serve as a witness against himself, or be subject to trial for the same offense twice, or be deprived of life, liberty, or property without due process of law.

FIRST AMENDMENT Prohibits Congress from enacting any law respecting an establishment of religion, prohibiting the free exercise of religion, abridging freedom of speech or the press, the right of peaceful assembly and the right to petition for a redress of grievances.

FOURTH AMENDMENT Provides that persons be secure as to their person and private belongings against unreasonable searches and seizures.

SIXTH AMENDMENT Provides the right to a speedy and public trial by impartial jury, the right to be informed of the accusation, the right to confront witnesses, and the right to have the assistance of counsel in all criminal prosecutions.

━■━

Illinois v. Gates

State (P) v. Criminal defendant (D)

462 U.S. 213 (1983).

NATURE OF CASE: Review of order granting motion to suppress.

FACT SUMMARY: The trial court suppressed certain contra-band found in a search made on Gates' (D) property because the warrant had been procured due to an anonymous tip of questionable reliability.

🏛️ **RULE OF LAW**
If corroborating evidence exists, a warrant may issue on the basis of a tip of questionable reliability.

FACTS: City police received an anonymous letter that the Gateses (D) were engaged in a narcotics enterprise. The letter was detailed but revealed nothing of the informant's reliability. State and federal agents began conducting surveillance upon the Gateses (D). At one point, Lance Gates (D) went on a brief trip to Florida. Based on the letter and Lance Gates's (D) trip to Florida, a warrant issued. A search of the Gateses' (D) car and home revealed narcotics and other contraband. At a suppression hearing, the trial court concluded that since the letter was anonymous and gave no indication for reliability of the informant, it was insufficient to provide a basis for a warrant. The contraband was suppressed. The Illinois Supreme Court affirmed, and the Supreme Court granted review.

ISSUE: If corroborating evidence exists, may a warrant issue on the basis of a tip of questionable reliability?

HOLDING AND DECISION: (Rehnquist, J.) Yes. If corroborating evidence exists, a warrant may issue on the basis of a tip of questionable reliability. This Court has established a "two-prong" analysis for warrants to issue on the basis of informant state-ments, one prong being reliability and the other being knowledge. Many courts, including the court below, have considered this to mean that both requirements must be shown independently. This is an improper analysis. Probable cause is a fluid analysis and is best assessed under a totality-of-the-circumstances approach. If an informant is known to be very reliable, probable cause may exist even if his knowledge is questionable. If the tipper seems very knowledgeable about relevant facts, less reliability needs to be shown. Here, the anonymous letter was quite detailed and was supported by Lance Gates's (D) activities and confirmed by agents' surveillance. This strong showing of knowledgeability rendered the lack of demonstrable reliability nonfatal to the warrant. Reversed.

CONCURRENCE: (White, J.) The corroboration went not only to knowledge but to reliability as well. Reliability remains a condition precedent to probable cause. The warrant should be upheld based on the two-prong analysis, which should continue to be the approach to evaluating probable cause.

DISSENT: (Stevens, J.) The letter and the agents' observations were insufficient to meet the twin tests of reliability and knowledge.

▶ *ANALYSIS*

The "two-prong" test arose out of the cases *Aguilar v. Texas*, 378 U.S. 108 (1964), and *Spinelli v. United States*, 383 U.S. 410 (1969). These cases reflected a concern that informants constituted an opportunity for abuse of discretion in the issuance of warrants. The two-prong test, repudiated by the Court in the present decision, was the Court's effort to address this perceived problem.

■—■

Quicknotes

WARRANT An order issued by a court directing an officer to undertake a certain act (e.g., arrest or search).

■—■

Ornelas v. United States

Criminal defendant (D) v. Federal government (P)

517 U.S. 690 (1996).

NATURE OF CASE: Appeal challenging the admissibility of narcotics evidence.

FACT SUMMARY: Ornelas (D) challenged the constitutionality of a police search of his car, wherein narcotics were found, because the search was made without a warrant and no probable cause existed for the search.

RULE OF LAW

The standard of appellate review for questions of reasonable suspicion and probable cause to make a warrantless search is de novo review.

FACTS: In December, 1992, veteran police officers specializing in drug enforcement conducted surveillance in a downtown Milwaukee motel's parking lot. The officers spotted an older GM car with California plates, a type of car often used by drug couriers. Ornelas (D) checked into the motel at 4:00 a.m. without a reservation. The officers then checked DEA records and Ornelas's (D) name appeared as a known drug suspect. The officers summoned a police drug-sniffing dog. Ornelas (D) emerged later, and the police approached the car, identifying themselves in the process. When asked if he had drugs in the car, Ornelas (D) said "no." When asked if the police could search the car, Ornelas (D) consented. The officers, who were experienced in searching cars for drugs, noticed the right rear armrest was loose and saw a rusty screw next to the armrest. The police removed the armrest and found drugs hidden inside. Ornelas (D) filed a pretrial motion to suppress the evidence, and the officers conceded that it was an investigatory stop and that probable cause was needed for the warrantless search. The magistrate hearing the motion found the officers had reasonable suspicion, but not probable cause. The magistrate denied the motion to suppress, however, on the grounds of inevitable discovery, due to the drug-sniffing dog's presence. The district court adopted the magistrate's opinion as to the reasonable suspicion, but found that the police had probable cause as well. The court of appeals reviewed the case following the standard of "clear error." The court found no clear error with respect to the reasonable suspicion decision, but required the district court to determine whether the police were credible witnesses in deciding the probable cause issue. The magistrate found the testimony credible, and the district court accepted the ruling, again finding that probable cause supported the search. The court of appeals affirmed, and Ornelas (D) appealed.

ISSUE: Should the standard of appellate review for questions of reasonable suspicion and probable cause to make a warrantless search be de novo review?

HOLDING AND DECISION: (Rehnquist, C.J.) Yes. The standard of appellate review for questions of reasonable suspicion and probable cause to make a warrantless search is de novo review. The review of issues surrounding reasonable suspicion and probable cause involve questions of both fact and law. Appellate review of such issues in this context should not be expressly deferred to the trial court's determination because such deference would leave unchecked wildly inconsistent results. Especially in warrantless search contexts, the need for appellate review is paramount. The Fourth Amendment highly favors searches conducted pursuant to a warrant and the police are more likely to obtain a warrant if the scrutiny applied to searches made pursuant to a warrant is less than that applied to warrantless searches. This is not to say that findings of historical fact and inferences made thereon by the trial court are not to be given significant weight in this review. The trial court is in the best position to make such determinations and an appeals court should give those determinations due weight. Here, the appellate court reviewed Ornelas's (D) case on a clear error standard, rather than on a de novo standard. The appellate court erred in its ruling and the judgments are vacated and remanded back to the court of appeals to review on a de novo basis. Vacated and remanded.

ANALYSIS

The case highlights certain Fourth Amendment search and seizure issues in the context of automobiles. While the Fourth Amendment usually requires police to obtain search warrants before conducting a search, the easy mobility of automobiles often permits searches without warrants if the police have probable cause to search the vehicle. In assessing whether probable cause exists, the appellate courts in their de novo review can look at the facts in their particular contexts and give due weight to the findings of the trail courts. Because the Fourth Amendment favors searches made pursuant to a warrant, the scrutiny warrantless searches will undergo will be greater than searches made pursuant to a warrant.

Continued on next page.

Quicknotes

FOURTH AMENDMENT Provides that persons be secure as to their person and private belongings against unreasonable searches and seizures.

■▬■

Maryland v. Pringle

State (P) v. Convicted drug possessor (D)

540 U.S. 366 (2003).

NATURE OF CASE: Appeal by state from reversal of conviction for cocaine possession.

FACT SUMMARY: Pringle (D) was arrested for cocaine possession when he was a front-seat passenger in a vehicle and the cocaine was found in the back seat. He argued that he did not have sufficient possession of the cocaine to show probable cause for his arrest, hence any confession resulting from such arrest would be invalid.

🏛 RULE OF LAW
The passenger of a vehicle, even if separated from the drugs, has sufficient constructive possession of drugs located in the vehicle to give rise to probable cause for the passenger's arrest.

FACTS: A police officer stopped an automobile for speeding. There were three occupants in the car. Pringle (D) was the front-seat passenger. When the driver opened the glove compartment to get the registration, the officer observed a large amount of rolled-up cash. The driver consented to a vehicle search, which yielded $763 from the glove-compartment and cocaine from behind the back-seat armrest. Pringle (D) and both other occupants were arrested. Pringle (D) waived his Miranda rights and confessed the cocaine belonged to him. The trial court denied Pringle's (D) motion to suppress the confession as fruit of an illegal arrest, holding the officer had probable cause for the arrest. Pringle (D) was convicted of cocaine possession, however the Maryland Court of Appeals reversed, holding that the mere finding of cocaine in the back armrest when Pringle (D) was simply a passenger in the front seat, failed to establish probable cause to arrest Pringle (D) for possession. Maryland (P) appealed.

ISSUE: Does the passenger of a vehicle, even if separated from the drugs, have sufficient constructive possession of drugs located in the vehicle to give rise to probable cause for the passenger's arrest?

HOLDING AND DECISION: (Rehnquist, C.J.) Yes. The passenger of a vehicle, even if separated from the drugs, has sufficient constructive possession of drugs located in the vehicle to give rise to probable cause for the passenger's arrest. Maryland law authorizes police officers to execute warrantless arrests, inter alia, for felonies committed in an officer's presence or where the officer has probable cause to believe a felony has been, or is being, committed. Here, the officer, upon recovering the plastic bags of cocaine, had probable cause to believe a felony had been committed. As to whether there was probable cause to believe Pringle (D) had committed that crime, Maryland law defines "possession" as the exercise of actual or constructive dominion over a thing by one or more persons. The probable cause standard is incapable of precise definition or quantification into percentages because it deals with probabilities and depends on the totality of the circumstances. In the instant case, Pringle (D) was one of three men riding in the car in the early morning hours when a large amount of rolled up cash and five baggies of cocaine were found. The cocaine was "accessible" to all three of the occupants, including Pringle (D). It was an entirely reasonable inference from these facts that any or all three of the occupants had knowledge of, and exercised dominion and control over, the cocaine. Thus, a reasonable officer could conclude there was probable cause to believe Pringle (D) committed the crime of possession of cocaine, either solely or jointly. Reversed and remanded.

▌ *ANALYSIS*

As the U.S. Supreme Court makes clear in Pringle, the probable cause standard is a practical, nontechnical conception that deals with the factual and practical considerations of everyday life on which reasonable and prudent persons, "not legal technicians," act. Probable cause is a "fluid concept"—turning on the assessment of probabilities in particular factual contexts, not readily, or even usually, reduced to a neat set of legal rules.

■═▮

Quicknotes

PROBABLE CAUSE   A reasonable basis for believing that a crime has been committed.

■═▮

United States v. Banks

Government (P) v. Convicted cocaine dealer (D)

540 U.S. 31 (2003).

NATURE OF CASE: Appeal by federal government from reversal of conviction for cocaine possession.

FACT SUMMARY: When federal and state agents, executing a warrant for a narcotics search of Banks's (D) apartment, waited 15 to 20 seconds before battering down his door, Banks (D) argued that this constituted such an unreasonably short time before forcing entry that it violated his Fourth Amendment search and seizure rights.

🏛 RULE OF LAW
When executing a search warrant, a 15-to-20-second wait before a forcible entry satisfies the Fourth Amendment.

FACTS: With information that Banks (D) was selling cocaine at home, federal and state agents obtained a warrant to search his apartment. As soon as they arrived in mid-afternoon, they called out "police search warrant" and rapped hard on the door. There was no indication whether anyone was at home. After waiting 15 to 20 seconds with no answer, the officers broke open the front door with a battering ram. Banks (D) was in the shower and testified that he heard nothing until the crash of the door. The search produced weapons, crack cocaine, and other evidence of drug dealing. Banks's (D) Fourth Amendment motion to suppress this evidence on the grounds the agents waited an unreasonably short time before forcing entry was denied. The district court denied the motion, and Banks (D) pleaded guilty, reserving the right to challenge the search on appeal. The Ninth Circuit reversed and ordered suppression of the evidence. The Government (P) appealed.

ISSUE: When executing a search warrant, does a 15-to-20-second wait before a forcible entry satisfy the Fourth Amendment?

HOLDING AND DECISION: (Souter, J.) Yes. When executing a search warrant, a 15-to-20-second wait before a forcible entry satisfies the Fourth Amendment. Exigency may develop in the period beginning when officers with a warrant knock to be admitted, and the issue then comes down to whether it was reasonable to suspect imminent loss of evidence after the 15 to 20 seconds the officers waited prior to forcing their way. Although here "this call is a close one," after 15 or 20 seconds without a response, the officers could fairly suspect that cocaine would be gone if they were reticent any longer. Indeed, Courts of Appeals have routinely held similar wait times to be reasonable in drug cases with similar facts including easily disposable evidence, and some courts have found even shorter times to be reasonable enough. As to Banks's (D) argument that he was in the shower, what is important is that the facts known to the police are what count in judging reasonable waiting time, and there is no indication that the police knew Banks (D) was in the shower and thus unaware of an impending search that he would otherwise have tried to frustrate. Furthermore, on the record in the instant case, what matters is the opportunity to get rid of cocaine, which a prudent dealer will keep near a commode or kitchen sink. In a case such as this, the exigent need of law enforcement "trumps" a resident's interest in avoiding all property damage. Officers seeking a stolen piano, on the other hand, may be able to spend more time to make sure they really need a battering ram. Reversed.

▶ ANALYSIS

The Fourth Amendment says nothing specific about formalities in executing a warrant's authorization, speaking to the manner of searching as well as to the legitimacy of searching at all simply in terms of the right to be secure against unreasonable searches and seizures. Although the notion of reasonable execution must therefore be fleshed out, the Supreme Court has done that case by case, largely avoiding categories and protocols for searches. Instead, the Court has treated reasonableness as a function of the facts of cases so various that no template is likely to produce sounder results than examining the totality of circumstances in a given case.

■=■

Quicknotes

FOURTH AMENDMENT Provides that persons be secure as to their person and private belongings against unreasonable searches and seizures.

■=■

Wilson v. Layne

Homeowner (P) v. Newspaper reporter and police (D)

526 U.S. 603 (1999).

NATURE OF CASE: Appeal from upholding police officers' defense of qualified immunity.

FACT SUMMARY: While attempting to execute an authorized arrest warrant against Dominic Wilson in his private residence, U.S. marshals and county police officers brought along members of the media. But the warrant was inadvertently executed at the home of Wilson's parents (P). The parents (P) brought civil suit against the police and the media representatives, arguing that bringing members of the media to observe and record execution of the warrant violated their Fourth Amendment rights.

🏛 RULE OF LAW
It is a violation of the Fourth Amendment for police to bring members of the media or other third parties into a home during execution of a warrant when such presence does not aid in execution of the warrant.

FACTS: While executing an arrest warrant against Dominic Wilson in a private home as part of a special national fugitive apprehension program to apprehend certain dangerous designated criminals, police officers invited representatives of the media to accompany them. Unknown to the police, the address provided by the police computer was not actually the residence of Dominic Wilson, but rather was the residence of his parents. The U.S. marshals and local police invited a reporter and photographer from the Washington Post to "ride-along" and attend the warrant's execution. During an ensuing altercation in the home, the newspaper photographer took several photographs. Wilson's parents (P) sued Layne (D), the newspaper reporter, and the law enforcement officials in their personal capacities for money damages, claiming that bringing members of the media to observe and record execution of the warrant violated their Fourth Amendment rights. While upholding the defense of qualified immunity as to the police officers, the federal court of appeals declined to decide whether the actions of the police violated the Fourth Amendment. Wilson (P) appealed.

ISSUE: Is it a violation of the Fourth Amendment for police to bring members of the media or other third parties into a home during execution of a warrant when such presence does not aid in execution of the warrant?

HOLDING AND DECISION: (Rehnquist, C.J.) Yes. It is a violation of the Fourth Amendment for police to bring members of the media or other third parties into a home during execution of a warrant when such presence does not aid in execution of the warrant. Although not every police action while inside a home must be explicitly authorized by the text of the warrant, the Fourth Amendment does require that police actions in execution of a warrant "be related to the objectives of the authorized intrusion." Here, certainly the presence of reporters inside the home was not related to the objectives of the authorized intrusion. The police concede that the reporters did not engage in the execution of the warrant, and did not assist the police in their task. The reporters therefore were not present for any reason related to the justification for police entry into the home: the apprehension of Dominic Wilson. The Washington Post reporters in the Wilsons' (P) home were working on a story for their own purposes. They were not present for the purpose of protecting the officers, much less the Wilsons (P). A private photographer was acting for private purposes as evidenced by the fact that the newspaper and not the police retained the photographs. Affirmed as to the police officers' defense of qualified immunity.

▶ ANALYSIS

As made clear in the *Wilson* decision, the possibility of good public relations for the police is simply not enough, standing alone, to justify the ride-along intrusion into a private home. Even the need for accurate reporting on police issues in general, explained the Supreme Court, bears no direct relation to the constitutional justification for the police intrusion into a home in order to execute a felony arrest warrant.

■■■■

Quicknotes

FOURTH AMENDMENT Provides that persons be secure as to their person and private belongings against unreasonable searches and seizures.

WARRANT An order issued by a court directing an officer to undertake a certain act (e.g., arrest or search).

■■■■

Mincey v. Arizona

Criminal defendant (D) v. State (P)

437 U.S. 385 (1978).

NATURE OF CASE: Appeal from murder, assault, and narcotics convictions.

FACT SUMMARY: Police officers performed a four-day, intensive warrantless search of an apartment following the shooting of an officer.

🏛 RULE OF LAW
States must meet a substantial burden to demonstrate an exceptional situation justifying a new exception to a warrant requirement under the Fourth and Fourteenth Amendments.

FACTS: On October 28, 1974, undercover officer Barry Headricks of the Metropolitan Area Narcotics Squad arranged to purchase a quantity of heroin from Rufus Mincey (D). Later that same day, Headricks returned to Mincey's (D) apartment accompanied by nine plainclothes policemen. As police entered the apartment, a volley of bullets was heard in the bedroom. Headricks, who had gone in ahead of the other officers, emerged from the bedroom badly wounded. He died a few hours later in the hospital. The police officers involved in the operation conducted a limited search for additional victims and called for backup. After additional officers arrived, the police performed an extensive, four-day search of Mincey's (D) apartment during which they seized 200–300 items. Mincey (D) was tried and convicted of murder, assault, and three counts of narcotics offenses. He appealed, contending that the evidence had been illegally seized. The Arizona Supreme Court held that a warrantless search of a homicide scene is permissible under the Fourth and Fourteenth Amendments.

ISSUE: Was the four-day, intensive warrantless search of Mincey's apartment constitutionally permissible?

HOLDING AND DECISION: (Stewart, J.) No. According to this Court's precedent, all warrantless searches are per se unconstitutional under the Fourth Amendment subject to a few delineated exceptions. The Arizona Supreme Court recognized an exception to the warrant requirement for homicide scenes. This exception falls outside of this Court's delineated exceptions to the warrant requirement. Although an argument can be made that this search falls under the exigent circumstances exception because the police needed to determine if there were other victims or a murderer on the premises, an exigent circumstances search must be strictly circumscribed. The search at issue in this case lasted for four days and was rather extensive, going far beyond the strictures of a exigent circumstances search.

▶ ANALYSIS

Mincey teaches that the warrantless search should end when the exigent circumstances end.

━━

Quicknotes

FOURTEENTH AMENDMENT Declares that no state shall make or enforce any law that shall abridge the privileges and immunities of citizens of the United States. No state shall deny to any person within its jurisdiction the equal protection of the laws.

FOURTH AMENDMENT Provides that persons be secure as to their person and private belongings against unreasonable searches and seizures.

━━

Welsh v. Wisconsin

Suspected drunk driver (D) v. State (P)

466 U.S. 740 (1984).

NATURE OF CASE: Appeal from conviction for driving or operating a motor vehicle while under the influence of an intoxicant.

FACT SUMMARY: Police entered Welsh's (D) home without a warrant, near where he left his car, and arrested him.

🏛 RULE OF LAW
The gravity of the suspected offense is a factor to be considered in determining whether the exigent circumstances exception to the Fourth Amendment may be invoked.

FACTS: Welsh (D), driving erratically, pulled off the road. A passerby who observed his behavior called the police; meanwhile, Welsh (D) exited his car and walked to his home a short distance away. Police arrived and proceeded to the house, where they found Welsh (D) naked in bed. They arrested him for a first offense of driving under the influence, a noncriminal violation subject to a civil forfeiture. Welsh (D) challenged the arrest on Fourth Amendment grounds, and the Supreme Court granted review.

ISSUE: Is the gravity of the suspected offense a factor to be considered in determining whether the exigent-circumstances exception to the Fourth Amendment may be invoked?

HOLDING AND DECISION: (Brennan, J.) Yes. The gravity of the suspected offense is a factor to be considered in determining whether the exigent circumstances exception to the Fourth Amendment may be invoked. Prior Supreme Court decisions have emphasized that exceptions to the warrant requirement are "few in number and carefully delineated." We hesitate to find exigent circumstances where the underlying offense is relatively minor. Wisconsin (P) has chosen to make the first offense for driving under the influence a traffic violation, which is not even a misdemeanor. Therefore, the need to enter Welsh's (D) home without a warrant to obtain a blood alcohol level does not rise to the level of exigent circumstances. The arrest of Welsh (D) was invalid. Case is remanded.

DISSENT: (White, J.) A test under which the existence of exigent circumstances turns on the perceived gravity of the crime would significantly hamper law enforcement and burden courts with pointless litigation concerning the nature and gradation of various crimes.

▶ ANALYSIS

The Court notes that a first offense for driving under the influence is a traffic offense. They do not, however, state that the police were aware that this was Welsh's (D) first such offense. The Court does observe that subsequent acts of driving under the influence are treated as more serious crimes. Given these circumstances, *Welsh* seems to suggest that perhaps the search would have been valid if the officers had later discovered that Welsh (D) was a habitual drunk driver.

Quicknotes

EXIGENT CIRCUMSTANCES Circumstances requiring an extraordinary or immediate response; an exception to the prohibition on a warrantless arrest or search when police officers believe probable cause to exist and there is no time for obtaining a warrant.

HOT PURSUIT The pursuit of a fleeing suspect, rendering police officers of the requirement to obtain a warrant before following him into protected area or before arrest.

FELONY MURDER The unlawful killing of another human being while in the commission of, or attempted commission of, specified felonies.

Illinois v. McArthur

State (P) v. Drug possessor (D)

531 U.S. 326 (2001).

NATURE OF CASE: Review of grant of motion to suppress evidence.

FACT SUMMARY: McArthur (D) moved to suppress evidence seized from his home on the basis that it was the "fruit" of an unlawful search.

🏛 RULE OF LAW
In determining whether a search is unreasonable and in violation of the Fourth Amendment, the court must balance the privacy-related and law enforcement-related concerns to determine whether the intrusion was reasonable.

FACTS: Tera McArthur asked two police officers to accompany her to the trailer where she and her husband, Charles (D), lived so that they could keep the peace while she retrieved some of her belongings. She informed the officers that Charles (D) had some drugs in the trailer. Charles (D) was restrained by the police while another officer went to obtain a search warrant. The officers obtained a search warrant and found a small amount of marijuana in the residence. Charles (D) was arrested and charged. He moved to suppress the evidence (pipe, box and marijuana) on the basis that it was the "fruit" of an unlawful seizure. The trial court granted the motion and the appellate court affirmed.

ISSUE: In determining whether a search is unreasonable and in violation of the Fourth Amendment, must the court balance the privacy-related and law enforcement-related concerns to determine whether the intrusion was reasonable?

HOLDING AND DECISION: (Breyer, J.) Yes. In determining whether a search is unreasonable and in violation of the Fourth Amendment, the court must balance the privacy-related and law enforcement-related concerns to determine whether the intrusion was reasonable. Here the restriction at issue was reasonable in light of the fact that the police had probable cause to believe McArthur's (D) trailer home contained evidence of a crime and contraband and that the police had time to speak to his wife and assess her reliability. The police also had good reason to believe that unless restrained, McArthur (D) would destroy the evidence. The police made reasonable efforts to reconcile law enforcement needs with the demands of personal privacy and imposed the restraint for only a limited time period of two hours. The restraint was compatible with the Fourth Amendment's requirements. Reversed and remanded.

CONCURRENCE: (Souter, J.) Since the law requires a warrant, officers need a fair chance to convey their probable cause to a magistrate and obtain one.

DISSENT: (Stevens, J.) Each of the Illinois jurists who participated in this decision correctly placed a higher value on the sanctity of the ordinary citizen's home than on the prosecution of this petty offense. They correctly viewed that interest—whether the home be a humble cottage, a second-hand trailer, or a stately mansion—as one meriting the most serious constitutional protection.

▶ ANALYSIS

In determining whether the Fourth Amendment is violated, the court must invoke a "reasonableness" inquiry. In general, seizures of personal property are presumptively unreasonable unless conducted pursuant to a warrant issued by a neutral magistrate after finding probable cause.

■■■

Quicknotes

CONTRABAND Items that are illegal to have in one's possession or to trade or produce.

FOURTH AMENDMENT Provides that persons be secure as to their person and private belongings against unreasonable searches and.

PROBABLE CAUSE A reasonable basis for believing that a crime has been committed.

WARRANT An order issued by a court directing an officer to undertake a certain act (e.g., arrest or search).

■■■

Arizona v. Hicks

State (P) v. Accused robber (D)

480 U.S. 321 (1987).

NATURE OF CASE: On certiorari from appellate court affirmation of grant of motion to suppress.

FACT SUMMARY: Police conducted a search of Hicks's (D) apartment, moving stereo equipment in order to observe the serial numbers.

🏛 RULE OF LAW
Physically moving a suspicious object in an individual's home to determine if it is incriminating evidence, without probable cause, during an unrelated warrantless search, is violative of the Fourth Amendment.

FACTS: Police entered Hicks's (D) apartment after a bullet was fired through the floor of the apartment, injuring a man below. One of the officers observed expensive stereo equipment which seemed out of place in the shabby surroundings. He moved the equipment in order to observe and record its serial numbers. It was later determined that the serial numbers matched those on equipment taken in an armed robbery, and a search warrant was issued and executed.

ISSUE: May a suspicious object in an individual's home be moved and inspected, without probable cause, during an unrelated warrantless search?

HOLDING AND DECISION: (Scalia, J.) No. Physically moving a suspicious object in an individual's home to determine if it is incriminating evidence, without probable cause, during an unrelated warrantless search, is violative of the Fourth Amendment. The moving of the turntable constituted an invasion of privacy unrelated to the objectives of the search for the shooter. Although the movement was slight, the difference between looking at a suspicious object in plain view and moving it even a few inches is more than trivial for purposes of the Fourth Amendment. Without probable cause, the officer may not search beyond what is already exposed to view. The judgment of the court of appeals is affirmed.

DISSENT: (Powell, J.) The distinction between looking at a suspicious object in plain view and moving it a few inches trivializes the Fourth Amendment.

DISSENT: (O'Connor, J.) On reasonable suspicion that an object in plain view is contraband, officers ought to be permitted to conduct a cursory inspection, such as was done here. Probable cause should be required in order to conduct a full-blown search.

▶ ANALYSIS

Justice Scalia rejected Justice O'Connor's "cursory inspection" theory, saying that such a vague standard would plunge police and judges into a "new thicket of Fourth Amendment law." He indicated that society's interests in privacy and the consistent administration of justice required a bright-line rule.

Quicknotes

SEIZURE The removal of property from one's possession due to unlawful activity or in satisfaction of a judgment entered by the court.

CONTRABAND Items that are illegal to have in one's possession or to trade or produce.

REASONABLE SUSPICION That which would cause an ordinary prudent person under the circumstances to suspect that a crime has been committed based on specific and articulable facts.

PROBABLE CAUSE A reasonable basis for believing that a crime has been committed.

Horton v. California

Convicted robber (D) v. State (P)

496 U.S. 128 (1990).

NATURE OF CASE: Appeal from conviction of robbery.

FACT SUMMARY: When officers searched Horton's (D) apartment for proceeds of an armed robbery, they seized weapons used in the robbery lying in plain view.

🏛 RULE OF LAW
Inadvertence is not a necessary condition of "plain view" seizures.

FACTS: Walker was accosted by two masked men who threatened him with weapons and robbed him. Walker identified Horton's (D) voice as that of one of the robbers. A search warrant was issued authorizing a search for the proceeds of the robbery, but not for the weapons allegedly used in the commission of the robbery. While searching Horton's (D) apartment, the police found the weapons in question in plain view and seized them. The trial court refused to suppress the evidence found in Horton's (D) home, and he was convicted of armed robbery. The California Court of Appeal affirmed, rejecting Horton's (D) argument that suppression of the evidence that had not been listed in the warrant was required because its discovery was not inadvertent. The California Supreme Court affirmed. The U.S. Supreme Court granted certiorari.

ISSUE: Is inadvertence a necessary condition of "plain view" seizures?

HOLDING AND DECISION: (Stevens, J.) No. Inadvertence is not a necessary condition of "plain view" seizures. Evenhanded law enforcement is best achieved by application of objective standards of conduct, rather than standards that depend upon the subjective state of mind of the officer. The fact that an officer is interested in an item of evidence and expects to find it in the course of a search should not invalidate its seizure if the search is confined in area and duration by the terms of the warrant or a valid exception to the warrant requirement. The suggestion that the inadvertence requirement is necessary to prevent the police from conducting general searches is not persuasive because that interest is already served by the requirements that no warrant issue unless it particularly describes the place to be searched and the persons or things to be seized. Here, the scope of the search was not enlarged in the slightest by the omission of any reference to the weapons in the warrant. Affirmed.

▶ ANALYSIS

In *Arizona v. Hicks*, 480 U.S. 321 (1987), police, during the execution of a search, moved stereo equipment that they suspected (but lacked probable cause to believe) was stolen in order to gain access to the serial numbers on the back of the equipment. The Supreme Court rejected the argument that the plain view doctrine authorized police to move the stereo equipment. It found that if an object is unrelated to the justification for the search and if police do not have probable cause to seize the object, they cannot use the plain view doctrine as an excuse for meddling with the object.

Quicknotes

PLAIN VIEW Exception to the requirement of a valid warrant for a search or seizure so long as the officer is lawfully in the location where the evidence is obtained and it is apparent that the thing seized is evidence.

EXIGENT CIRCUMSTANCES Circumstances requiring an extraordinary or immediate response; an exception to the prohibition on a warrantless arrest or search when police officers believe probable cause to exist and there is no time for obtaining a warrant.

AFFIDAVIT A declaration of facts written and affirmed before a witness.

California v. Acevedo

State (P) v. Convicted drug possessor (D)

500 U.S. 565 (1991).

NATURE OF CASE: Review of denial of motion to suppress evidence in a narcotics prosecution.

FACT SUMMARY: Police searched a container in Acevedo's (D) vehicle, despite a lack of probable cause to search the whole vehicle.

 RULE OF LAW
Police do not need probable cause to search an entire vehicle to search a container found therein.

FACTS: Police "staked out" the apartment of an individual known to have recently imported marijuana. Acevedo (D) was seen to enter this apartment and leave carrying a brown paper bag that appeared full. The police stopped his vehicle, opened his bag, and found marijuana. Acevedo (D) was prosecuted for possession. His motion to suppress was denied, and he pled guilty. On appeal, the California Court of Appeal held that the evidence should have been suppressed as the fruit of an illegal search. The California Supreme Court declined review. The State (P) appealed and the Supreme Court granted certiorari.

ISSUE: Do police need probable cause to search an entire vehicle to search a container found therein?

HOLDING AND DECISION: (Blackmun, J.) No. Police do not need probable cause to search an entire vehicle to search a container found therein. This Court has held that police, if probable cause exists to search a vehicle, may search a closed container therein. However, the Court has also held that search of a container found requires a warrant, even if found in a vehicle. This distinction was based on the notion that a container carries a high expectation of privacy. In practice, however, numerous flaws in these rules have become evident. The line between probable cause to search a vehicle and probable cause to search only a container therein is fuzzy at best and has presented continuing confusion in law enforcement. Waste of law enforcement manpower has resulted, as police often elect to search an entire vehicle when they know or suspect that contraband is only in one container therein. Consequently, the legal dichotomy formulated by this Court has led to police being required to conduct a more intrusive search to justify a less intrusive one. Finally, the rule against opening containers not part of a general vehicle search in reality provides no significant protection of privacy, as police can impound the container and obtain a warrant. In view of these considerations, the better rule, adopted here, is that

officers may search an auto and any containers therein when they have probable cause to believe contraband is contained anywhere therein. Here, the police had probable cause to believe marijuana was in the paper bag, so the warrantless search was valid. Reversed.

CONCURRENCE: (Scalia, J.) The warrantless search of a closed container, outside a privately owned building, is reasonable under the Fourth Amendment as long as there is probable cause.

DISSENT: (Stevens, J.) When authorities have probable cause to believe that a closed container conceals incriminating materials, and this container is placed in an automobile, they may seize, but not search, this container until a warrant has been issued.

ANALYSIS

Most searches require a warrant; for the most part, warrantless searches are per se invalid. Autos and movable containers are the exception to the rule because of their movability. The Supreme Court has been trying for many years to define the limits of warrantless searches in this area, the present case being such an effort.

Quicknotes

PROBABLE CAUSE A reasonable basis for believing that a crime has been committed.

Wyoming v. Houghton

State (P) v. Criminal defendant (D)

526 U.S. 295 (1999).

NATURE OF CASE: Review of reversal of criminal conviction for felony drug possession.

FACT SUMMARY: Houghton (D) alleged that her Fourth Amendment rights had been violated when police searched her purse, which they found inside a car in which she had been a passenger.

🏛 RULE OF LAW
Police officers with probable cause to search a car may inspect passengers' belongings found in the car that are capable of concealing the object of the search.

FACTS: A Wyoming police officer stopped a car for speeding and discovered that the driver of the car had a syringe in his pocket that he admitted he used for drugs. The officer then searched the passenger compartment of the car for contraband. On the back seat, he found a purse that belonged to Houghton (D), the driver's girlfriend, who was a passenger in the car. Drug paraphernalia and methamphetamine were found in the purse, and fresh needle-track marks were found on Houghton's (D) arms. Houghton (D) was placed under arrest, and she was charged with felony possession of methamphetamine. After a hearing, the trial court denied her motion to suppress all evidence from the purse as obtained in violation of the Fourth and Fourteenth Amendments. She was convicted and appealed. The Wyoming Supreme Court reversed, holding that the search of Houghton's (D) purse violated the Fourth and Fourteenth Amendments because the officer knew or should have known that the purse did not belong to the driver, but to one of the passengers, and because there was no probable cause to search the passengers' personal effects and no reason to believe that contraband had been placed within the purse. The State (P) appealed, and the Supreme Court granted certiorari.

ISSUE: May police officers with probable cause to search a car inspect passengers' belongings found in the car that are capable of concealing the object of the search?

HOLDING AND DECISION: (Scalia, J.) Yes. Police officers with probable cause to search a car may inspect passengers' belongings found in the car that are capable of concealing the object of the search. If probable cause justifies the search of a lawfully stopped vehicle, it justifies the search of every part of the vehicle and its contents that may conceal the object of its search. It is uncontested in the present case that the police officers had probable cause to believe there were illegal drugs in the car. Even if the historical evidence were thought to be equivocal, the balancing of the relative interests weighs decidedly in favor of allowing searches of a passengers' belongings. In balancing the competing interests to determine reasonableness under the Fourth Amendment, the practical realities militate in favor of the needs of law enforcement and against a personal-privacy interest that is ordinarily weak. Reversed.

DISSENT: (Stevens, J.) In all prior cases that apply the automobile exception to the Fourth Amendment's warrant requirement, either the defendant was the operator of the vehicle and in custody of the object of the search, or no question was raised as to the defendant's ownership or custody. In this case, instead of adhering to the settled distinction between drivers and passengers, the court fashions a new rule that is based on a distinction between property contained in clothing worn by a passenger and property contained in a passenger's briefcase or purse. Instead of applying ordinary Fourth Amendment principles to this case, the majority extends the automobile warrant exception to allow searches of passenger belongings based on the driver's misconduct.

▶ ANALYSIS

The Fourth Amendment protects the right of the people to be secure in their persons, houses, papers, and effects, against unreasonable searches and seizures. In determining whether a particular governmental action violates this provision, the majority inquired first as to whether the action was regarded as an unlawful search or seizure under the common law when the Amendment was framed. Where that inquiry yields no answer, the search or seizure must be evaluated under traditional standards of reasonableness.

━━■

Quicknotes

FOURTH AMENDMENT Provides that persons be secure as to their person and private belongings against unreasonable searches and seizures.

PLAIN VIEW Exception to the requirement of a valid warrant for a search or seizure so long as the officer is lawfully in the location where the evidence is obtained and it is apparent that the object seized is evidence.

PROBABLE CAUSE A reasonable basis for believing that a crime has been committed.

━━■

Atwater v. City of Lago Vista

Driver (P) v. City (D)

532 U.S. 318 (2001).

NATURE OF CASE: Appeal from grant of summary judgment in civil rights claim stemming from arrest for misdemeanor traffic violation.

FACT SUMMARY: Atwater (P) claimed that her arrest for a misdemeanor seatbelt violation violated her Fourth Amendment rights against warrantless searches and seizures.

🏛 RULE OF LAW
The Fourth Amendment does not forbid a warrantless arrest for a minor criminal offense, such as a misdemeanor seatbelt violation punishable only by a fine.

FACTS: Atwater (P) was driving in a pickup truck with her three-year-old son and five-year-old daughter in the front seat. None of them was wearing a seatbelt. Texas law made it a misdemeanor for a driver, in a car equipped with a seatbelt, not to wear a seatbelt or not to secure any small child riding in the front seat with one. She ultimately pled no contest to the seatbelt charge and paid the fine. She then filed a 42 U.S.C. § 1983 action against the police officer (D), the City of Lago Vista (D), and the chief of police (D), alleging her Fourth Amendment rights were violated. The district court granted summary judgment for the City of Lago Vista (D), concluding the claim was meritless. A panel of the court of appeals reversed, but the court en banc vacated the previous decision and affirmed the summary judgment.

ISSUE: Does the Fourth Amendment forbid a warrantless arrest for a minor criminal offense, such as a misdemeanor seatbelt violation punishable only by a fine?

HOLDING AND DECISION: (Souter, J.) No. The Fourth Amendment does not forbid a warrantless arrest for a minor criminal offense, such as a misdemeanor seatbelt violation punishable only by a fine. We confirm what prior cases have suggested, that probable cause applies to all arrests. There is no need to apply a balancing test of interests involved in the particular situation. If an official has probable cause to believe that an individual has committed even a very minor criminal offense in his presence he may arrest the offender without violating the Fourth Amendment. Affirmed.

DISSENT: (O'Connor, J.) The Court's position is inconsistent with the Fourth Amendment's guarantees. A custodial arrest, such as the one here, is a seizure. When it is affected without a warrant, the Fourth Amendment requires such search to be reasonable. The record here shows that Atwater's (P) arrest was unreasonable. The police officer (D) was not justified by law or reason in his decision to arrest Atwater (P) rather than to give her a citation, and severely infringed Atwater's (P) liberty and privacy interests.

▶ ANALYSIS

Atwater (P) argued that common law principles prohibited police officers from making warrantless misdemeanor arrests except in cases of "breach of the peace," a narrow category only including nonfelony offenses "involving or tending toward violence." The Court rejects this argument stating that neither the legislative history of the Fourth Amendment nor subsequent decisions supported this position.

■■■■

Quicknotes

COMMON LAW A body of law developed through the judicial decisions of the courts as opposed to the legislative process.

FOURTH AMENDMENT property from one's possession due to unlawful activity or in satisfaction of a judgment entered by the court.

MISDEMEANOR Any offense that does not constitute a felony, which is generally less severe and for which a lesser punishment is imposed.

WARRANT An order issued by a court directing an officer to undertake a certain act (e.g., arrest or search).

■■■■

Chimel v. California

Convicted burglar (D) v. State (P)

395 U.S. 752 (1969).

NATURE OF CASE: Appeal from a burglary conviction.

FACT SUMMARY: California (P) contended it could search Chimel's (D) entire premises pursuant to his lawful arrest there.

⚖ RULE OF LAW
A search incident to a lawful arrest is limited to the suspect's person and the area within which he could reach for a weapon or evidence.

FACTS: Chimel (D) was arrested in the living room of his home on a burglary charge. The police, without a warrant, searched the entire premises and finally found the evidence of the burglary in the master bedroom. They justified the search as pursuant to the lawful arrest. Chimel (D) moved to suppress on the basis the search was constitutionally limited to his area of control. The motion was denied and the California Supreme Court upheld the conviction. The U. S. Supreme Court granted certiorari.

ISSUE: Is a search conducted incident to a lawful arrest limited to the suspect's person and the area within which he can reach for a weapon or destroy evidence?

HOLDING AND DECISION: (Stewart, J.) Yes. A search incident to a lawful arrest is limited to the person and the area within which he could grab a weapon or destroy evidence. The search is to allow the officer to protect himself and preserve evidence. It does not extend to extremities of the premises where the suspect could never obtain a weapon or destroy evidence. Thus the search of the bedroom was not lawful without a warrant or consent and the evidence should have been suppressed. Reversed.

DISSENT: (White, J.) When there is probable cause to search and there are exigent circumstances making it "impracticable" to obtain a search warrant, a warrantless search is reasonable under the Fourth Amendment. Such an exigent circumstance is supplied by the fact of an arrest. Almost always, there is a strong possibility that if officers leave the scene of the arrest to obtain a warrant, confederates of the arrestee will remove that evidence for which the officers had probable cause to search. It is, therefore, unreasonable, assuming that there is probable cause to search the premises where a person is lawfully arrested, to require the police to obtain a search warrant.

▶ ANALYSIS

Some commentators, including Mr. Justice White, have criticized the holding in this case on the basis it does not meet with the requirements of reality. The officers in this case should have obtained a search warrant under this holding, yet to have done so would have allowed the defendant or accomplices to remove or destroy the evidence.

Quicknotes

CERTIORARI A discretionary writ issued by a superior court to an inferior court in order to review the lower court's decisions; the Supreme Court's writ ordering such review.

FOURTH AMENDMENT Provides that persons be secure as to their person and private belongings against unreasonable searches and seizures.

WARRANT An order issued by a court directing an officer to undertake a certain act (e.g., arrest or search).

Thornton v. United States

Drug and firearms defendant (P) v. Federal government (D)

124 S.Ct. 2127 (2004).

NATURE OF CASE: Appeal from denial of a motion to suppress evidence.

FACT SUMMARY: When a police officer, after lawfully arresting Marcus Thornton (D) who had just alighted from his vehicle, searched the interior of the vehicle and found incriminating evidence, Thornton (D) contended that, under *New York v. Belton*, it is only when an officer makes a lawful custodial arrest of an "occupant" of a vehicle that the Fourth Amendment allows a search of the vehicle's interior.

RULE OF LAW
So long as an arrestee is a recent occupant of a vehicle, officers may search that vehicle incident to the arrest.

FACTS: A suspicious police officer observed Marcus Thornton (D) drive his vehicle into a parking lot and exit the vehicle. The officer accosted Thornton (D) and informed him his license tags did not match the vehicle he was driving. Thornton (D) agreed to a pat down; the officer found drugs, placed Thornton (D) under arrest, and searched the interior of the vehicle where he found a handgun under the driver's seat. The district court denied Thornton's (D) motion to suppress evidence of the gun. Thornton (D) was convicted of drug and gun charges. The court of appeals affirmed, and Thornton (D) appealed.

ISSUE: So long as an arrestee is a recent occupant of a vehicle, may officers search that vehicle incident to the arrest?

HOLDING AND DECISION: (Rehnquist, C.J.) Yes. So long as an arrestee is a recent occupant of a vehicle, officers may search that vehicle incident to the arrest. In *New York v. Belton*, 453 U.S. 454 (1981), this Court held that when an officer makes a lawful custodial arrest of an occupant of an automobile, the Fourth Amendment allows a search of the passenger compartment. Today we hold that *Belton* governs even when an officer does not make the vehicle search until the person has left the vehicle. In all relevant aspects, the arrest of a suspect who is next to a vehicle presents identical concerns regarding officer safety and the destruction of evidence as the arrest of one who is inside the vehicle. An officer may search a suspect's vehicle under *Belton* only if the suspect is arrested. A custodial arrest is fluid and the danger to the police officer flows from the fact of the arrest, and its attendant proximity, stress, and uncertainty. The stress is no less merely because the arrestee exited his or her car before the officer initiated contact, nor is an arrestee less likely to attempt to lunge for a weapon or to destroy evidence if he or she is outside of, but still in control of, the vehicle. In either case, the officer faces a highly volatile situation. It would make little sense to apply two different rules to what is, at bottom, the same situation. Furthermore, in some circumstances it may be safer and more effective for officers to conceal their presence from a suspect until he or she has left the vehicle; certainly that is a judgment officers should be free to make without jeopardizing their ability to maintain their own safety or to prevent evidence destruction. Affirmed.

CONCURRENCE: (O'Connor, J.) Lower court decisions seem now to treat the ability to search a vehicle incident to the arrest of a recent occupant as a police entitlement rather than as an exception justified by the rationales of *Chimel v. California*, 395 U.S. 752 (1969).

CONCURRENCE: (Scalia, J.) If *Belton* searches are justifiable, it is not because the arrestee might grab a weapon or evidentiary item from the car, but simply because the car might contain evidence relevant to the crime for which he was arrested. Here, Thornton (D) was lawfully arrested for a drug offense, and it was reasonable for the officer to believe that further contraband might be found in the vehicle from which he had just alighted and which was still in the vicinity at the time of the arrest. I would affirm on that ground.

DISSENT: (Stevens, J.) The only genuine justification for extending *Belton* to cover search of a vehicle after the arrestee has exited, is the interest in uncovering potentially valuable evidence. Such a goal must give way to the citizen's constitutionally protected interest in privacy when there is already in place a well-defined rule limiting the permissible scope of a search of an arrested pedestrian.

ANALYSIS

Not all contraband in the passenger compartment or other interior part of a vehicle is likely to be readily accessible to a recent occupant. However, in *Thornton*, the firearm and the passenger compartment in general were no more inaccessible than were the contraband and the passenger compartment in *Belton*. The need for a clear rule, readily understood by police officers and not depending on differing estimates of what items were or were not within reach of an arrestee at any particular moment, justifies the sort of generalization which *Belton* enunciated.

Knowles v. Iowa

Convicted drug dealer (D) v. State (P)

525 U.S. 113 (1998).

NATURE OF CASE: Review of a state supreme court decision affirming denial of motion to suppress evidence.

FACT SUMMARY: Knowles (D) moved to suppress evidence gathered when he was stopped by an Iowa police officer (P) who issued a citation and conducted a full search of the car.

🏛 RULE OF LAW
Officers may not conduct a full search of a car and driver when the police elect to issue a citation instead of making a custodial arrest.

FACTS: Knowles (D) was stopped by an Iowa police officer for speeding. The officer issued a citation and then conducted a full search of the car. Under Iowa law, officers may issue citations in lieu of arrest, and this does not affect their authority to conduct an otherwise lawful search. When a bag of marijuana and a pot pipe were found under the driver's seat, Knowles (D) was arrested and charged with state drug law violations. At trial, Knowles (D) moved to suppress the evidence, arguing that the search could not be sustained under the search incident to arrest exception, since he had not been under arrest. The trial court denied the motion to suppress and found Knowles (D) guilty. The Supreme Court of Iowa affirmed by a divided vote. The U.S. Supreme Court granted certiorari.

ISSUE: May officers conduct a full search of a car and driver when the police elect to issue a citation instead of making a custodial arrest?

HOLDING AND DECISION: (Rehnquist, C.J.) No. Officers may not conduct a full search of a car and driver when the police elect to issue a citation instead of making a custodial arrest. The two historical rationales for the search incident to arrest exception are the need to disarm the suspect in order to take him into custody and the need to preserve evidence for later use at trial. The threat to officer safety from issuing a traffic citation is a good deal less than in the case of a custodial arrest. Once Knowles (D) was stopped for speeding and issued a citation, no further evidence was necessary to prosecute that offense, so there was no need to discover or preserve any evidence. Since the police officer had neither Knowles's (D) consent nor probable cause to conduct the search, and the requirements for a search incident to arrest were not met, the search was not justified. Reversed and remanded.

▌ ANALYSIS

The court in this case reversed the Iowa Supreme Court's interpretation of Iowa law. The state code had been interpreted to permit a search incident to citation. The bright-line rule from *United States v. Robinson*, 414 U.S. 218 (1973), permitting a full field search as incident to an arrest, was not expanded to include incidents where no custodial arrest had been made.

■═■

Quicknotes

FOURTH AMENDMENT Provides that persons be secure as to their person and private belongings against unreasonable searches and seizures.

PROBABLE CAUSE A reasonable basis for believing that a crime has been committed.

TERRY STOP A search of a person suspected of intending to commit a crime that is conducted by patting down the clothes of the person; the search must be limited to the reason for which the individual was lawfully stopped.

■═■

Terry v. Ohio

Criminal defendant (D) v. State (P)

392 U.S. 1 (1968).

NATURE OF CASE: Review of order denying motion to suppress in prosecution for carrying concealed weapons.

FACT SUMMARY: Terry (D), who was frisked by a police officer, contended that such a procedure could not have been performed absent probable cause to arrest.

🏛 RULE OF LAW
Police may stop and frisk an individual who they reasonably suspect may be armed and dangerous, even if probable cause to arrest is not present.

FACTS: McFadden, a police detective of 35 years' experience, was patrolling his beat on foot when he observed Terry (D) and another man repeatedly strolling by a store, looking in, and then walking away. This continued for over 10 minutes. McFadden formed the opinion that they were casing the store. He approached them and asked for identification. When their responses proved evasive, McFadden spun Terry (D) against a wall. Frisking him, he found a gun. Terry (D) was charged with carrying a concealed weapon. His motion to suppress was denied, and the state supreme court affirmed. The U.S. Supreme Court granted review.

ISSUE: May police stop and frisk an individual whom they reasonably suspect may be armed and dangerous, even if probable cause to arrest is not present?

HOLDING AND DECISION: (Warren, C.J.) Yes. Police may stop and frisk an individual whom they reasonably suspect may be armed and dangerous, even if probable cause to arrest is not present. Competing values are at issue here. On the one hand, the rapidly increasing dangerousness on city streets has created the need for flexible responses on the part of law enforcement. On the other hand, the authority of the police to search a person must be limited to situations when probable cause is present for the Fourth Amendment to have any meaning. Superimposed on this analysis is the limited ability of the judiciary to control day-to-day situations on city streets. The exclusionary rule can only go so far in controlling police conduct. When it cannot do so, its reasons for existence cease. The point of departure for analysis is that the Fourth Amendment's reasonableness requirement remains central. The reasonableness of a stop and frisk depends upon weighing the governmental interest in police and bystander security against a possibly armed criminal and every citizen's interest against police interference. This Court believes that a proper balance between these interests is struck by a rule allowing the minimally intrusive stop and frisk for weapons when an officer suspects, on an objectively reasonable level, that a person may be armed and dangerous. Here, Terry's (D) conduct was sufficiently suggestive of an intent to rob that McFadden's belief in this regard was reasonable. The stop, therefore, did not constitute a Fourth Amendment violation. Affirmed.

CONCURRENCE: (Harlan, J.) Once circumstances justify a confrontation with a citizen, the right to frisk naturally flows therefrom.

CONCURRENCE: (White, J.) A person cannot be compelled to cooperate if addressed by an officer, and such refusal cannot in itself furnish a basis for arrest.

DISSENT: (Douglas, J.) Nothing less than probable cause can justify forcible detention of an individual.

▶ ANALYSIS

The exclusionary rule is found nowhere in the Constitution. It was created by the Court as a prophylactic measure to advance the rights found in the Fourth Amendment. In the present case, the Court reasoned that when the rule could no longer serve its prophylactic purpose, which it believed to be the case here, it should not be imposed.

Quicknotes

FOURTH AMENDMENT Provides that persons be secure as to their person and private belongings against unreasonable searches and seizures.

TERRY STOP A search of a person suspected of intending to commit a crime that is conducted by patting down the clothes of the person; the search must be limited to the reason for which the individual was lawfully stopped.

Florida v. J.L.

State (P) v. Criminal defendant (D)

529 U.S. 266 (2000).

NATURE OF CASE: Appeal from conviction for carrying a concealed firearm.

FACT SUMMARY: J.L. (D) was searched and convicted for carrying a concealed weapon on the basis of an anonymous tip that he would be standing in a particular location carrying the weapon.

> **RULE OF LAW**
> An anonymous tip that a person is carrying a gun is not sufficient to justify a police officer's stop and frisk of that person.

FACTS: An anonymous caller reported to Miami-Dade Police that a young black male standing at a particular bus stop and wearing a plaid shirt was carrying a gun. Two officers were instructed to respond. They approached J.L. (D), frisked him, and seized a gun from his pocket. J.L. (D) was charged with carrying a concealed firearm without a license and with possessing a firearm while under the age of 18. He moved to suppress the gun as the fruit of an unlawful search and the trial court granted the motion. The Florida Supreme Court affirmed.

ISSUE: Is an anonymous tip that a person is carrying a gun sufficient to justify a police officer's stop and frisk of that person?

HOLDING AND DECISION: (Ginsburg, J.) No. An anonymous tip that a person is carrying a gun is not sufficient to justify a police officer's stop and frisk of that person. The Florida Supreme Court stated that tips may form the basis for reasonable suspicion only if accompanied by specific indicia of reliability. Here the tip lacked the moderate indicia of reliability. The anonymous call provided no predictive information and left the police without any means of testing the informant's knowledge or credibility. That the allegation proved to be true does not prove that the officers had a reasonable basis for suspecting that J.L. (D) was engaging in unlawful conduct. The reasonableness of official suspicion must be measured by what the officers knew before commencing the search. Florida (P) argued the tip was reliable since it described the suspect's visible attributes accurately. While an accurate description of a subject's readily observable location and appearance is reliable in helping the police to identify the person the tipster means to accuse, it does not show that the tipster had knowledge of concealed criminal activity. Florida (P) also argued that there should be a "firearm exception" to

the standard Terry analysis. The court declines to accept this proposition. Affirmed.

> ▶ **ANALYSIS**
>
> Terry's rule allows police searches on the basis of reasonable suspicion rather than demanding that officers meet the higher standard of probable cause.

■══■

Quicknotes

TERRY STOP A search of a person suspected of intending to commit a crime that is conducted by patting down the clothes of the person; the search must be limited to the reason for which the individual was lawfully stopped.

■══■

Illinois v. Wardlow

State (P) v. Convicted felon (D)

528 U.S. 119 (2000).

NATURE OF CASE: Appeal from conviction for unlawful use of a weapon by a felon.

FACT SUMMARY: Wardlow (D) sought to suppress introduction of a .38-caliber handgun at trial on the basis that the gun was recovered during an unlawful stop and frisk.

🏛 RULE OF LAW
Flight from police is sufficient to support a finding of reasonable suspicion and to justify a police officer's further investigation.

FACTS: Officers Nolan and Harvey were working as uniformed officers in the specials operations section of the Chicago Police Department. They observed Wardlow (D) standing next to a building holding an opaque bag. When he saw the officers, he fled. The officers eventually cornered him and conducted a pat-down search for weapons. During the frisk, Nolan felt a hard object and opened the bag to discover a .38-caliber handgun with five live rounds of ammunition. The officers arrested Wardlow (D). The trial court denied Wardlow's (D) motion to suppress, concluding the gun was recovered during a lawful stop and frisk, and convicted Wardlow (D) of unlawful use of a weapon by a felon. The appellate court reversed on the basis that Nolan did not have reasonable suspicion sufficient to justify an investigative stop under *Terry v. Ohio*. The Illinois Supreme Court agreed and the U.S. Supreme Court granted review.

ISSUE: Is flight from police sufficient to support a finding of reasonable suspicion justifying a police officer in further investigation?

HOLDING AND DECISION: (Rehnquist, C.J.) Yes. Flight from police is sufficient to support a finding of reasonable suspicion justifying a police officer in further investigation. This case is governed by this Court's analysis in *Terry*. Nolan and Harvey were among eight other officers in a four-car caravan converging on an area known for drug trafficking. While an individual's presence in an area of expected criminal activity is not sufficient, without more, to support a reasonable, particularized suspicion that the person is committing a crime, the officers may take into consideration the relevant characteristics of a location in determining whether the circumstances are sufficiently suspicious to warrant further investigation. Moreover, nervous, evasive behavior is another pertinent factor in determining reasonable suspicion, such as

Wardlow's (D) unprovoked flight upon seeing the police. Thus Nolan was justified in suspecting Wardlow (D) was involved in criminal activity and in investigating further. Reversed.

CONCURRENCE AND DISSENT IN PART: (Stevens, J.) The state (P) asks the Court to announce a per se rule authorizing the temporary detention of anyone who flees at the mere sight of a police officer, while Wardlow (D) asks the Court to adopt the opposite per se rule—that the fact that a person flees upon seeing the police can never justify a temporary investigative stop. While I agree with the Court's rejection of both per se rules, the testimony of the officer who seized Wardlow (D) does not support the conclusion that he had reasonable suspicion to make the stop.

▶ ANALYSIS

Compare the result in this case with that in *Florida v. J.L.*, 529 U.S. 266 (2000). There the police responded to an anonymous call that a young black male would be at a particular location, wearing particular clothing and carrying a gun. While nothing in the youth's behavior aroused suspicion, the police officer frisked him and discovered a gun. The Court held that an "anonymous tip" was insufficient to establish reasonable suspicion justifying the police to make an investigatory stop.

■—■

Quicknotes

REASONABLE SUSPICION That which would cause an ordinary prudent person under the circumstances to suspect that a crime has been committed based on specific and articulable facts.

TERRY STOP A search of a person suspected of intending to commit a crime that is conducted by patting down the clothes of the person; the search must be limited to the reason for which the individual was lawfully stopped.

■—■

Whren v. United States

Criminal defendant (D) v. Federal government (P)

517 U.S. 806 (1996).

NATURE OF CASE: Appeal challenging admissibility of drugs seized during traffice stop.

FACT SUMMARY: Whren (D) challenged the constitutionality of a police search of his car, wherein narcotics were found, when the police stopped him for a traffic violation.

🏛 RULE OF LAW
The temporary detention of a motorist who the police have probable cause to believe has committed a civil traffic violation is consistent with the Fourth Amendment.

FACTS: On June 10, 1993, plainclothes vice-squad officers patrolled a "high drug area" of Washington, D.C. The police saw Whren (D) sitting at a stop sign in a truck for an unusually long time. When the police approached, Whren (D) turned right without signaling and sped off at an "unreasonable" speed. When the police stopped Whren (D), they looked in the car and saw bags of crack cocaine. When Whren (D) was arrested on narcotics charges, he challenged the legality of the stop, stating the police had no probable cause to search the car. Whren (D) claimed the police's reasons for the stop—traffic violations—were pretextual and that in this circumstance, a more strict, "objective officer" rule should govern whether the search was legal. The district court convicted Whren (D) of the narcotics charges and the appellate court affirmed. Whren (D) appealed.

ISSUE: Is the temporary detention of a motorist who the police have probable cause to believe has committed a civil traffic violation inconsistent with the Fourth Amendment's prohibition against unreasonable seizures?

HOLDING AND DECISION: (Scalia, J.) No. The temporary detention of a motorist who the police have probable cause to believe has committed a civil traffic violation is not inconsistent with the Fourth Amendment. Here, Whren (D) had violated traffic laws and, as such, the police had the right to stop him to give him a citation. The fact that such violations occur routinely does not warrant a different standard as to whether the search was constitutional. Even though the police were plainclothes officers, they still had the right to stop a motorist who violates traffic laws. An officer's motive does not automatically invalidate objectively justifiable behavior under the Fourth Amendment. Intentional discrimination in the application of a law is a Fifth Amendment equal protec-

tion question, not a Fourth Amendment search and seizure question, and does not apply to the case at hand. Searches are subject to a reasonableness standard, but when probable cause has existed, balancing tests have been applied only where the search and seizure has been extraordinary. Here, the traffic violation warranted the probable cause, and the police properly seized the narcotics in plain view. Affirmed.

▎ANALYSIS

This case highlights certain Fourth Amendment search and seizure issues in the context of automobiles. While the Fourth Amendment usually requires police to obtain search warrants before conducting a search, the easy mobility of automobiles often permits searches without warrants if the police have probable cause to search the vehicle. Occasions where warrantless searches have been allowed involved searches incident to arrest and searches to prevent the loss of evidence. See *Application of Kiser*, 419 F.2d 1134 (8th Cir. 1969); *Carroll v. U.S.*, 267 U.S. 132 (1925).

■▬■

Quicknotes

PROBABLE CAUSE A reasonable basis for believing that a crime has been committed.

AUTOMOBILE STOP A police officer may stop an automobile and conduct a search of the vehicle without a valid warrant if he has probable cause to believe the vehicle contains evidence of a crime or contraband.

■▬■

Chicago v. Morales

City (P) v. Loitering-ordinance challenger (D)

527 U.S. 41 (1999).

NATURE OF CASE: Supreme Court review of state court ruling on constitutionality of city ordinance.

FACT SUMMARY: City (P) appealed after Morales (D) successfully challenged an anti-gang ordinance passed by the City of Chicago (P) on the basis that the wording of the statute defining "loitering" was so vague as to make the statute unconstitutional.

🏛 RULE OF LAW
A statute providing penalties for criminal conduct is unconstitutionally vague if it fails to give sufficient notice regarding the type of conduct prohibited.

FACTS: Morales (D) and others were accused as "criminal street gang members" under a new ordinance passed by the City of Chicago (P) prohibiting persons from "loitering" with one another in public places. A city (P) commission solicited witness testimony and made a series of findings suggesting that an increase in street activity was a primary cause of the escalation in violent and drug-related crimes and that a common function of loitering was to enable a street gang to establish control over particular areas. In addition, the commission discovered that loitering by street gang members in public places intimidated law-abiding citizens and limited access to these areas by creating a "justifiable fear for the safety of persons and property" in the areas where loitering took place. In response, the City (P) passed the Gang Congregation Ordinance, which created a criminal offense punishable by a fine of up to $500, as well as imprisonment and community service, for "loitering" by suspected street gang members in public places. The statute defined four elements of the crime of "loitering": first, a police officer must reasonably believe that at least two or more persons present in a public place are gang members; second, these persons must be "loitering" by remaining in one place with no apparent purpose; third, the officer must order these persons to disperse; and finally, the order to disperse must be disobeyed by the suspected gang members. Morales (D) challenged the ordinance on the basis that it broadly covered a significant amount of additional activity beyond what should be interpreted as "loitering" and was therefore unconstitutionally vague. The state supreme court concluded the ordinance was unconstitutionally vague because it did not provide specific limits on the discretion of police officers to determine what conduct constituted "loitering", and the city (P) filed for review of that determination.

ISSUE: Is a statute which provides penalties for criminal conduct unconstitutionally vague if it fails to give sufficient notice regarding the type of conduct prohibited?

HOLDING AND DECISION: (Stevens, J.) Yes. A statute providing penalties for criminal conduct is unconstitutionally vague if it fails to give sufficient notice regarding the type of conduct prohibited. Clearly, a law directly prohibiting intimidating conduct similar to that described by the city commission is constitutional on its face. However, such a law may still be found unconstitutionally vague for two reasons: first, the law fails to provide the type of notice that permits ordinary persons to understand the conduct prohibited; and second, the wording of the law encourages arbitrary and discriminatory enforcement. Citizens should not have to speculate as to the meaning of a law. The requirement of notice is not met here because the order to disperse takes places before an officer knows whether the prohibited conduct has occurred, and is therefore an unjustifiable impairment of liberty if the loiterer is harmless and innocent. In addition, the statute establishes only minimal guidelines for law enforcement to follow. Police officers may exercise absolute discretion when assessing a group of bystanders for dispersal. The City (P) asserts that the statute provides limitations on a police officer's discretion because it does not permit a dispersal order to issue if a person has an apparent purpose or until the officer reasonably believes that "loitering" is taking place. However, these limitations are insufficient because they do not directly address the degree of discretion an officer may exercise. The ability to assess a "loitering" situation is only subjectively limited by the officer's own evaluation of the circumstances. The Illinois Supreme Court's ruling that the statute in question is unconstitutional was correctly concluded, and is therefore affirmed.

CONCURRENCE: (O'Connor, J.) The ordinance is unconstitutionally vague, and that is a sufficient ground to affirm. There is no need to consider the other issues briefed by the parties. Furthermore, the majority's holding has a narrow scope and Chicago (P) has reasonable alternatives, including other laws on the books, to combat gang violence.

CONCURRENCE: (Kennedy, J.) The ordinance would reach a broad range of innocent conduct and, therefore, it is

Continued on next page.

not saved by the requirement that the citizen must first disobey a police order to disperse before there is a violation. Although some police commands will subject a citizen to prosecution for disobeying whether or not the citizen knows why the order is given, it does not follow that any unexplained police order must be obeyed without notice of the lawfulness of the order.

CONCURRENCE: (Breyer, J.) The ordinance is unconstitutional because nongang members are subject to the ordinance and the range of conduct that the police may prohibit is unlimited. Moreover, a police officer is delegated the authority to determine what constitutes an apparent purpose and what does not. The officer is thus given too much discretion, in every case, to decide whom to order to move on and in what circumstances.

DISSENT: (Scalia, J.) The majority has erroneously transposed the burden of proof by requiring the plaintiffs to show that the ordinance is valid in all its applications when they should have required the defendants to show that it is invalid in all is applications. Furthermore, the ordinance is not vague because the ordinance subjects an individual to a criminal penalty for refusing to obey a dispersal order after there has been adequate notice that the conduct is prohibited. In this case, the offenders knew that they could be arrested for failing to obey a dispersal order because an officer had told them to disperse from loitering. When she returned later, they still had not dispersed and were thus arrested for violating her order. In addition, contrary to the majority's opinion, there is no constitutionally protected right for a person to remain in a public place of his choice. It was not considered an essential attribute of liberty at the time of the framing of the Constitution or the adoption of the Fourteenth Amendment. The burden to establish that loitering is not a fundamental liberty should not be placed on the plaintiff. Moreover, a police officer should be able to issue an order without necessarily having precise standards for that order; otherwise no urban society would be able to function. Furthermore, enforcement of the law is not arbitrary or discriminatory because the criteria for issuing a dispersal order has sufficient specificity. To issue such an order, criteria resembling probable cause standards must be met and the ordinance requires a person to remain in an area without a reason for being there. Lastly, although there may be other laws on the books, the offenders tend to end their conduct when the police are in sight but return to it once officers have left the area, therefore, the other laws are not sufficient to cure the problem.

DISSENT: (Thomas, J.) Gang activity is a major problem in many areas. Prior to enacting the subject ordinance, the city council held hearings on the problems of gang loitering. Con-

cerned citizens testified regarding the detrimental impact that gangs were having on their lives. The ordinance was enacted in an attempt to cure the ills of loitering gangs. The ordinance does not infringe upon a liberty interest because laws against loitering have been around since the founding of the colonies and have remained in one form or another to the present day. Furthermore, the ordinance does not offer too much discretion to a police officer, but rather enables an officer to fulfill his peace-keeping function. Part of that role is to order people who threaten the public peace to disperse. An officer must apply some discretion while accomplishing this goal and the law cannot constrain his every action. The ordinance provides the appropriate amount of guidance to the officer.

▌*ANALYSIS*

Justice Stevens's opinion suggests that the Gang Congregation Ordinance could have been worded optimally to include conduct that was apparent, such as the effort by gang members to publicize the gang's dominance over a certain area. Use of this phrasing explicitly would have satisfied constitutional concerns of specificity; however, the Court ironically noted that the absence of this descriptive language not only expanded the statute's inclusion of harmless behavior, but excluded those exact circumstances where the statute would have played a critical role in addressing the intended problem.

■■■■

Quicknotes

FOURTEENTH AMENDMENT Declares that no state shall make or enforce any law which shall abridge the privileges and immunities of citizens of the United States.

VAGUENESS AND OVERBREADTH Characteristics of a statute that make it difficult to identify the limits of the conduct being regulated.

■■■■

Indianapolis v. Edmond

City (D) v. Class action plaintiffs (P)

531 U.S. 32 (2000).

NATURE OF CASE: Class action challenging constitutionality of vehicle checkpoints.

FACT SUMMARY: Motorists (P) challenged the constitutional validity of city-imposed vehicle checkpoints as violative of the Fourth Amendment's prohibition against unlawful searches and seizures.

RULE OF LAW
Where a vehicle checkpoint program is designed primarily to uncover evidence of criminal wrongdoing, such program constitutes an unlawful search and seizure in violation of the Fourth Amendment.

FACTS: The City of Indianapolis (D) began to operate vehicle checkpoints in an effort to intercept unlawful drugs. Checkpoint locations were selected weeks in advance, based on certain considerations such as area crime statistics and traffic flow. Edmond (P) and Palmer (P) were each stopped at such a narcotics checkpoint. They filed a lawsuit on behalf of themselves and the class of all motorists who had been stopped or were subject to being stopped in the future at the checkpoints. They claimed the roadblocks violated the Fourth Amendment and the search and seizure provision of the state constitution, and they moved for a preliminary injunction. The district court denied, holding the Fourth Amendment was not violated. The court of appeals reversed, and the U.S. Supreme Court granted certiorari.

ISSUE: When a vehicle checkpoint program is designed primarily to uncover evidence of criminal wrongdoing, does such program constitute an unlawful search and seizure in violation of the Fourth Amendment?

HOLDING AND DECISION: (O'Connor, J.) Yes. When a vehicle checkpoint program is designed primarily to uncover evidence of criminal wrongdoing, such program constitutes an unlawful search and seizure in violation of the Fourth Amendment. Our checkpoint cases have recognized only limited exceptions to the general rule that a seizure must be accompanied by some measure of individualized suspicion. When law enforcement authorities pursue primarily general crime-control purposes at checkpoints such as these, such stops may only be justified because of some measure of individualized suspicion. Because the primary purpose of the program was indistinguishable from its general interest in crime control, the checkpoints violate the Fourth Amendment. Affirmed.

DISSENT: (Rehnquist, C.J.) The program in issue here complies with previous decisions regarding roadblock seizures. It is constitutionally irrelevant that the law enforcement also hoped to intercept narcotics.

DISSENT: (Thomas, J.) Prior decisions compel upholding the program at issue here, although those cases may not have been correctly decided. A program of indiscriminate stops of individuals not suspected of wrongdoing is not consistent with the intent of the Fourth Amendment.

ANALYSIS

The Fourth Amendment requires that searches be "reasonable" in order to be held valid. A search is presumptively unreasonable if there is a lack of probable cause. A special category of searches are excluded from the reasonable requirement where they are required to serve "special needs, beyond the normal need for law enforcement." The Court has upheld such special needs as border control and sobriety checkpoints, while rejecting discretionary, suspicion-less spot checks of drivers' licenses and registrations. The constitutionality of any such program is based on a balancing test between the interests at stake and the program's effectiveness.

Quicknotes

FOURTH AMENDMENT Provides that persons be secure from unreasonable searches and seizures as regards their person and private belongings.

PROBABLE CAUSE A reasonable basis for believing that a crime has been committed.

SEIZURE The removal of property from one's possession due to unlawful activity or in satisfaction of a judgment entered by the court.

Illinois v. Lidster

State (P) v. DUI Convict (D)

540 U.S. 419 (2004).

NATURE OF CASE: Appeal by state from suppression of evidence obtained during a vehicle checkpoint stop.

FACT SUMMARY: When Robert Lidster's (D) minivan was randomly stopped during an information-seeking highway checkpoint stop of vehicles, and Lidster (D) was found to be drunk and convicted of drunk driving, he argued that in the absence of any individualized suspicion of crime, the stop was without reasonable cause and violated the Fourth Amendment.

> ## RULE OF LAW
> Information-seeking highway stops do not per se violate the Fourth Amendment.

FACTS: Late one night an unknown hit-and-run motorist struck and killed a 70-year-old bicyclist. A week later, at the same time of night, the police set up a highway checkpoint designed to attempt to obtain more information about the accident. All cars were stopped for 10 to 15 seconds and the occupants asked whether they had seen anything happen in the area the previous week, and each was handed a flyer about the hit-and-run incident. When Robert Lidster's (D) minivan was stopped, the officer smelled alcohol on his breath, administered a sobriety test, and arrested Lidster (D) for drunk driving. Lidster (D) was convicted of the charge in state trial court, which rejected Lidster's (D) argument that evidence of the crime was obtained through use of a vehicle checkpoint stop which violated the Fourth Amendment. The Illinois intermediate appellate court reached the opposite conclusion, and the Illinois Supreme Court agreed. The state appealed.

ISSUE: Do information-seeking highway stops per se violate the Fourth Amendment?

HOLDING AND DECISION: (Breyer, J.) No. Information-seeking highway stops do not per se violate the Fourth Amendment. Special law enforcement concerns will sometimes justify highway stops without individualized suspicion. Moreover, the context here (seeking information from the public) is one in which, by definition, the concept of individualized suspicion has little role to play. Like certain other forms of police activity, such as crowd control or public safety, an information-seeking stop is not the kind of event that involves suspicion of the relevant individual. Furthermore, information-seeking highway stops are less likely to provoke anxiety or to prove intrusive. The police are not likely to ask questions designed to elicit self-incriminating information.

Citizens will often react positively when police simply ask for their help as responsible citizens to give whatever information they may have to aid in law enforcement. Further, the law ordinarily permits police to seek the voluntary cooperation of members of the public in the investigation of a crime. While the importance of soliciting the public's assistance is offset to some degree by the need to stop a motorist to obtain that help, such difference is not, however, important enough to justify an individualized-suspicion rule. Finally, an individualized-suspicion rule is not needed to prevent an unreasonable proliferation of police checkpoints. Practical considerations, such as limited police resources and community hostility related to traffic tie-ups, seem likely to inhibit any such proliferation. Most important, here the information-seeking stop interfered only minimally with liberty of the sort the Fourth Amendment seeks to protect. The checkpoint stop was constitutional. Reversed.

CONCURRENCE AND DISSENT: (Stevens, J.) Motorists who confront a roadblock are required to stop and to remain stopped for as long as the officers choose to detain them, and motorists may find such stops alarming. Furthermore, the likelihood that questioning a random sample of drivers will yield useful information about a hit-and-run accident that occurred a week earlier is speculative at best.

▶ *ANALYSIS*

As the Court makes clear in *Lidster*, the mere fact that a presumption of unconstitutionality does not apply in the instant case, does not mean that the stop is automatically, or even presumptively constitutional. It simply means that the Court must judge its reasonableness, hence its constitutionality, on the basis of the individual circumstances. In judging reasonableness, the Court will look to the gravity of the public concerns, the degree to which the seizure advances the public interest, and the severity of the interference with individual liberty.

■━■

Quicknotes

AUTOMOBILE STOP A police officer may stop an automobile and conduct a search of the vehicle without a valid warrant if he has probable cause to believe the vehicle contains evidence of a crime or contraband.

FOURTH AMENDMENT Provides that persons be secure as to their person and private belongings against unreasonable searches and seizures.

■━■

Ferguson v. Charleston

Cocaine users (D) v. Municipality (P)

532 U.S. 67 (2001).

NATURE OF CASE: Appeal from finding that warrantless and nonconsensual drug tests were reasonable.

FACT SUMMARY: Ten women (D), maternity patients, were arrested after testing positive in routine prenatal tests for cocaine use and brought suit challenging the practice of urine drug tests as unconstitutional searches.

🏛 RULE OF LAW
A state hospital's performance of a diagnostic test to obtain evidence of a patient's criminal conduct for law enforcement purposes is an unreasonable search if the patient has not consented to the procedure.

FACTS: The Medical University of South Carolina (MUSC) adopted a program (Policy M-7) whereby its staff would identify pregnant patients suspected of drug abuse and require a patient to be tested for cocaine use if she met certain criteria. Police were to be notified of those who tested positive, and the patient arrested. Petitioners were ten women (D) who received obstetrical care at MUSC and who were arrested after testing positive for cocaine. The women (D) challenged the validity of the policy, claiming the warrantless and nonconsensual drug tests conducted for criminal investigation purposes were unconstitutional searches. A jury found for the City (P) and the women (D) appealed.

ISSUE: Is a state hospital's performance of a diagnostic test to obtain evidence of a patient's criminal conduct for law enforcement purposes an unreasonable search if the patient has not consented to the procedure?

HOLDING AND DECISION: (Stevens, J.) Yes. A state hospital's performance of a diagnostic test to obtain evidence of a patient's criminal conduct for law enforcement purposes is an unreasonable search if the patient has not consented to the procedure. While state hospital employees, like other citizens, may have a duty to provide the police with evidence of criminal conduct that they inadvertently acquire in the course of their routine treatment, when they undertake to obtain such evidence from the patient for the specific purpose of incriminating him, they have a special obligation to make sure the patient is fully informed of his constitutional rights, consistence with the requirements of a knowing waiver. Even though here the motive asserted was benign, this cannot justify a departure from Fourth Amendment prohibitions against nonconsensual, warrantless and suspicionless searches. While

drug abuse is a serious problem, the gravity of the threat is not dispositive of what means law enforcement may employ. Reversed and remanded to determine whether the searches were conducted with the patients' informed consent.

CONCURRENCE: (Kennedy, J.) The search procedure here cannot be sustained under the Fourth Amendment. The hospital acted as an institutional arm of law enforcement for purposes of carrying out the search policy and, while it may have served legitimate needs unrelated to law enforcement, it also had a penal character with far greater connections to law enforcement than other searches sustained under the Court's special-needs rationale.

DISSENT: (Scalia, J.) The police conduct here does not violate the Fourth Amendment's prohibition of unreasonable searches and seizures. Fourth Amendment law provides that a search that has been consented to is not unreasonable. Here there is no contention that the urine samples were extracted forcibly. This Court has never held that lawfully obtained material that a person voluntarily entrusts to one person cannot be given by that person to the police and used for whatever evidence it may contain.

▶ ANALYSIS

Note that the Court distinguishes this case from prior "special needs" cases on the basis that in prior cases the "special need" asserted as a justification for absence of a warrant was separate from the state's interest in law enforcement. Here the essential feature of the policy was the "use of law enforcement to coerce the patients into substance abuse treatment."

Quicknotes

FOURTH AMENDMENT Provides that persons be secure as to their person and private belongings against unreasonable searches and seizures.

SEARCH An inspection conducted in order to obtain evidence to be utilized for the prosecution of a crime.

WAIVER The intentional or voluntary forfeiture of a recognized right.

WARRANT An order issued by a court directing an officer to undertake a certain act (e.g., arrest or search).

Tennessee v. Garner

State (D) v. Civil rights plaintiff (P)

471 U.S. 1 (1985).

NATURE OF CASE: Review of order reversing defense verdict in federal civil rights action.

FACT SUMMARY: Tennessee's (D) law permitting the use of deadly force to apprehend any fleeing felony suspect was challenged as unconstitutional.

🏛 RULE OF LAW
Deadly force may not be used to apprehend a fleeing felony suspect unless there is probable cause to believe that the suspect poses a significant threat to the safety of others.

FACTS: Tennessee (D) state law permitted police officers to use deadly force to stop any fleeing felony suspect. Edward Garner, suspected of having just burglarized a house, was shot and killed while attempting to flee. He was unarmed and gave no appearance thereof. His father, Garner (P), brought an action for damages in district court under 42 U.S.C. § 1983, contending that the officer's acts violated his son's civil rights. The district court held the Tennessee (D) law constitutional and entered a defense verdict. The court of appeals reversed, and the Supreme Court granted review.

ISSUE: May deadly force be used to apprehend a fleeing suspect if there is no probable cause to believe that the suspect poses a significant threat to the safety of others?

HOLDING AND DECISION: (White, J.) No. Deadly force may not be used to apprehend a fleeing suspect unless there is probable cause to believe that the suspect poses a significant threat to the safety of others. Apprehension of a suspect is a "seizure" covered by the Fourth Amendment. The reasonableness of any seizure thereunder involves the balancing of the individual's personal interests against those of the government. With respect to deadly force, the individual's interest in remaining alive is obvious. The government's interest in effective law enforcement is equally clear. Deadly force does not always advance this interest. First, it can interfere with judicial determination of guilt or innocence. Also, statistics show that successful apprehensions are not noticeably higher in states that allow use of deadly force than in those that do not. It is true that, at common law, deadly force could be used to apprehend any felony suspect. However, at common law, all felonies were punishable by death, so killing a fleeing suspect was more commensurate with the ultimate punishment. Such is not the case today. In summation, only when a suspect poses significant threat to the safety of others is governmental interest in apprehension so great as to warrant deadly force. Here, the decedent did not pose such a threat, so deadly force was not warranted. Affirmed.

▶ ANALYSIS

In early times, felonies were limited to certain very serious crimes, such as murder, burglary, and rape, and were always punishable by death. Today, a felony is usually defined by the amount of time in prison one can receive for committing the crime, usually one or two years, depending upon the jurisdiction. Consequently, as societal attitudes toward the nature and degree of punishment have changed over the centuries, the Court did not feel constrained to incorporate the common law in existence at the time of the Fourth Amendment's adoption into its analysis.

■=■

Quicknotes

DEADLY FORCE That degree of force that is likely to result in death or great bodily injury.

FOURTH AMENDMENT Provides that persons be secure as to their person and private belongings against unreasonable searches and seizures.

SEIZURE The taking of property by unlawful activity or in satisfaction of a judgment entered by the court.

■=■

Graham v. Connor

Civil rights plaintiff (P) v. Officer (D)

490 U.S. 386 (1989).

NATURE OF CASE: Appeal from grant of directed verdict in 42 U.S.C. § 1983 claim of excessive force.

FACT SUMMARY: Police officers were physically abusive in making an investigatory stop, seizure, and arrest of a free citizen.

RULE OF LAW

All claims that law enforcement officers have used excessive force—deadly or not—in the course of arrest, investigatory stop, or other seizure of a free citizen should be analyzed under the Fourth Amendment and its "reasonableness" standard.

FACTS: Dethorne Graham (P), a diabetic, was suffering from an insulin reaction when he contacted a friend, Berry, to take him to the convenience store to purchase some juice to counteract the attack. Upon entering the store, Graham (P) noted how busy the store was and how long the line was and made a quick decision to go to another friend's house instead. Thus, Graham (P) rushed out of the store and into Berry's waiting car. Police officer Connor (D) witnessed this, and, suspicious about Graham's activities within the store, followed Graham (P) and Berry. About one-half mile from the store, Connor made an investigatory stop. Berry explained that Graham (P) was a diabetic and was having an episode, but Connor (D) ignored his pleas to get Graham (P) some sugar. Connor (D) ordered the two men to wait while he determined what, if anything, occurred at the convenience store. While Connor (D) returned to his car to call for backup assistance, Graham (P) ran twice around the car and finally sat down on the curb, where he passed out. Backup officers arrived on the scene amid the confusion, rolled Graham (P) over on the sidewalk, and cuffed him. They later dragged him over to a cruiser, slammed his head against its hood twice, and threw him headfirst into the cruiser. The officers eventually learned that nothing had occurred at the convenience store and drove Graham (P) home. Graham (P) sustained a broken foot, cuts on his wrists, an injured shoulder, and a ringing in his ears from his encounter with police. He filed a § 1983 claim against the officers for excessive force. The district court found no excessive force and granted the officers' motion for directed verdict. The Court of Appeals for the Fourth Circuit affirmed.

ISSUE: What constitutional standard governs a free citizen's claim that law enforcement officials used excessive force in the course of making an arrest, investigatory stop, or other seizure of his person?

HOLDING AND DECISION: (Rehnquist, C.J.) The Court of Appeals erred in applying the four-part due process test. All claims that law enforcement officers have used excessive force—deadly or not—in the course of arrest, investigatory stop, or other seizure of a free citizen should be analyzed under the Fourth Amendment and its "reasonableness" standard, which requires balancing the intrusion on an individual's Fourth Amendment rights against the countervailing government interests at issue. The reasonableness of a particular use of force must be judged from the perspective of an officer on the scene. An officer's evil intentions will not make a Fourth Amendment violation out of an objectively reasonable use of force. Vacated and remanded for reconsideration of the issue under the Fourth Amendment "reasonableness" standard.

ANALYSIS

Graham rejects using an officer's subjective intent as part of Fourth Amendment analysis in excessive force cases.

Quicknotes

FOURTH AMENDMENT Provides that persons be secure as to their person and private belongings against unreasonable searches and seizures.

Schneckloth v. Bustamonte

Court (P) v. Accused forger (D)

412 U.S. 218 (1973).

NATURE OF CASE: Review of grant of federal writ of habeas corpus.

FACT SUMMARY: Bustamonte (D) contended that consent to search an automobile had not been voluntary because the person giving consent had not been told that he had a right to decline consent.

> 🏛 **RULE OF LAW**
> To be voluntary, consent to a search need not include a police admonition that consent may be withheld.

FACTS: Police stopped an auto for having a nonfunctioning headlight. The only occupant with a license, Alcala, informed the police that it was his brother's car. The officer asked if he could search the car. Alcala consented and cooperated in opening the trunk and glove compartment. Inside, certain forged checks were found. Bustamonte (D), a passenger, was charged with possessing a check with intent to defraud. He moved to suppress the checks, contending that consent to search had not been voluntary. The motion was denied, and he was convicted. This was affirmed on appeal. Bustamonte (D) filed a habeas corpus action. The district court denied the writ, but the Ninth Circuit reversed, holding that for a search consent to be voluntary, the consenting party had to be informed that consent could be withheld. The Supreme Court granted review.

ISSUE: To be voluntary, must consent to a search include a police admonition that consent may be withheld?

HOLDING AND DECISION: (Stewart, J.) No. To be voluntary, consent to a search need not include a police admonition that consent may be withheld. The notion of "voluntariness" is vague at best, and what exactly constitutes voluntary action will largely depend upon a person's philosophical perspective. In light of the difficulty in quantifying the meaning of voluntariness, the best approach in deciding whether it exists is on a case-by-case basis, examining all relevant factors, such as environment and level of coercion. No single criterion should be controlling. It is true that in some areas a "knowing" waiver is required, such as a waiver of counsel or custodial interrogation. However, these are situations in which the fairness of a trial is implicated. A Fourth Amendment search simply does not raise the implications of an unfair trial as does an absence of counsel or the circumstances of custodial interrogation. Consequently, no hard test for ascertaining voluntariness is appropriate. Here, the trial court's finding that Alcala's consent was voluntary appears to be supported by substantial evidence. Reversed.

DISSENT: (Marshall, J.) Consent involves a choice by a person to forgo his right to be free from police intrusion. Such a decision cannot realistically be called "choice" if the actor doesn't know he has the right to withhold consent.

▶ **ANALYSIS**

The basic Fourth Amendment principle is that a search requires a warrant. When a search involved not a warrant but consent, it is up to the prosecution to prove consent. What was at issue in the present case was what must be demonstrated to prove consent.

■==■

Quicknotes

AUTOMOBILE STOP A police officer may stop an automobile and conduct a search of the vehicle without a valid warrant if he has probable cause to believe the vehicle contains evidence of a crime or contraband.

FOURTH AMENDMENT Provides that persons be secure as to their person and private belongings against unreasonable searches and seizures.

■==■

Ohio v. Robinette

State (P) v. Drug suspect (D)

519 U.S. 33 (1996).

NATURE OF CASE: Appeal from reversal of a criminal conviction.

FACT SUMMARY: Robert Robinette (D) argued that his consent to a search of his vehicle was not constitutionally valid under the Fourth Amendment since he was never advised that he was "free to go."

🏛 RULE OF LAW
The Fourth Amendment does not require that a lawfully seized defendant must be advised he is "free to go" before his consent to search will be deemed voluntary.

FACTS: Robert Robinette (D) was clocked at 69 miles per hour in a 45 mile per hour zone, and pulled over. The officer ran a computer check which revealed Robinette (D) had no previous violations. The officer asked Robinette (D) if he could search the car and was given consent. The search revealed illegal drugs. The Ohio Court of Appeals held that the search resulted from an unlawful detention. The Ohio Supreme Court affirmed, holding that to meet state and federal constitutional standards, citizens stopped for traffic offenses must be clearly informed by the detaining officer when they are free to go after a valid detention before the officer may attempt to engage in a consensual interrogation or search. The State (P) appealed.

ISSUE: Does the Fourth Amendment require that a lawfully seized defendant must be advised he is "free to go" before his consent to search will be deemed voluntary?

HOLDING AND DECISION: (Rehnquist, C.J.) No. The Fourth Amendment does not require that a lawfully seized defendant must be advised he is "free to go" before his consent to search will be deemed voluntary. The touchstone of the Fourth Amendment is reasonableness. Reasonableness, in turn, is measured in objective terms by examining the totality of the circumstances. In applying this test, the Court has consistently eschewed bright-line rules, instead emphasizing the fact-specific nature of the reasonableness inquiry. The proper inquiry in Fourth Amendment cases necessitates a consideration of all the circumstances surrounding the encounter. While knowledge of the right to refuse consent is one factor to be taken into account, the government need not establish such factor as the sine qua non of an effective consent. Just as it would be thoroughly impractical to impose on the normal consent search the detailed requirements of an effective warning, so too it would be unrealistic to require police officers always to inform detainees that they are free to go before a consent to search may be deemed voluntary. Reversed.

▌ ANALYSIS

As the Supreme Court in *Robinette* makes clear, the Fourth Amendment test for a valid consent is that the consent be voluntary, and voluntariness is a question of fact to be determined from all the circumstances. The Supreme Court, in Fourth Amendment consent cases, has expressly disavowed any "litmus-paper test" or "single sentence rule," in recognition of the endless variations in the facts and circumstances implicating the Fourth Amendment.

■═■

Quicknotes

FOURTH AMENDMENT Provides that persons be secure as to their person and private belongings against unreasonable searches and seizures.

■═■

United States v. Leon

Federal government (P) v. Criminal defendant (D)

468 U.S. 897 (1984).

NATURE OF CASE: Appeal from grant of motion to suppress in prosecution for possessing and distributing narcotics.

FACT SUMMARY: The Government (P) contended that evidence obtained from a defective search warrant should not be excluded when the police relied in good faith on that warrant.

RULE OF LAW
Evidence will not be excluded when police rely in good faith on a defective search warrant.

FACTS: vPolice officers received a tip from an informant of unproven reliability that two of the defendants were selling narcotics. An experienced narcotics investigator prepared an application for a search warrant and an affidavit that related information from the tip and the investigation. The application was reviewed, and a facially valid warrant was issued. The subsequent search revealed narcotics, and Leon (D) and the other defendants were indicted for various drug offenses. The district court granted Leon's (D) motion to suppress because the affidavit was insufficient to establish probable cause. However, the court made clear that the investigator had acted in good faith. The court of appeals affirmed. The Government (P) appealed solely on the question of whether the exclusionary rule should be modified so as not to bar the admission of evidence seized in reasonable, good-faith reliance on a search warrant that is subsequently held to be defective.

ISSUE: Should evidence be excluded where police rely in good faith on a defective search warrant?

HOLDING AND DECISION: (White, J.) No. Evidence will not be excluded where police rely in good faith on a defective search warrant. The marginal or nonexistent benefits produced by suppressing evidence obtained in objectively reasonable reliance on a subsequently invalidated search warrant cannot justify the substantial costs of exclusion. The investigator's application for a warrant clearly was supported by much more than a "bare bones" affidavit. The affidavit related the results of an extensive investigation and, as the divided panel of the court of appeals made clear, provided evidence sufficient to create disagreement among thoughtful and competent judges as to the existence of probable cause. Under these circumstances, the officers' reliance on the magistrate's determination of probable cause was objectively reasonable, and, thus, exclusion was inappropriate. Reversed.

CONCURRENCE: (Blackmun, J.) Any judgment about the effect of the exclusionary rule in a particular class of cases necessarily is a short-term one. In the future, if the good-faith exception to the exclusionary rule results in a material change in police compliance with the Fourth Amendment, today's holding may need to be reconsidered.

DISSENT: (Brennan, J.) The full impact of the Court's regrettable decision will not be felt until the Court attempts to extend this rule to situations in which the police have conducted a warrantless search solely on the basis of their own judgment about the existence of probable cause and exigent circumstances. In contrast with more financially costly and difficult measures of fighting crime, the erosion of Fourth Amendment standards has no monetary cost, but lost rights constitute a different kind of price.

▶ ANALYSIS

One of the keys to the majority's conclusion is its belief that the prospective deterrent effect of the exclusionary rule operates only in those situations in which police officers, when deciding whether to go forward with some particular search, have reason to know that their planned conduct will violate the requirements of the Fourth Amendment. When police officers act in good faith on a warrant, no such deterrent effect of the exclusionary rule exists.

■=■

Quicknotes

FOURTH AMENDMENT Provides that persons be secure as to their person and private belongings against unreasonable searches and seizures.

GOOD FAITH EXCEPTION TO WARRANT REQUIREMENT The exception to the rule that evidence obtained as the result of an unlawful search and seizure is nevertheless admissible at trial if the officers had a reasonable, good faith belief that they acted pursuant to legal authority.

WARRANT An order issued by a court directing an officer to undertake a certain act (e.g., arrest or search).

■=■

Minnesota v. Carter

State (P) v. Criminal defendant (D)

525 U.S. 83 (1998).

NATURE OF CASE: Appeal from an order holding that an illegal search had occurred.

FACT SUMMARY: When a police officer saw people packaging cocaine through a window and later arrested the occupants of the apartment, they alleged that their Fourth Amendment rights had been violated and sought to have the evidence excluded

RULE OF LAW

An overnight guest in a home may claim the protection of the Fourth Amendment, but one who is merely present with the consent of the householder may not.

FACTS: A confidential informant told the police that when walking by the window of a ground floor apartment, he had seen people putting a white powder into bags. The police officer looked through the same window, saw the men, and notified headquarters to prepare affidavits for a search warrant. When Carter (D) and Johns (D) left the building, they were arrested while in a motor vehicle, and cocaine was later found in the vehicle and in the apartment. Carter (D) and Johns (D) had never been in that apartment before and had been there for approximately 2 hours to package the cocaine. Carter (D) and Johns (D) were convicted of state drug offenses. The trial court held that since they were only temporary out-of-state visitors, they could not challenge the legality of the government intrusion into the apartment, and that the police officer's observation through the window was not a "search" within the meaning of the Fourth Amendment. The state supreme court reversed, holding that Carter (D) and Johns (D) had "standing" because they had a legitimate expectation of privacy in the invaded place, and that the officer's observation constituted an unreasonable "search" of the apartment. Minnesota (P) appealed.

ISSUE: If an overnight guest in a home may claim the protection of the Fourth Amendment, may one who is merely present with the consent of the householder also do so?

HOLDING AND DECISION: (Rehnquist, C.J.) No. An overnight guest in a home may claim the protection of the Fourth Amendment, but one who is merely present with the consent of the householder may not. The purely commercial nature of the transaction engaged in here, the relatively short time on the premises, and the lack of any previous connection between Carter (D), Johns (D), and the householder, all lead to the conclusion that their situation is closer to that of one simply permitted on the premises rather than that of an overnight guest. Therefore, any search that may have occurred did not violate their Fourth Amendment rights. Reversed.

CONCURRENCE: (Scalia, J.) Whereas it is plausible to regard a person's overnight lodging as at least his "temporary" residence, it is entirely impossible to give that characterization to an apartment that he uses to package cocaine.

CONCURRENCE: (Kennedy, J.) Almost all social guests have a legitimate expectation of privacy, and hence protection against unreasonable searches, in their host's home. In this case, Carter (D) and Johns (D) have established nothing more than a fleeting and insubstantial connection with Thompson's home.

CONCURRENCE: (Breyer, J.) The police officer's observation made from a public area outside the curtilage of the residence did not violate Carter's (D) Fourth Amendment rights. The officer did not engage in what the constitution forbids, namely, an unreasonable search.

DISSENT: (Ginsburg, J.) The court's decision undermines not only the security of short-term guests but also the security of the home resident herself. When a homeowner chooses to share the privacy of her home and her company with a short-term guest, both host and guest have exhibited an actual (subjective) expectation of privacy, and that expectation is one that our society is prepared to recognize as reasonable.

ANALYSIS

Property used for commercial purposes is treated differently for Fourth Amendment purposes than residential property. While Carter (D) and Johns (D) were present in a "home," it was not their home. Only the Dissent argued that a short-term guest in a home should share his host's shelter against unreasonable searches and seizures. Since there was no violation of the Fourth Amendment, the evidence seized by the police was used against Carter (D) and Johns (D).

Quicknotes

EXPECTATION OF PRIVACY Requirement that in order to invoke the Fourth Amendment's protection against unreasonable searches and seizures, the individual must have a reasonable

Continued on next page.

expectation of privacy in respect to the location searched or thing seized.

FOURTH AMENDMENT Provides that persons be secure as to their person and private belongings against unreasonable searches and seizures.

SEARCH An inspection conducted in order to obtain evidence to be utilized for the prosecution of a crime.

SEIZURE The removal of property from one's possession due to unlawful activity or in satisfaction of a judgment entered by the court.

Wong Sun v. United States

Criminal defendant (D) v. Federal government (P)

371 U.S. 471 (1963).

NATURE OF CASE: On certiorari from appellate court judgment upholding conviction for dealing in heroin.

FACT SUMMARY: Wong Sun's (D) codefendant was unlawfully arrested and made incriminating statements to police.

🏛 RULE OF LAW
Statements made by a defendant directly as the result of lawless police conduct are inadmissible against the defendant.

FACTS: Federal agents went to the laundry operated by Wong Sun's (D) codefendant, James Wah Toy. Toy told the agent that he was not open for business and to come back. The agent identified himself as a narcotics agent, and Toy ran into his living quarters at the back of the laundry. The agents broke open the door, followed Toy into his bedroom, and arrested him. A search of the premise revealed no narcotics. Toy told the agents that he and another man had been smoking some heroin the night before and told him where the other man lived. Toy and two others were indicted on drug charges, and his statements to the agents in his bedroom were admitted against him.

ISSUE: May statements made by a defendant directly as the result of lawless police conduct be admitted against the defendant?

HOLDING AND DECISION: (Brennan, J.) No. Statements made by a defendant directly as the result of lawless police conduct are inadmissible against the defendant. The Court of Appeals held that there was neither reasonable grounds nor probable cause for Toy's arrest. We have held that physical evidence obtained during an unlawful invasion must be excluded. Today we hold that verbal evidence that derives so immediately from an unlawful entry is no less the fruit of the poisonous tree than the more tangible fruits of the unwarranted intrusion. There was no intervening independent act to purge the illegality of its taint; therefore the judgment of the Court of Appeals is reversed and the case is remanded.

▶ ANALYSIS

Wong Sun (D) made a confession as well, but his confession took place when he voluntarily returned several days after being arraigned to make the statement. Given his in-

dependent intervening voluntary act, the Court held that the taint of Toy's unlawful arrest was purged as to Wong Sun's (D) confession.

◼◼◼

Quicknotes

EXCLUSIONARY RULE A rule precluding the introduction at trial of evidence unlawfully obtained in violation of the federal constitutional safeguards against unreasonable searches and seizures.

◼◼◼

Murray v. United States

Criminal defendant (D) v. Federal government

487 U.S. 533 (1988).

NATURE OF CASE: Appeal from a conviction for marijuana possession.

FACT SUMMARY: Murray (D) contended that marijuana seized in his warehouse, initially discovered during an illegal search but subsequently acquired through an independent and lawful search warrant, should be excluded.

🏛 RULE OF LAW
Evidence found for the first time during the execution of a valid and untainted search warrant is admissible if it is discovered pursuant to an independent source.

FACTS: Police officers made an illegal warrantless entry into a warehouse where they observed bales of marijuana. Some officers stayed at the warehouse, keeping it under surveillance, while others obtained a search warrant. In seeking the warrant, the officers made no mention of the illegal entry and did not rely on any observations made during the entry. After obtaining the warrant, the officers searched the warehouse and seized the marijuana. Murray (D) and the other defendants unsuccessfully objected to the use of the evidence against them on the grounds that the officers should have told the magistrate of the illegal entry and that the illegal entry tainted the warrant. Following his conviction, Murray (D) appealed.

ISSUE: Is evidence found for the first time during the execution of a valid and untainted search warrant admissible if it is discovered pursuant to an independent source?

HOLDING AND DECISION: (Scalia, J.) Yes. Evidence found for the first time during the execution of a valid and untainted search warrant is admissible if it is discovered pursuant to an independent source. If the officers' decision to seek the warrant was prompted by what they had seen during the initial entry, or if information obtained during that entry was presented to the magistrate and affected his decision to issue the warrant, the search pursuant to the warrant would not have been an independent source. The district court found that the officers did not reveal their warrantless entry or their observations of the marijuana to the magistrate. The court did not, however, explicitly find that the agents would have sought a warrant if they had not earlier entered the warehouse. This was error; a determination of whether the warrant-authorized search was an independent source of the challenged evidence should have been made. Vacated and remanded.

▶ ANALYSIS

Justice Marshall argued that where the police cannot point to some historically verifiable fact demonstrating that the subsequent search pursuant to a warrant was wholly unaffected by the prior illegal search, a per se rule of inadmissibility should be adopted. It would be difficult for the trial court to verify, or the defendant to rebut, an assertion by officers that they always intended to obtain a warrant, regardless of the results of the illegal search. The testimony of the officers conducting the illegal search is the only direct evidence of intent, and the defendant will be relegated simply to arguing that the officers should not be believed.

Quicknotes

INDEPENDENT SOURCE Pertaining to facts derived from another source, independent of those contained in a defective warrant.

PROBABLE CAUSE A reasonable basis for believing that a crime has been committed.

FRUIT OF POISONOUS TREE Doctrine that evidence obtained as a result of illegal procedures is inadmissible at trial.

United States v. Havens

Federal government (P) v. Drug importer (D)

446 U.S. 620 (1980).

NATURE OF CASE: Appeal from reversal of conviction for cocaine possession.

FACT SUMMARY: When Havens (D) denied on direct examination ever having been involved in smuggling drugs, the Government (P), on cross-examination, asked him if he had knowledge of having in his luggage a certain T-shirt, which it then introduced for impeachment purposes despite its having been the fruit of an illegal search and seizure.

> ### 🏛 RULE OF LAW
> Evidence suppressed by an illegal search and seizure may be used to impeach a defendant's false trial testimony, given in response to proper cross-examination, when the evidence does not squarely contradict the defendant's testimony on direct examination.

FACTS: Havens (D) was charged with importing and possessing cocaine after a Miami customs officer searched McLeroth, Havens's (D) companion, and found cocaine sewed into makeshift pockets in a T-shirt he was wearing under his clothing. McLeroth implicated Havens (D), who had already cleared customs, in the illegal activity. After Havens (D) was arrested, his luggage was seized and illegally searched without a warrant. The only thing found was a T-shirt with pieces cut out. Those pieces matched the pieces that had been sewn on to McLeroth's T-shirt, which were used to hide the cocaine. On direct examination, Havens (D) denied McLeroth's allegations that Havens (D) supplied him with the altered T-shirt and denied ever having been involved in drug smuggling. On cross-examination, Havens (D) denied knowledge of the T-shirt. The Government (P) then introduced the T-shirt to rebut his credibility. Havens (D) was convicted, but the court of appeals reversed, holding that illegally obtained evidence could be used only to impeach a statement made on direct examination.

ISSUE: May evidence suppressed by an illegal search and seizure be used to impeach a defendant's false trial testimony, given in response to proper cross-examination, when the evidence does not squarely contradict the defendant's testimony on direct examination?

HOLDING AND DECISION: (White, J.) Yes. Evidence suppressed by an illegal search and seizure may be used to impeach a defendant's false trial testimony, given in response to proper cross-examination, when the evidence does

not squarely contradict the defendant's testimony on direct examination. The cross-examination about the T-shirt and luggage was closely connected with matters explored during direct examination. The Government (P) called attention to Havens's (D) answers on direct and then asked whether he had anything to do with sewing the cotton patches on McLeroth's T-shirt. Thus, the Government (P) did not "smuggle in" the impeaching opportunity in the course of cross-examination, and the ensuing impeachment did not violate Havens's (D) constitutional rights. Reversed.

▶ ANALYSIS

Justice Brennan feared that the majority's approach to the exclusionary rule would obscure the difference between judicial decision-making and legislative or administrative policy-making. In addition, he also feared the denigration of the Fourth Amendment's and Fifth Amendment's unique status as constitutional protections by treating the privileges as mere incentive schemes. The majority, on the other hand, placed the consequences to society as a whole from not allowing impeachment under the circumstances on a higher level than discouraging the use of illegally seized evidence when that evidence relates only to peripheral matters, the thought being that police will not be encouraged by this exception to engage in unlawful search and seizures.

■=■

Quicknotes

FIFTH AMENDMENT Provides that no person shall be compelled to serve as a witness against himself, or be subject to trial for the same offense twice, or be deprived of life, liberty, or property without due process of law.

FOURTH AMENDMENT Provides that persons be secure as to their person and private belongings against unreasonable searches and seizures.

■=■

Anderson v. Creighton

FBI agent (D) v. Tort plaintiff (P)

483 U.S. 635 (1987).

NATURE OF CASE: Appeal from a Bivens claim for money damages.

FACT SUMMARY: An FBI agent conducted a warrantless search of a family's house for a suspected bank robber.

🏛 RULE OF LAW
Whether an official may be held personally liable for an allegedly unlawful official action depends on the "objective legal reasonableness" of the action.

FACTS: On November 11, 1983, FBI agent Russell Anderson (D) and other state and federal law enforcement officers conducted a warrantless search of the Creighton family home. The search was conducted because Anderson (D) believed that Vadaain Dixon, a suspected bank robber, would be found within the confines of the Creighton (P) home. Dixon was not present in the home. The Creightons (P) filed a claim in a Minnesota state court for money damages under the Fourth Amendment. Anderson (D) removed to federal district court and there filed a motion for summary judgment. The district court granted it on the ground that the search was lawful: Anderson (D) had probable cause to search the Creighton (P) home, and his failure to obtain a warrant was justified by the presence of exigent circumstances. The court of appeals held that Anderson (D) was not entitled to summary judgment on qualified immunity grounds because the right Anderson (D) was alleged to have violated was clearly established.

ISSUE: Was Anderson (D) entitled to summary judgment on grounds of qualified immunity?

HOLDING AND DECISION: (Scalia, J.) Yes. The court of appeals incorrectly interpreted the standard for qualified immunity. An official's action is protected by qualified immunity unless, in light of the pre-existing law, the unlawfulness of the activity is apparent. Law enforcement officers making the difficult determination of whether a particular search is objectively legally reasonable should no more be held personally liable in damages than should officials making analogous determinations in other areas of law. Vacated and remanded.

DISSENT: (Stevens, J.) The majority errs in expanding qualified immunity to the degree that federal agents may ignore the limitations of probable cause and warrant requirements with impunity.

▶ ANALYSIS

Creighton stands for the proposition that damages are available against a police officer who has violated the Fourth Amendment only when that officer has behaved with gross negligence.

■■■

Quicknotes

FOURTH AMENDMENT Provides that persons be secure as to their person and private belongings against unreasonable searches and seizures.

■■■

Los Angeles v. Lyons

City (D) v. Equity plaintiff (P)

461 U.S. 95 (1983).

NATURE OF CASE: Appeal from a claim seeking an injunction.

FACT SUMMARY: A motorist stopped by police was injured when he was subjected to an allegedly unjustified choke hold.

RULE OF LAW

Past wrongs do not necessarily amount to a real and immediate threat of future injury which is necessary to make a case or controversy that justifies equitable relief.

FACTS: At 2:00 a.m. on October 6, 1976, Adolph Lyons (P) was stopped by police for a traffic or vehicle code violation. Although Lyons (P) offered no resistance or threat whatsoever, the officers, without provocation, seized him and applied a choke hold. Lyons (P) was rendered unconscious by the officers' actions and sustained damage to his larynx. On February 7, 1977, Lyons (P) filed a complaint against the City (D). This complaint sought a preliminary and permanent injunction barring the use of choke holds.

ISSUE: Do Lyons's (P) injuries at the hands of police justify injunctive relief?

HOLDING AND DECISION: (White, J.) No. Lyons's (P) standing to seek the injunction requested depends on whether he was likely to suffer future injury from the use of choke holds by police officers. The fact that officers stopped and injured Lyons (P) with a choke hold on October 6 does not establish that they will again stop him for a traffic violation or any offense. To obtain the injunction he seeks, Lyons (P) must allege he will have another encounter with the police and that all police officers in Los Angeles always choke any citizen with whom they happen to have an encounter or that the city ordered or authorized the police to act in this manner. The equitable remedy of injunction is unavailable absent a showing of irreparable injury. Lyons (P), because he cannot demonstrate a real or immediate threat that he will be subject to a future choke hold at the hands of Los Angeles police, cannot show irreparable injury. Thus, injunctive relief is inappropriate in this case.

▶ ANALYSIS

Lyons effectively pushes claimants in actions against police or municipalities toward damage actions and away from systematic relief against police departments or municipalities.

Quicknotes

INJUNCTIVE RELIEF A court order issued as a remedy, requiring a person to do, or prohibiting that person from doing, a specific act.

CHAPTER 6

The Fifth Amendment

Quick Reference Rules of Law

Kastigar v. United States

Contemnor (D) v. Federal government (P)

406 U.S. 441 (1972).

NATURE OF CASE: Action to quash contempt citation.

FACT SUMMARY: After being given prosecutorial immunity, Kastigar (D) still refused to testify before a grand jury on Fifth Amendment grounds.

🏛 RULE OF LAW
Testimony may be compelled if immunity from prosecution is granted; no Fifth Amendment violation occurs.

FACTS: Kastigar (D) was subpoenaed to testify before a grand jury. The U.S. attorney obtained prosecutorial immunity for Kastigar (D) since he felt that the Fifth Amendment would be invoked. Kastigar (D) refused to testify anyway, invoking the Fifth Amendment. Kastigar (D) was cited for contempt and imprisoned. Kastigar (D) appealed alleging that prosecutorial immunity was not coextensive with Fifth Amendment rights.

ISSUE: Is the protection afforded by prosecutorial immunity coextensive with the protection of the Fifth Amendment so that a party may be compelled to testify?

HOLDING AND DECISION: (Powell, J.) Yes. First, prosecutorial immunity from any statements made before the grand jury prevents the prosecution for anything but perjury. Therefore there is no self-incrimination with respect to any present or future criminal proceedings and the privilege is inapplicable. When the privilege cannot be raised, the state may compel testimony in grand jury hearings. If the protection offered by prosecutorial immunity is coextensive with that of the Fifth Amendment, the contempt citation must stand. Kastigar (D) alleged that full transactional immunity must be granted to be coextensive with the privilege against self-incrimination. Prosecutorial immunity merely grants immunity for the subject of the testimony or its fruits. No absolute immunity is granted for future prosecutions. The proscription of the use of the testimony or evidence in any future criminal prosecution is coextensive with Fifth Amendment protection. The immunity bars the use of the information for any leads. The contempt citation is affirmed.

DISSENT: (Marshall, J.) Use immunity does not prevent future prosecution for crimes admitted during the compelled testimony. All the prosecution must do to bring a subsequent action is show that the information was obtained from inde-

pendent sources. Merely placing a heavy burden on the prosecution does not adequately protect the defendant. There is too great a possibility for abuse.

▶ ANALYSIS

In the companion case, *Zicarelli v. New Jersey State Commission of Investigation*, 406 U.S. 472 (1972), the Court upheld a similar state use statute. There was also upheld a requirement of responsive answers. Immunity would not be enlarged by unresponsive answers which tended to enlarge the scope of the immunity by including other wrongdoing. A state may grant immunity and the testimony cannot be used in another state or in a federal prosecution. *Murphy v. Waterfront Common*, 378 U.S. 52 (1964).

Quicknotes

FIFTH AMENDMENT Provides that no person shall be compelled to serve as a witness against himself, or be subject to trial for the same offense twice, or be deprived of life, liberty, or property without due process of law.

PROSECUTORIAL IMMUNITY Statutory protection afforded to a witness against prosecution as a result of his testimony.

Baltimore City Department of Social Services v. Bouknight

City social services (P) v. Parent (D)

493 U.S. 549 (1990).

NATURE OF CASE: Appeal from reversal of a contempt order.

FACT SUMMARY: Bouknight (D) contended that the contempt order issued by the juvenile court for her to produce her child violated her Fifth Amendment privilege against self-incrimination.

🏛 **RULE OF LAW**
A parent, who is the custodian of a child pursuant to a court order, may not invoke the Fifth Amendment privilege against self-incrimination to resist an order of the juvenile court to produce the child.

FACTS: Bouknight (D) was under suspicion for abusing her child, Maurice. Baltimore Social Services (P) obtained a court order removing Maurice from Bouknight's (D) care. Shortly thereafter, Bouknight (D) regained custody of Maurice but under the continuing oversight of Baltimore Social Services (P). Eight months later, fearing for Maurice's safety, Baltimore Social Services (P) returned to juvenile court, stating that Bouknight (D) did not cooperate with caseworkers, violated the terms of the protective order, and could not provide adequate care for her child in general. The court then granted the petition to remove Maurice from Bouknight's (D) control for placement in foster care. Bouknight (D), however, failed to produce her child or say where he was. The court, fearing for Maurice's safety, issued a bench warrant for Bouknight's (D) appearance. After refusing again to produce her child, Bouknight (D) was found in contempt of court and ordered jailed until she produced the child. The juvenile court rejected Bouknight's (D) claim that the contempt order violated her Fifth Amendment rights. The court of appeals reversed, and this appeal followed.

ISSUE: May a parent, who is the custodian of a child pursuant to a court order, invoke the Fifth Amendment privilege against self-incrimination to resist an order of the juvenile court to produce the child?

HOLDING AND DECISION: (O'Connor, J.) No. A parent, who is the custodian of a child pursuant to a court order, may not invoke the Fifth Amendment privilege against self-incrimination to resist an order of the juvenile court to produce the child. A person may not claim the Fifth Amendment's protection based upon the incrimination that may result from the contents or nature of the thing demanded. Bouknight (D), therefore, cannot claim the privilege based upon anything that the examination of Maurice might reveal nor can she assert the privilege upon the theory that compliance would assert that the child produced is in fact Maurice (a fact that the state could readily establish). The possibility that a production order will compel testimonial assertions that may prove incriminating does not, in all contexts, justify invoking the privilege to resist production. Concern for Maurice's safety was the reason for the order to produce him. The government demand for production of the very public charge entrusted to a custodian was made for compelling reasons unrelated to criminal law enforcement and as part of a broadly applied regulatory regime. In these circumstances, Bouknight (D) could not invoke the privilege to resist the order to produce Maurice. Reversed.

DISSENT: (Marshall, J.) The fact that the state throws a wide net in seeking information does not mean that it can demand from the few persons whose Fifth Amendment rights are implicated that they participate in their own criminal prosecutions. Rather, when the state demands testimony from its citizens, it should do so with an explicit grant of immunity.

▶ *ANALYSIS*

Justice Marshall also proposed a different analysis from that of the majority. Justice Marshall believed that an individualized inquiry is preferable because it allows the privilege to turn on the concrete facts of a particular case, rather than on abstract characterizations concerning the nature of a regulatory scheme. However, for case-by-case analysis to work, some clear guidelines are needed so that consistent and predictable results will be achieved.

■═■

Quicknotes

FIFTH AMENDMENT Provides that no person shall be compelled to serve as a witness against himself, or be subject to trial for the same offense twice, or be deprived of life, liberty, or property without due process of law.

PRIVILEGE AGAINST SELF-INCRIMINATION A privilege guaranteed by the Fifth Amendment to the federal Constitution in a criminal proceeding for communications made by an accused and protecting an accused or witness from having to give testimony that may incriminate himself.

■═■

Massiah v. United States

Convicted drug possessor (D) v. Federal government (P)

377 U.S. 201 (1964).

NATURE OF CASE: Review of conviction for narcotics possession.

FACT SUMMARY: While free on bail following his indictment and arraignment, Massiah (D) made incriminating statements to an accomplice who had secretly agreed with authorities to act as an informer.

🏛 RULE OF LAW
After the accused has been indicted, the Sixth Amendment forbids the use at trial of incriminating statements deliberately elicited from the accused by government agents in the absence of counsel.

FACTS: Massiah (D) was arrested, arraigned, and indicted for possession of narcotics. He retained a lawyer, pleaded not guilty, and was released on bail. In the same indictment naming Massiah (D), Colson was charged with conspiracy to sell narcotics. Without Massiah's (D) knowledge, Colson agreed to cooperate with federal agents in their investigation of Massiah (D) and have a radio transmitter installed in his car so that federal agents could overhear conversations taking place there. During one such conversation with Colson, Massiah (D) made incriminating statements. The district court admitted the statements at trial, which resulted in Massiah's (D) conviction. The court of appeals affirmed, and Massiah (D) appealed.

ISSUE: Does the Sixth Amendment forbid the use at trial of incriminating statements deliberately elicited from an accused by government agents after the accused has been indicted and in the absence of counsel?

HOLDING AND DECISION: (Stewart, J.) Yes. The Sixth Amendment forbids the use at trial of incriminating statements deliberately elicited from an accused by government agents after the accused has been indicted and in the absence of counsel. Under the Fourteenth Amendment, the right of an accused to counsel in a state criminal adversarial proceeding commences no later than upon indictment of the accused. A contrary ruling might deny an accused "effective representation by counsel at the only stage when legal aid and advice would help him." The Sixth Amendment's specific guarantee of the right to assistance of counsel applies directly to this federal proceeding. The interrogation need not take place in a police station. For the rule to have any efficacy, it must also apply to the indirect and surreptitious interrogation conducted here. This is especially true since Massiah (D) was more seriously imposed upon in that he did not even know he was being interrogated. The continued investigation of Massiah (D) following his indictment was within Sixth Amendment strictures but the introduction at trial of the incriminating statements deliberately elicited from Massiah (D) by authorities in the absence of his counsel was not. Reversed.

DISSENT: (White, J.) Since the new rule would exclude all admissions made to the police, no matter how voluntary and reliable, the requirement of counsel's presence or approval would seem to rest upon the probability that counsel would foreclose any admissions at all. This is nothing more than a thinly disguised constitutional policy of minimizing or entirely prohibiting the use in evidence of voluntary out-of-court admissions and confessions made by the accused. The Court's newly fashioned exclusionary principle goes far beyond the constitutional privilege against self-incrimination, which neither requires nor suggests the barring of voluntary pretrial admissions. A wiser rule that should be used, instead of the one announced by the majority, is to consider the absence of counsel as one of several factors by which voluntariness is to be judged.

▶ ANALYSIS

In *Massiah*, the Supreme Court, for the first time, held that the right to counsel arises prior to trial in a criminal proceeding. The Sixth Amendment right to counsel at trial discussed in *Massiah* must be clearly distinguished from the prophylactic right to counsel during interrogation articulated in *Miranda*. In fact, *Massiah*, decided in 1964, preceded *Miranda* by two years.

■=■

Quicknotes

SIXTH AMENDMENT Provides the right to a speedy and public trial by impartial jury, the right to be informed of the accusation, the right to confront witnesses, and the right to have the assistance of counsel in all criminal prosecutions.

■=■

Miranda v. Arizona

Criminal defendant (D) v. State (P)

384 U.S. 436 (1966).

NATURE OF CASE: Appeal from a conviction of kidnapping and rape.

FACT SUMMARY: Miranda (D) contended that his written and oral confessions should not be admitted into evidence because he was not advised of his right to consult with an attorney and to have one present during the interrogation.

🏛 RULE OF LAW
A defendant's statement may not be offered into evidence if it results from custodial interrogation of the defendant by the government unless warnings under the Fifth Amendment have been given to the defendant.

FACTS: The police arrested Miranda (D) for kidnapping and rape and took him to the police station, where he was identified by a complaining witness. The officers then took Miranda (D) to an interrogation room to answer some questions. The officers did not advise Miranda (D) that he had the right to have an attorney present. Two hours later, the officers obtained a written confession from Miranda (D). At the top of the statement was a typed paragraph stating that the confession was made voluntarily, without threats or promises of immunity, and with full knowledge of his legal rights. At his trial, the written confession was admitted into evidence over Miranda's (D) objection, and the officers testified to the prior oral confession made by Miranda (D) during the interrogation. Miranda (D) was found guilty, and he appealed, arguing that he should have been informed of his right to have an attorney present during interrogation.

ISSUE: Unless warnings under the Fifth Amendment have been given to the defendant, may a defendant's statement be offered into evidence if it results from custodial interrogation of the defendant by the government?

HOLDING AND DECISION: (Warren, C.J.) No. A defendant's statement may not be offered into evidence if it results from custodial interrogation of the defendant by the government unless warnings under the Fifth Amendment have been given to the defendant. The defendant must be informed, prior to custodial interrogation, that he has the right to remain silent, anything he says can be used against him at trial, he has the right to the assistance of a lawyer, and if he cannot afford a lawyer, the government will provide him with one. Custodial interrogation shall be defined as questioning initiated by law enforcement officers after a person has been taken into custody or otherwise deprived of his freedom of action in any significant way. The defendant may waive these rights, provided the waiver is made voluntarily, knowingly, and intelligently. If, however, he indicates in any manner and at any stage of the process that he wishes to consult with an attorney before speaking, there can be no questioning. Likewise, the defendant may stop the questioning at any time and ask for an attorney. In addition, if an interrogation takes place without the presence of an attorney and a statement is taken, a heavy burden rests on the government to demonstrate that the defendant knowingly and intelligently waived his rights. From the testimony of the officers and by the admission of Arizona (P), it is clear that Miranda (D) was not in any way apprised of his right to consult with an attorney and to have one present during his interrogation, nor was his right not to be compelled to incriminate himself effectively protected in any other manner. Without these warnings, the statements were inadmissible. The mere fact that he signed a statement which contained a typed-in clause stating that he had "full knowledge" of his "legal rights" does not approach the knowing and intelligent waiver required to relinquish constitutional rights. Reversed.

We also reverse three companion cases today decided with *Miranda: Vignera v. New York; Westover v. United States; California v. Stewart.* In all three, there was no evidence that the accused was ever advised of his constitutional rights prior to being interrogated by the police and ultimately making a confession or incriminating statement. In dealing with custodial interrogation, this Court will not presume that a defendant has been effectively apprised of constitutional rights on a record that does not show that any warnings have been given or that any effective alternative has been employed. Nor can a knowing and intelligent waiver of these rights be assumed on a silent record.

DISSENT: (Harlan, J.) In this particular case, there is no basis to extend the Fifth Amendment's privilege to confessions at police stations. Historically, the privilege against self-incrimination did not bear at all on the use of extra-legal confessions. Moreover, extension of this principal has already occurred under the due process standard governing confessions. Furthermore, the new rule as defined by the majority is not compelled by Fifth Amendment precedent or the Assistance of Counsel Clause of the Sixth Amendment. The rule's precedents

Continued on next page.

should have no bearing on police interrogation but should rather point to judicial proceedings. The Fifth Amendment has never been thought to forbid all pressure to incriminate one's self in relevant situations and precise knowledge of one's rights is not a settled prerequisite under the Fifth Amendment. In addition, in regard to public policy, police questioning allowable under due process precedents may inherently entail some pressure on the suspect and may take advantage of his weaknesses or ignorance. Until today's ruling, however, the role of the Constitution was to sift out undue pressure. The majority's rule at least impairs, and may end up wholly frustrating, law enforcement. The ruling requires an express waiver, an end to questioning upon a suspect's request, and the suggestion of counsel for the suspect which practically invites an end to the interrogation. Moreover, the majority portrays the evils of police questions in exaggerated terms. In the present case, Miranda (D) confessed within two hours of interrogation without any force, threats, or promises. His confession was obtained during a brief daytime interrogation conducted by two officers and without evidence of coercion. The Constitution cannot be read to exclude such a confession obtained by an interrogation which had a legitimate purpose, no perceptible unfairness, and little risk of injustice.

DISSENT: (White, J.) The Court's holding is neither compelled nor even strongly suggested by the language of the Fifth Amendment, is at odds with American and English legal history, and involves a departure from precedent. Further, the rule announced today will greatly weaken the effectiveness of the criminal justice system.

▌ ANALYSIS

The majority stressed that all confessions are not inadmissible and remain a proper element in law enforcement. There is no requirement that police stop a person who enters a police station and states that he wishes to confess to a crime. Volunteered statements of any kind are not barred by the Fifth Amendment, and their admissibility is not affected by the majority's holding in *Miranda*.

■══■

Quicknotes

CUSTODIAL INTERROGATION The questioning of a suspect by police while in custody.

FIFTH AMENDMENT Provides that no person shall be compelled to serve as a witness against himself, or be subject to trial for the same offense twice, or be deprived of life, liberty, or property without due process of law.

■══■

Rhode Island v. Innis

State (P) v. Criminal defendant (D)

446 U.S. 291 (1980).

NATURE OF CASE: Review of reversal of conviction for murder.

FACT SUMMARY: Innis (D) contended that a police officer's comments were made in order to elicit a response by Innis (D), thereby interrogating him, in violation of Miranda.

🏛 RULE OF LAW

There is no interrogation where comments by one officer to another officer about the dangerousness of the crime elicit a response from the suspect.

FACTS: Innis (D) was arrested for the gunshot murder of a taxicab driver and the armed robbery of another taxicab driver. The robbery victim identified Innis (D) in a photograph at the police station and told the police that Innis (D) used a sawed-off shotgun to rob him. When the police picked up Innis (D), he was unarmed. Three different officers advised Innis (D) of his Miranda rights. Innis (D) stated that he understood his rights and wanted to speak with a lawyer. Three different officers were assigned to drive Innis (D) to the police station, and their captain told them not to question, intimidate, or coerce Innis (D) in any way. While en route, one of the officers stated to the others that there were a lot of handicapped children in the area and voiced his concern that they might find the gun and hurt themselves. Innis (D) interrupted the conversation and told the officers he would show them where the gun was. Innis (D) was driven back to the spot where he was arrested and again given the Miranda warning by the captain. Innis (D) then told the captain the location of the gun. The Rhode Island Supreme Court held that the police's statements constituted interrogation and suppressed Innis's (D) statements. Rhode Island (P) appealed.

ISSUE: Is there an interrogation where comments by one officer to another officer about the dangerousness of the crime elicit a response from the suspect?

HOLDING AND DECISION: (Stewart, J.) No. There is no interrogation where comments by one officer to another officer about the dangerousness of the crime elicit a response from the suspect. The term "interrogation" under Miranda refers not only to express questioning but also to any words or actions on the part of the police that the police should know are reasonably likely to elicit an incriminating response from the suspect. Given the fact that the entire conversation appears to have consisted of no more than a few offhand remarks, it cannot be said that the officers should have known that it was reasonably likely that Innis (D) would so respond. This is not a case where the police carried on a lengthy conversation in the presence of the suspect or where the officer's comments particularly "evocative." Reversed.

DISSENT: (Stevens, J.) In order to give full protection to a suspect's right to be free from any interrogation at all, the definition of "interrogation" must include any police statement or conduct that has the same purpose or effect as a direct question. Statements that appear to call for a response from the suspect, as well as those that are designed to do so, should be considered interrogation.

▌ ANALYSIS

According to Justice Stevens, if the officer directly asked Innis (D) in the form of a question where the shotgun was so handicapped children could be protected, there would then have been an interrogation. It would appear that in determining whether there was an interrogation, the totality of the circumstances must be examined. Factors to be considered include the nature of the statements, the surroundings where they are made, and the duration of the statements, among others.

■=■

Quicknotes

MIRANDA RULE A required warning given before any questioning by law enforcement authorities can take place. Individuals in custody receive warnings regarding their privilege against self incrimination, right to remain silent, and right to be represented by an attorney.

MIRANDA WARNINGS Specified warnings that must be communicated to a person prior to a custodial interrogation; in the absence of the communication of such warnings, any communications made during the interrogation are inadmissible at trial.

■=■

Illinois v. Perkins

State (P) v. Inmate (D)

496 U.S. 292 (1990).

NATURE OF CASE: Appeal from suppression of statements in prosecution for murder.

FACT SUMMARY: Perkins (D) contended that statements made to an undercover officer in jail should be suppressed because his Fifth Amendment privilege against self-incrimination was violated under the terms in *Miranda*.

🏛 RULE OF LAW
Miranda warnings are not required when the suspect is unaware that he is speaking to a law enforcement officer and gives a voluntary statement.

FACTS: Parisi, an undercover agent, was placed in the cell of Perkins (D), who was incarcerated on charges unrelated to the subject of the agent's investigation. Parisi's investigation arose from information given to him about an unsolved murder by Charlton, a former cellmate of Perkins (D). Charlton claimed that Perkins (D) told him in detail about a murder he had committed while the two of them were incarcerated together. Parisi and Charlton posed as prisoners and were placed in the same cellblock where Perkins (D) was being held. Soon thereafter, Parisi and Charlton got Perkins (D) to describe at length the events of the murder in question. Parisi did not give Miranda warnings before the conversation. Perkins (D) was charged with murder. Perkins (D) moved to suppress the statements made to Parisi in the jail. The trial court granted the motion to suppress, and the state of Illinois (P) appealed. The appellate court of Illinois affirmed, holding that *Miranda v. Arizona*, 384 U.S. 436 (1966), prohibits all undercover contacts with incarcerated suspects that are reasonably likely to elicit an incriminating response. Illinois (P) appealed.

ISSUE: Are Miranda warnings required when the suspect is unaware that he is speaking to a law enforcement officer and gives a voluntary statement?

HOLDING AND DECISION: (Kennedy, J.) No. Miranda warnings are not required when the suspect is unaware that he is speaking to a law enforcement officer and gives a voluntary statement. Conversations between suspects and undercover agents do not implicate the concerns underlying *Miranda*. The essential ingredients of a "police-dominated atmosphere" and compulsion are not present when an incarcerated person speaks freely to someone whom he believes to be a fellow inmate. Coercion is determined from the perspective of the suspect. When a suspect considers himself in the company of cellmates and not officers, the coercive atmosphere is lacking. Ploys to mislead a suspect or lull him into a false sense of security that do not rise to the level of compulsion or coercion to speak are not within Miranda's concerns. Therefore, Perkins's (D) statements were voluntary, and there was no federal obstacle to their admissibility at trial. Reversed and remanded.

CONCURRENCE: (Brennan, J.) While the majority has not correctly characterized *Miranda* in its entirety, the majority is correct that when a suspect does not know that his questioner is a police agent, such questioning does not amount to "interrogation" in an "inherently coercive" environment so as to require application of Miranda. However, the Constitution does not condone the method by which the police extracted the confession in this case, and a claim could be raised that the confession was obtained in violation of the Due Process Clause.

DISSENT: (Marshall, J.) Because Perkins (D) was interrogated by police while he was in custody, *Miranda* requires that the officer inform him of his rights. *Miranda* was not concerned solely with police coercion. It dealt with any police tactics that may operate to compel a suspect in custody to make incriminating statements without full awareness of his or her constitutional rights. The compulsion proscribed by *Miranda* includes deception by the police.

▶ ANALYSIS

The majority distinguishes this case from *Mathis v. United States*, 391 U.S. 1 (1968), where an inmate in a state prison was interviewed by an Internal Revenue Service agent about possible tax violations. No Miranda warnings were given before questioning. The Court held that the suspect's incriminating statements were not admissible at his subsequent trial on tax fraud charges. The difference between the two cases lies in the fact that the suspect in *Mathis* was aware that the interviewing agent was a government official and, therefore, might feel coerced.

Continued on next page.

Quicknotes

DUE PROCESS CLAUSE Clauses found in the Fifth and Fourteenth Amendments to the United States Constitution providing that no person shall be deprived of "life, liberty, or property, without due process of law."

MIRANDA WARNINGS Specified warnings that must be communicated to a person prior to a custodial interrogation; in the absence of the communication of such warnings, any communications made during the interrogation are inadmissible at trial.

■═■

Moran v. Burbine

Government official (P) v. Convicted murderer (D)

475 U.S. 412 (1986).

NATURE OF CASE: Appeal from grant of motion to suppress a murder confession.

FACT SUMMARY: The court of appeals granted the trial court's denial of Burbine's (D) motion to suppress his murder confession made after a valid waiver of his right to an attorney because the police failed to inform him of his attorney's preconfession communications.

🏛 RULE OF LAW
A pre-arraignment confession preceded by an otherwise valid waiver is not tainted by unrelated police misconduct.

FACTS: After his arrest on a burglary charge, Burbine (D) validly waived his right to an attorney prior to confessing to an unrelated murder of a woman. This confession, however, was preceded, unbeknownst to Burbine (D), by his attorney's attempt to contact him, whereby the officer answering the phone stated to the attorney that Burbine (D) would not be questioned. Later, prior to Burbine's (D) murder trial in state court, he moved to suppress his confession. The state court denied the motion, which was affirmed on appeal by the Rhode Island Supreme Court. After unsuccessfully petitioning the U.S. district court for a writ of habeas corpus, Burbine (D) appealed to the First Circuit Court of Appeals, which reversed and granted his motion. Moran (P), on behalf of Rhode Island, appealed.

ISSUE: Is a pre-arraignment confession preceded by an otherwise valid waiver tainted by unrelated police misconduct?

HOLDING AND DECISION: (O'Connor, J.) No. A pre-arraignment confession preceded by an otherwise valid waiver is not tainted by unrelated police misconduct. This rule follows from examining the underlying purpose of the Miranda rules and striking a proper balance between the competing interests Miranda recognizes. In respect to the former, the purpose of these rules is to dissipate the compulsion inherent in interrogation and, in so doing, guard against abridgment of a defendant's Fifth Amendment rights. Clearly, a rule that focuses on conduct bearing no relevance at all to the degree of compulsion experienced by the defendant during interrogation would ignore both Miranda's mission and its only source of legitimacy. In respect to the latter, given Miranda's recognition of the need for police questioning as an effective law enforcement measure as weighed against the need to provide

a defendant with some protections against such an inherently coercive process, a rule requiring additional protection for conduct unrelated to this process would both be unnecessary for the protection of the Fifth Amendment privilege and injurious to legitimate law enforcement. In the instant case, since the police misconduct centered around activity unrelated to Burbine's (D) otherwise valid murder confession and since it did not offend the Fourteenth Amendment's guarantee of fundamental fairness, Burbine's (D) motion to suppress his confession was wrongly granted by the court of appeals. Reversed and remanded.

DISSENT: (Stevens, J.) Settled principles about construing waivers of constitutional rights and about the need for strict presumptions in custodial interrogations, as well as a plain reading of the Miranda opinion itself, overwhelmingly support the conclusion that a suspect's waiver of his right to counsel is invalid if police refuse to inform him of his counsel's communications.

▶ ANALYSIS

In Michigan v. Mosley, 423 U.S. 96 (1975), Mosley, who had been arrested in connection with certain robberies, was briefly interrogated; he then invoked his right to remain silent, at which point the interrogation ceased. Sometime later, a different police officer interrogated Mosley about a homicide. The second officer advised Mosley of his rights, obtained a waiver, and secured incriminating information. The Court found that Mosley's rights had not been violated, holding that Miranda does not literally mean that a person who has invoked his "right to silence" can never again be subjected to custodial interrogation by any police officer at any time or place on any subject.

■▬■

Quicknotes

CUSTODIAL INTERROGATION The questioning of a suspect by police while in custody.

FIFTH AMENDMENT Provides that no person shall be compelled to serve as a witness against himself, or be subject to trial for the same offense twice, or be deprived of life, liberty, or property without due process of law.

Continued on next page.

MIRANDA RULE A required warning given before any questioning by law enforcement authorities can take place. Individuals in custody receive warnings regarding their privilege against self incrimination, right to remain silent, and right to be represented by an attorney.

MIRANDA WARNINGS Specified warnings that must be communicated to a person prior to a custodial interrogation; in the absence of the communication of such warnings, any communications made during the interrogation is inadmissible at trial.

Dickerson v. United States

Criminal defendant (D) v. Federal government (P)

530 U.S. 428 (2000).

NATURE OF CASE: Appeal from denial of motion to suppress statement based on Miranda violation.

FACT SUMMARY: Dickerson (D) sought to suppress a statement he made while in an FBI field office prior to being given his Miranda warnings.

⚖ RULE OF LAW
When a decision of the court involves interpretation and application of the Constitution, Congress may not legislatively supercede such decision.

FACTS: Dickerson (D) was indicted for bank robbery and conspiracy to commit bank robbery. Before trial he moved to suppress a statement he made at an FBI field office on the ground that he had not received Miranda warnings before being interrogated. The district court granted the motion, and the government (P) took an interlocutory appeal to the court of appeals, which reversed, stating that 18 U.S.C. § 3501 was satisfied since the statement was made voluntarily. Dickerson (D) appealed.

ISSUE: When a decision of the court involves interpretation and application of the Constitution, may Congress legislatively supercede such decision?

HOLDING AND DECISION: (Rehnquist, C.J.) When a decision of the court involves interpretation and application of the Constitution, Congress may not legislatively supercede such decision. *Miranda* and its progeny govern the admissibility of statements made during custodial interrogation in both state and federal courts. Section 3501 provides that the admissibility of a custodial suspect's statements should depend on whether they are voluntarily made. Prior to *Miranda*, the admissibility of a suspect's confession was evaluated under a voluntariness test. The requirement of voluntariness was based on the Fifth Amendment right against self-incrimination and the Due Process Clause of the Fourteenth Amendment. The Court's decisions in *Miranda* and *Malloy* changed the focus of the due process inquiry. In *Malloy*, the Court held that the Fifth Amendment's Self-Incrimination Clause is incorporated into the Due Process Clause of the Fourteenth Amendment and this applies to the states. In *Miranda*, the Court recognized that the coercion inherent in custodial interrogation makes it difficult to determine whether a statement is voluntary or involuntary and heightens the risk of self-incrimination. Section 3501 was enacted two years after the decision in *Miranda* and was intended by Congress to overrule the Court's decision

in that case. The issue is whether Congress has the constitutional authority to do so. While Congress retains the ultimate authority to modify or set aside any judicially created rules of evidence and procedure that are not required by the Constitution, it may not legislatively supercede the Court's decisions that interpret and apply the Constitution. *Miranda* is a constitutional decision. The Court specifically stated that it was intended "to explore some facets of the problems of applying the privilege against self-incrimination to in-custody interrogation and to give concrete constitutional guidelines for law enforcement agencies and courts to follow." The decision is otherwise replete with references to constitutional rules and standards. *Miranda* announced a constitutional rule that Congress may not supercede legislatively. Reversed.

DISSENT: (Scalia, J.) *Marbury v. Madison* held that an Act of Congress will not be enforced if what it prescribes violates the Constitution. The majority opinion fails to state, however, that what § 3501 prescribes, the use of a voluntary confession at trial, violates the Constitution.

▶ ANALYSIS

The Court also relies on the principle of stare decisis as weighing heavily against overruling *Miranda*, since Miranda warnings have become "embedded in routine police practice to the point where the warnings have become part of our national culture." Justice Scalia rejects such rationale on the basis that the court rules are both "mutable and modifiable" and that they "must make sense."

■▬■

Quicknotes

FOURTEENTH AMENDMENT DUE PROCESS CLAUSE Provides that protections mandated by the U.S. Constitution and observed by the federal government are equally applicable, and therefore must be observed by the States.

MIRANDA WARNINGS Specified warnings that must be communicated to a person prior to a custodial interrogation; in the absence of the communication of such warnings, any communications made during the interrogation are inadmissible at trial.

■▬■

Missouri v. Seibert

State (P) v. Murder suspect (D)

124 S.Ct. 2601 (2004).

NATURE OF CASE: Appeal from reversal of a murder conviction.

FACT SUMMARY: Patrice Seibert (D) argued that since her murder confession was obtained by the police technique of interrogating in successive, unwarned and warned phases, known as "question-first," the requirements of *Miranda* were violated.

🏛 RULE OF LAW
The police technique of interrogating in successive, unwarned and warned phases violates the requirements of *Miranda*.

FACTS: In questioning Patrice Seibert (D), a murder suspect, the police interrogator employed a widely used interrogation technique known as "question-first" in which the interrogator questions the suspect first, then gives the Miranda warnings, and then repeats the questioning until the interrogator obtains the confession or incriminating statement which the suspect has already previously provided. After employing this technique of interrogating in successive, unwarned and warned phases, Seibert (D) confessed to murder prior to her warnings and then again after being given the warnings. The trial court suppressed Seibert's (D) pre-warning confession but admitted her post-warning confession. She was convicted of murder. The Missouri Supreme Court reversed, holding that here where the interrogation was "nearly continuous," the second statement was clearly "the product of the invalid first statement" and should have been suppressed. Missouri (P) appealed.

ISSUE: Does the police technique of interrogating in successive, unwarned and warned phases violate the requirements of *Miranda*?

HOLDING AND DECISION: (Souter, J.) Yes. The police technique of interrogating in successive, unwarned and warned phases violates the requirements of *Miranda*. *Miranda* addressed interrogation practices likely to disable an individual from making a free and rational choice about speaking and held that a suspect must be "adequately and effectively" advised of the choice the Constitution guarantees. The object of the "question-first" technique here utilized against Seibert (D) was to render Miranda warnings ineffective by waiting for a particularly opportune time to give them, after the suspect had already confessed. Just as no talismanic incantation is required to satisfy *Miranda*'s strictures, it would be absurd to think that mere recitation of the litany suffices to satisfy *Miranda* in every conceivable circumstance. The issue when interrogators question first and warn later is thus whether the warnings reasonably convey to a suspect his Miranda rights. Unless the warnings could place a suspect who has just been interrogated in a position to make an informed choice as to whether to speak, there is no practical justification for accepting the formal warnings as compliance with *Miranda*, or for treating the second stage of interrogation as distinct from the first, unwarned and inadmissible segment. By any objective measure, applied to circumstances exemplified here, it is likely that if the interrogators employ the technique of withholding warnings until after interrogation succeeds in eliciting a confession, the warnings will be ineffective in preparing the suspect for successive interrogation, close in time and similar in content. Accordingly, the question-first tactic effectively threatens to thwart *Miranda*'s purpose of reducing the risk that a coerced confession would be admitted. Affirmed.

CONCURRENCE: (Breyer, J.) Courts should exclude the "fruits" of the initial unwarned questioning unless the failure to warn was in good faith.

CONCURRENCE: (Kennedy, J.) Not every violation of *Miranda* requires suppression of the evidence obtained. The scope of the *Miranda* suppression remedy depends on a consideration of whether admission of the evidence under the circumstances would frustrate *Miranda*'s "central concerns and objectives."

DISSENT: (O'Connor, J.) Because here the isolated fact of the interrogating officer's intent could not have had any bearing on Seibert's (D) capacity to comprehend and knowingly relinquish her right to remain silent, it could not by itself affect the voluntariness of her confession.

▶ ANALYSIS

As the Supreme Court makes clear in *Seibert*, the reason for the increased popularity of the question-first method of interrogation is to obtain a confession the suspect would not make if he understood his rights at the outset. The underlying police assumption, which is accurate, is that with one confession in hand before the warnings, the interrogator can usually count on getting a duplicate. It is unrealistic,

Continued on next page.

explained the Court, to treat two bouts of integrated and proximately conducted questioning as independent interrogations subject to independent evaluation simply because Miranda warnings formally punctuate them in the middle.

■═■

Quicknotes

CUSTODIAL INTERROGATION The questioning of a suspect by police while in custody.

MIRANDA RULE A required warning given before any questioning by law enforcement authorities can take place. Individuals in custody receive warnings regarding their privilege against self incrimination, right to remain silent, and right to be represented by an attorney.

MIRANDA WARNINGS Specified warnings that must be communicated to a person prior to a custodial interrogation; in the absence of the communication of such warnings, any communications made during the interrogation are inadmissible at trial.

■═■

United States v. Patane

Federal government (P) v. Possessor of illegal firearm (D)

124 S.Ct. 2620 (2004).

NATURE OF CASE: Appeal from suppression of physical evidence in criminal case.

FACT SUMMARY: When a police officer seized Samuel Patane's (D) pistol from his bedroom during an arrest, after being given Patane's (D) permission to do so, Patane (D) was subsequently indicted for possession of an illegal firearm. Pantane (D) argued that since he was not given full Miranda warnings, the pistol should be suppressed as a "physical fruit" of the poisonous tree.

> 🏛 **RULE OF LAW**
> The Self-Incrimination Clause is not violated by the admission into evidence of the physical fruit of a voluntary statement.

FACTS: Upon arresting Samuel Patane (D) at his residence for violating a restraining order, a police officer attempted to advise Patane (D) of his Miranda rights but got no further than the right to remain silent. At that point, Patane (D) interrupted, asserting that he knew his rights, whereupon the warnings were not completed. The police officer asked Patane (D) about an illegal Glock pistol he believed Patane (D) possessed. Pantane (D) told the police officer the pistol was in his bedroom and gave permission to seize it. Pantane (D) was indicted for possession of the pistol. The court of appeals affirmed the district court's suppression of the pistol, and the Government (P) appealed.

ISSUE: Is the Self-Incrimination Clause violated by the admission into evidence of the physical fruit of a voluntary statement?

HOLDING AND DECISION: (Thomas, J.) No. The Self-Incrimination Clause is not violated by the admission into evidence of the physical fruit of a voluntary statement. The police do not necessarily violate Miranda rights by negligent or even deliberate failures to provide a suspect with the full panoply of Miranda warnings. Potential violations occur, if at all, only upon the admission of unwarned statements into evidence at trial. At that point, the exclusion of unwarned statements is a complete and sufficient remedy for any perceived *Miranda* violation. Thus, unlike unreasonable searches under the Fourth Amendment or actual violations of the Due Process Clause or the Self-Incrimination Clause, there is, with respect to mere failures to warn, nothing to deter. There is therefore no reason to apply the "fruit of the poisonous tree" doctrine. It is not for this Court to impose its preferred police practices

on either federal law enforcement officials or their state counterparts. Characterization of *Miranda* as a constitutional rule does not lessen the need to maintain the closest possible fit between the Self-Incrimination Clause and any judge-made rule designed to protect it. Here, there is no such fit because the introduction of the nontestimonial fruit of a voluntary statement (the pistol) does not implicate the Self-Incrimination Clause. The admission of such fruit presents no risk that a defendant's coerced statements will be used against him or her at a criminal trial. There is simply no need to extend (and therefore no justification for extending) the prophylactic rule of *Miranda* to this context. Reversed.

CONCURRENCE: (Kennedy, J.) In light of the important probative value of reliable physical evidence, it is doubtful that exclusion can be justified by a deterrence rationale sensitive to both law enforcement interests and a suspect's rights during an in-custody interrogation.

DISSENT: (Souter, J.) In closing their eyes to the consequences of giving an evidentiary advantage to those who ignore *Miranda*, the majority adds an important inducement for interrogators to ignore the rule in that case. While there is a price for excluding evidence, the Fifth Amendment is worth a price.

DISSENT: (Breyer, J.) The "fruit of the poisonous tree" should be extended to cases such as this.

▶ **ANALYSIS**

As *Patane* makes clear, the Miranda rule is not a code of police conduct, and police do not necessarily violate the Constitution (or even the Miranda rule, for that matter) by mere failures to warn. Because various prophylactic rules (including the Miranda rule) necessarily sweep beyond the actual protections of the Self-Incrimination Clause, the Supreme Court has consistently taken the position that any further extension of these rules must be justified by its necessity for the protection of the actual right against compelled self-incrimination. It is for this reason, for example, that statements taken without Miranda warnings (though not actually compelled) can be used to impeach a defendant's testimony at trial.

■■■■

Continued on next page.

Quicknotes

MIRANDA RULE A required warning given before any questioning by law enforcement authorities can take place. Individuals in custody receive warnings regarding their privilege against self incrimination, right to remain silent, and right to be represented by an attorney.

MIRANDA WARNINGS Specified warnings that must be communicated to a person prior to a custodial interrogation; in the absence of the communication of such warnings, any communications made during the interrogation are inadmissible at trial.

PRIVILEGE AGAINST SELF-INCRIMINATION A privilege guaranteed by the Fifth Amendment to the federal Constitution in a criminal proceeding for communications made by an accused and protecting an accused or witness from having to give testimony that may incriminate himself.

■■■

Brewer v. Williams

Government official (P) v. Convicted murderer (D)

430 U.S. 387 (1977).

NATURE OF CASE: Appeal of grant of writ of habeas corpus after murder conviction.

FACT SUMMARY: Following his arraignment, Williams (P) told police where to find his victim's body after police initiated a discussion on the importance of a Christian burial.

🏛 RULE OF LAW
Once adversary proceedings have commenced against an individual, he has a right to legal representation when the government interrogates him.

FACTS: Williams (D), charged with murdering a little girl in Des Moines, turned himself in to the Davenport police. He was arraigned in Davenport and requested an attorney. The police sent to pick Williams (D) up were instructed not to talk to him about the case without an attorney present. On the drive, Detective Leaming, who knew Williams (D) was religious, initiated a discussion on the importance of a Christian burial for the victim. After the "Christian burial speech," Williams (D) took Detective Leaming to the girl's body. Williams (D) was convicted of murder despite his counsel's efforts to suppress all evidence relating to Williams's (D) statements during the ride. Williams (D) petitioned for a writ of habeas corpus claiming that the statements and attendant evidence were obtained in violation of his Sixth Amendment right to counsel and should have been excluded at trial. The district court agreed. The appellate court affirmed, and Brewer (P), on behalf of Iowa, appealed.

ISSUE: Once adversary proceedings have commenced against an individual, does he have a right to legal representation when the government interrogates him?

HOLDING AND DECISION: (Stewart, J.) Yes. Once adversary proceedings have commenced against an individual, he has a right to legal representation when the government interrogates him. Williams (D) was entitled to counsel at the time he made the incriminating statements, and there can be no serious doubt that Detective Leaming set out to elicit information from Williams (D) just as surely as if he had formally interrogated him. Further, there was no evidence that Williams (D) waived his right to counsel. Williams's (D) consistent reliance upon the advice of counsel and his statements that he would only talk to police with an attorney present refuted any suggestion of waiver. Despite Williams's (D) express and implicit assertions of his right to counsel, Detective

Leaming proceeded to elicit incriminating statements from Williams (D). This evidence violated *Miranda* and was inadmissible. Affirmed.

DISSENT: (Burger, C.J.) This decision carries the exclusionary rule to an absurd extent, punishing the public for the mistakes and misdeeds of law enforcement officers instead of punishing the officer directly.

▶ ANALYSIS

While both the Fifth Amendment and the Sixth Amendment seek to protect a criminal defendant from illegal interrogation, the significant difference between the Sixth Amendment right to counsel and the Fifth Amendment right against self-incrimination is that the Sixth Amendment right attaches after the initiation of formal proceedings. The right to counsel applies to any adversarial proceeding, as well as to noncustodial settings such as eliciting information from a suspect who is free on bail. This right may be waived only if the waiver is knowing, voluntary, and intelligent. The state has the burden of establishing waiver.

■=■

Quicknotes

FIFTH AMENDMENT Provides that no person shall be compelled to serve as a witness against himself, or be subject to trial for the same offense twice, or be deprived of life, liberty, or property without due process of law.

MIRANDA RULE A required warning given before any questioning by law enforcement authorities can take place. Individuals in custody receive warnings regarding their privilege against self incrimination, right to remain silent, and right to be represented by an attorney.

PRIVILEGE AGAINST SELF-INCRIMINATION A privilege guaranteed by the Fifth Amendment to the federal Constitution in a criminal proceeding for communications made by an accused and protecting an accused or witness from having to give testimony that may incriminate himself.

SIXTH AMENDMENT Provides the right to a speedy and public trial by impartial jury, the right to be informed of the accusation, the right to confront witnesses, and the right to have the assistance of counsel in all criminal prosecutions.

■=■

Michigan v. Jackson

State (P) v. Criminal defendant (D)

475 U.S. 625 (1986).

NATURE OF CASE: Appeal of grant of motion to exclude confession in murder prosecution.

FACT SUMMARY: Bladel (D) and Jackson (D), two defendants being separately arraigned on unrelated murder charges, sought to suppress voluntary confessions given after they had requested counsel but before counsel had been provided to them.

🏛 RULE OF LAW
Police may not initiate any interrogation after a defendant asserts his right to counsel at an arraignment or similar proceeding without a valid waiver of the defendant's right to counsel.

FACTS: Bladel (D) and Jackson (D) were arrested on unrelated murder charges. At their arraignments, both men requested that counsel be appointed for them. Subsequently, after being read their Miranda rights but before counsel was provided for them, both men voluntarily confessed. At both Bladel's (D) and Jackson's (D) trials, the trial court overruled objections to the admissibility of their post-arraignment confessions, finding that their Sixth Amendment right to counsel had not been abridged. In both cases, the appellate court affirmed. However, in Bladel's (D) case the appellate court reconsidered and reversed. The Michigan Supreme Court held that the post-arraignment statements in both cases should have been suppressed, noting that the Sixth Amendment right to counsel attached at the time of the arraignments when both men requested counsel.

ISSUE: May police initiate any interrogation after a defendant asserts his right to counsel at an arraignment or similar proceeding without a valid waiver of the defendant's right to counsel?

HOLDING AND DECISION: (Stevens, J.) No. Police may not initiate any interrogation after a defendant asserts his right to counsel at an arraignment or similar proceeding without a valid waiver of the defendant's right to counsel. *Edwards v. Arizona*, 451 U.S. 477 (1981), stands for the proposition that an accused person in custody who has asked for the assistance of counsel is not subject to further interrogation by police unless the accused initiates further conversation. This rule applies with even greater force after a suspect has been arraigned. After the "suspect" has become the "accused," the constitutional right to the assistance of counsel is of paramount importance. The State's (P) suggestion that requests for counsel should be construed to apply only to representation in formal legal proceedings is without merit. Every reasonable presumption against the waiver of fundamental constitutional rights should be indulged. The burden of proof was on the State (P) to show a valid waiver was obtained. No such showing was made. Affirmed.

DISSENT: (Rehnquist, J.) The prophylactic rule of *Edwards*, designed to protect a defendant's right under the Fifth Amendment not to be compelled to incriminate himself, does not meaningfully apply to the Sixth Amendment.

▶ ANALYSIS

The Court has continued to blur the line between the Fifth Amendment privilege against self-incrimination and the Sixth Amendment right to counsel. In *Patterson v. Illinois*, 478 U.S. 285 (1988), the Court held that the giving of Miranda warnings was sufficient to warn the accused of his Sixth Amendment right to counsel. The Court went on to say that a waiver given after such warnings also constituted a knowing and voluntary waiver of the Sixth Amendment right to counsel. Under this decision, then, a waiver of a defendant's Fifth Amendment rights is effectively a waiver of his Sixth Amendment rights.

■=■

Quicknotes

FIFTH AMENDMENT Provides that no person shall be compelled to serve as a witness against himself, or be subject to trial for the same offense twice, or be deprived of life, liberty, or property without due process of law.

SIXTH AMENDMENT Provides the right to a speedy and public trial by impartial jury, the right to be informed of the accusation, the right to confront witnesses, and the right to have the assistance of counsel in all criminal prosecutions.

■=■

CHAPTER 7

Investigating the Complex Crimes

Quick Reference Rules of Law

Scott v. United States

Criminal defendant (D) v. Federal government (P)

436 U.S. 128 (1978).

NATURE OF CASE: Appeal from a determination on a motion to suppress.

FACT SUMMARY: Federal agents intercepted all phone conversations over a particular phone for a period of one month.

🏛 RULE OF LAW
Subjective intent alone does not make otherwise lawful conduct illegal or unconstitutional.

FACTS: In January of 1970, government officials (P) applied for authorization to wiretap a telephone registered to Geneva Jenkins. The supporting affidavit alleged there was probable cause to believe nine individuals, all named, were participating in a conspiracy to import and distribute narcotics in the Washington, D.C., area. The district court granted the application on January 24, 1970. Interception began that day and continued, pursuant to a judicially authorized extension, until February 24, 1970. Upon cessation of the interceptions, search and arrest warrants were executed which led to the arrest of 22 persons and the indictment of 14. Before trial, the defendants moved to suppress all intercepted calls. After extensive discovery and hearings, the district court held that the agents failed to comply with the minimization requirement contained in the wiretap order and ordered suppression of the intercepted conversations and all derivative evidence. The Court of Appeals for the District of Columbia Circuit reversed and remanded.

ISSUE: Did the officers violate 18 U.S.C. § 2518(5) (1976 ed.) by failing to minimize the interception of irrelevant conversations?

HOLDING AND DECISION: (Rehnquist, J.) No. The subjective intent of an officer does not invalidate the action taken by the officer as long as the circumstances, viewed objectively, justify that action. As for petitioners' statutory argument that the wiretap statute requires that agents make good-faith efforts at minimization of interceptions of communications not otherwise subject to interception under the statute, the language in the statute suggests that an officer's intent is not of paramount concern. Because the statute requires that wiretapping or surveillance be "conducted" so as to minimize the interception of nonpertinent calls, it is clear that Congress was concerned with agents' actions rather than motives. Affirmed.

DISSENT: (Brennan, J.) The reasoning of the majority is flawed in several ways. First, it disregards the explicit congressional command that the wiretap should be conducted so as to minimize the interception of nonpertinent calls. Second, it foolishly accepts the post hoc conjectures of the Government (P) as to how the agent would have acted had he exercised his judgment. Finally, the majority's decision gives agents the authority to disregard the directives of the statute.

▶ ANALYSIS

The touchstone of the analysis in *Scott* is objective reasonableness. The court will not look into the subjective intent of the officers.

■■■■

Jacobson v. United States

Convicted child pornographer (D) v. Federal government (P)

503 U.S. 540 (1992).

NATURE OF CASE: Appeal of conviction for receiving child pornography.

FACT SUMMARY: Jacobson (D) claimed the Government (P) had entrapped him into violating a child pornography law.

🏛 RULE OF LAW
Where government actions create a person's disposition to commit a crime, and then the government suggests the crime which that person commits, it is entrapment.

FACTS: At a time when it was legal, Jacobson (D) ordered from an adult bookstore two magazines picturing nude boys, though he later testified he thought he was ordering photos of young men over 17. Congress subsequently passed the Child Protection Act of 1984, criminalizing receipt by mail of sexually explicit depictions of children. The Postal Service found Jacobson's (D) name on the store's mailing list and began mailing Jacobson (D) letters and questionnaires from fictitious research and lobbying organizations and a fake pen pal. The mailings discussed and asked about Jacobson's (D) tastes in pornography and views on censorship. Each time he answered, the next mailing was fit more to his tastes. After two years, the Customs Service, through a fake company, sent Jacobson (D) a child pornography brochure. He placed an order, but it was never filled. The Postal Service, using a fake company, sent Jacobson (D) a letter decrying censorship and claiming the media and government were trying to keep its material out of the country. Jacobson (D) requested a catalogue, from which he later ordered child pornography. Jacobson (D) was arrested upon controlled delivery of the magazine. He unsuccessfully raised an entrapment defense and was convicted under the 1984 Act. The court of appeals affirmed, and Jacobson (D) appealed.

ISSUE: Where government actions create a person's disposition to commit a crime, and then the government suggests the crime which that person consents, is it entrapment?

HOLDING AND DECISION: (White, J.) Yes. Where government acts create a person's disposition to commit a crime, and then the government suggests the crime that person commits, it is entrapment. Jacobson (D) had become predisposed to break the law by the time he ordered a magazine from the Government (P). However, the Government (P) did not prove this disposition was not the product of years of Government (P) targeting. The magazines Jacobson (D) ordered from the bookstore were legal when bought. Evidence of predisposition to do what was once legal is not sufficient to show predisposition to do what now is illegal, since most people obey laws they disagree with. Jacobson's (D) claim that he did not know he was ordering photos of minors from the bookstore was unchallenged. His answers to Government (P) mailings showed predisposition to view child pornography and to support a given agenda through lobbying groups but did not support an inference of predisposition to commit the alleged crime. The strong arguable inference is that by waving the banner of individual rights and disparaging efforts to restrict pornography, the Government (P) excited Jacobson's (D) interest in banned materials and exerted substantial pressure on him to fight censorship by obtaining such materials. The government may not play on an innocent man's weaknesses and beguile him into committing crimes he would not commit otherwise. Reversed.

DISSENT: (O'Connor, J.) Both times the Government (P) offered Jacobson (D) a chance to buy pornography he responded enthusiastically. Thus, a reasonable jury could find a predis-position to commit the crime. Predisposition should be assessed as of the time the government suggested the crime, not when the government first became involved; the government does not need a reasonable suspicion before it can investigate. Moreover, the two-year investigation of Jacobson (D) involved no threats, coercion, or "substantial pressure" to commit the crime. Finally, the Government (P) did not have to prove Jacobson (D) was predisposed to break the law, only that he was predisposed to receive child pornography. The 1984 Act does not require specific intent to break the law, only knowing receipt. Since the requirement of predisposition is designed to eliminate the entrapment defense for those who would have committed the crime absent government inducement, the elements of predisposition should track the elements of the crime.

▶ ANALYSIS

The Court follows the subjective test for entrapment, i.e., whether the defendant was predisposed to commit the crime, as opposed to the objective test, i.e., whether police conduct created a substantial risk that an innocent person

Continued on next page.

would commit the crime. However, as the dissent points out, the Court's main concern "is that the Government went too far and `abused' the `processes of detection and enforcement' by luring an innocent person to violate the law." Jacobson illustrates how the subjective and objective tests are blurred in application. In analyzing an entrapment claim, courts must look to the conduct of both the defendant and the police.

■══■

Quicknotes

ENTRAPMENT An act by public officers that induces a defendant into committing a criminal act.

■══■

United States v. Dionisio

Federal government (P) v. Subpoenaed defendant (D)

410 U.S. 1 (1973).

NATURE OF CASE: Appeal from judgment for civil contempt.

FACT SUMMARY: Dionisio (D) refused to give voice exemplars to the grand jury.

RULE OF LAW

Both the initial compulsion of a person to appear before a grand jury and a subsequent directive to make a voice recording are not unreasonable seizures within the meaning of the Fourth Amendment.

FACTS: Approximately 20 persons, including Dionisio (D), were subpoenaed before the grand jury to give voice exemplars for comparison with recorded conversations taken pursuant to a court-ordered surveillance. Dionisio (D) refused to give a voice exemplar, claiming protection under the Fourth and Fifth Amendments. The district judge ordered Dionisio (D) to give a voice exemplar. When Dionisio (D) refused, he was held in civil contempt and was committed to custody until he obeyed the order or until the expiration of 18 months. The court of appeals reversed.

ISSUE: Do voice exemplars, required to be given to a grand jury to be used for comparison with recorded conversations, violate a defendant's Fourth Amendment rights?

HOLDING AND DECISION: (Stewart, J.) No. Voice exemplars, required to be given to a grand jury to be used for comparison with recorded conversations, do not violate a defendant's Fourth Amendment right. First, a subpoena to appear before a grand jury is not a seizure of the person. It is the obligation of every person to appear and give evidence before the grand jury. It is an orderly, lawful process without social stigma and under the supervision of a judge. The fact that 20 persons were subpoenaed for the same reason is constitutionally irrelevant. Second, the order to give a voice exemplar was not a seizure under the meaning of the Fourth Amendment. What a person knowingly exposes to the public is not protected. Physical characteristics of voice, as opposed to content of conversations, are not reasonably expected to be private. Therefore, there is no need for the grand jury to determine reasonableness prior to ordering the exemplar where there is no other Fourth Amendment violation. To so require would impede the grand jury's proper function. Reversed.

DISSENT: (Marshall, J.) The only recognized exception in prior cases from Fourth Amendment coverage involved grand jury subpoenas requiring individuals to appear and testify. There is no basis for extending that exception when we move beyond the realm of grand jury investigations limited to testimonial inquiries, as in this case. The danger that law enforcement officials may seek to usurp the grand jury process to secure incriminating evidence from a suspect through the simple expedient of a subpoena arises and would, if the Fourth Amendment was held inapplicable here, allow law enforcement to accomplish indirectly what it would not be able to constitutionally accomplish directly.

ANALYSIS

In *Davis v. Mississippi*, 394 U.S. 721, the court held that an unlawful seizure could not be used to obtain fingerprints to be used to determine whether a person is the suspected criminal. *Dionisio* allows the grand jury to do exactly that on the rationale that a subpoena is not a seizure and that voice prints are not a seizure. The grand jury is thus in a position to gain real evidence from a potential defendant prior to any finding of probable cause.

Quicknotes

FIFTH AMENDMENT Provides that no person shall be compelled to serve as a witness against himself, or be subject to trial for the same offense twice, or be deprived of life, liberty, or property without due process of law.

FOURTH AMENDMENT Provides that persons be secure as to their person and private belongings against unreasonable searches and seizures.

GRAND JURY A group summoned to investigate, inform, and accuse persons of crimes when sufficient evidence exists to do so.

SUBPOENA A mandate issued by court to compel a witness to appear at trial.

In re Sealed Case No. 99-3091

Contempt proceeding

192 F.3d 995 (1999).

NATURE OF CASE: Review of an interlocutory appeal.

FACT SUMMARY: The district court ordered the Office of Independent Counsel (OIC) to show cause why the OIC should not be held in contempt for violating the grand jury secrecy rule.

🏛 RULE OF LAW
Prosecutors' statements about their investigations implicate Rule 6(e) only when the statements directly reveal grand jury matters.

FACTS: On January 31, 1999, the Senate was trying President William J. Clinton on articles of impeachment. During trial, the *New York Times* published a front page article entitled "Starr is Weighing Whether to Indict Sitting President." The article detailed plans on the part of the independent counsel to indict Clinton on charges of perjury, obstruction of justice, and lying under oath in his Jones deposition in January 1998 and in his grand jury testimony in August. The following day, the White House and Clinton jointly filed in district court a motion for an order to show cause why the OIC, or individuals therein, should not be held in contempt for disclosing grand jury material in violation of Federal Rule of Criminal Procedure 6(e). The OIC responded that the *Times* article merely rehashed old news reports and did not constitute "matters occurring before the grand jury." After an internal leak investigation by the FBI, the OIC abandoned its argument that OIC was not the source of the information disclosed in the *Times* article. Concerned by these developments, the district court ordered Bakaly, Counselor to the Independent Counsel, and the OIC to show cause why they should not be held in civil contempt for violation of Rule 6(e). The district court scheduled a consolidated show-cause hearing, ordered the FBI and the OIC to produce in camera all their relevant investigative reports, and required FBI agents involved in the investigation to appear to testify. The district court ordered the proceedings be closed and ex parte. The OIC and Bakaly asked the district court to certify for interlocutory appeal the question of the proper scope of Rule 6(e). The district court denied the request. The district court later issued an order appointing the Department of Justice (DOJ) to serve as prosecutor of the contempt charge against Bakaly and the OIC. The DOJ asked the court to withdraw its referral of the OIC for prosecution, stating that Rule 6(e) only applies to individuals, the OIC cannot be held vicariously liable for acts of its staff, and the OIC

is entitled to sovereign immunity. The OIC objected to being named as a criminal defendant, also raising the sovereign immunity argument. The OIC seeks summary reversal of the district court's order to show cause why the OIC should not be held in contempt for violating the grand jury secrecy rule. The OIC also seeks summary reversal of the district court's order appointing the DOJ as prosecutor of OIC in a criminal contempt proceeding.

ISSUE: Do prosecutors' statements about their investigations violate Rule 6(e) when they fail to directly reveal grand jury matters?

HOLDING AND DECISION: (Per curiam) No. Rule 6(e) protects against the revelation of "matters before the jury." The disclosure of information coincidentally before the grand jury that can be revealed in such a way that its revelation would not explicate the inner workings of the grand jury is not prohibited under Rule 6(e). Prosecutors' statements about their investigations implicate Rule 6(e) only when they directly reveal grand jury matters. Internal deliberations of prosecutors that do not directly reveal grand jury proceedings are not Rule 6(e) material. The disclosure that a group of OIC prosecutors "believe" that an indictment should be brought at the end of impeachment proceedings does not violate Rule 6(e). The statements revealed in the *Times* article do not implicate the grand jury. The fact that the article revealed a time frame for seeking the indictment does not make the statements ones that are "occurring before the grand jury." This disclosure simply reveals a desire on the part of some OIC prosecutors to seek an indictment at a particular time but not what is "likely to occur." The *Times* excerpt does not constitute a violation of Rule 6(e). Reversed and remanded with instructions to dismiss the Rule 6(e) contempt proceeding against the OIC.

▶ *ANALYSIS*

Rule 6(e) provides little guidance on the government's secrecy obligations when prosecutors simultaneously develop a case in the grand jury and pursue other investigative options outside of the grand jury's presence.

■══■

Quicknotes

GRAND JURY A group summoned to investigate, inform, and accuse persons of crimes when sufficient evidence exists to do so.

■══■

United States v. United States District Court

Attorney General (P) v. District court (D)

407 U.S. 297 (1972).

NATURE OF CASE: Appeal from court order requiring government disclosure of wiretap evidence obtained without prior judicial approval.

FACT SUMMARY: When the Attorney General, without obtaining a warrant or prior judicial approval, conducted wiretap surveillance on three individuals under federal investigation for destruction of federal property, the three individuals argued that their Fourth Amendment rights had been violated.

> 🏛 **RULE OF LAW**
> The federal government may not constitutionally authorize electronic surveillance in internal security matters without prior judicial approval.

FACTS: The federal Government (P) charged three defendants with conspiracy to destroy government property; one of them was charged with the dynamite bombing of the CIA office in Ann Arbor, Michigan. At pretrial, the defendants moved to compel the government to disclose certain electronic surveillance information and to conduct a hearing to determine whether this information "tainted" the evidence on which the indictment was based. The Attorney General had approved the wiretaps. However, no warrant or prior judicial approval was ever sought or obtained for the wiretaps. The district court held the surveillance violated the Fourth Amendment and ordered the Government (P) to make full disclosure of the overheard conversations. The court of appeals affirmed, and the Government (P) appealed.

ISSUE: May the federal government constitutionally authorize electronic surveillance in internal security matters without prior judicial approval?

HOLDING AND DECISION: (Powell, J.) No. The federal government may not constitutionally authorize electronic surveillance in internal security matters without prior judicial approval. Fourth Amendment freedoms cannot properly be guaranteed if domestic security surveillances may be conducted solely within the discretion of the Executive Branch. The Fourth Amendment does not contemplate the executive officers of government as neutral and disinterested magistrates. Their duty and responsibility are to enforce the laws, to investigate, and to prosecute. Those charged with this investigative and prosecutorial duty should not be the sole judges of when to utilize constitutionally sensitive means in pursuing their tasks. It may well be that, here, surveillance of the conversations was reasonable and would readily have gained prior judicial approval. However, this Court has never sustained a search upon the sole ground that officers reasonably expected to find evidence of a particular crime and voluntarily confined their activities to the least intrusive means consistent with that end. The Fourth Amendment contemplates a prior judicial judgment, not the risk that executive decisions may be reasonably exercised. This judicial role accords with our basic constitutional doctrine that individual freedoms will best be preserved through a separation of powers and division of functions among the different branches and levels of government. We do not think a case has been made for a departure from Fourth Amendment standards; the circumstances do not justify complete exemption of domestic security surveillance from prior judicial scrutiny. We reject the Government's (P) argument that internal security matters are too subtle and complex for judicial evaluation. Nor do we believe prior judicial approval will fracture the security essential to official intelligence gathering. Affirmed.

▶ *ANALYSIS*

As the Supreme Court makes clear, official surveillance, whether its purpose be criminal investigation or ongoing intelligence gathering, risks infringement of constitutionally protected privacy of speech. Security surveillances are especially sensitive because of the inherent vagueness of the domestic security concept, the necessarily broad and continuing nature of intelligence gathering, and the temptation to utilize such surveillances to oversee political dissent. The Supreme Court emphasized that the instant case involved only the domestic aspects of national security and that the Court was not addressing, and expressed no opinion as to, the issues which may be involved with respect to activities of foreign powers or their agents.

■■■

Quicknotes

FOURTH AMENDMENT Provides that persons be secure as to their person and private belongings against unreasonable searches and seizures.

■■■

CHAPTER 8

The Charging Decision

Quick Reference Rules of Law

Inmates of Attica Correctional Facility v. Rockefeller

Present and former inmates (P) v. Governor (D)

477 F.2d 375 (2d Cir. 1973).

NATURE OF CASE: Appeal from the dismissal of a complaint seeking a writ of mandamus.

FACT SUMMARY: Present and former prisoners, as well as the mother of an inmate killed in an inmate uprising, and a New York State Assemblyman filed a complaint seeking to compel state and federal officials to investigate civil rights violations at the Attica Correctional Facility.

 RULE OF LAW
The judiciary may not compel the prosecution of a crime.

FACTS: A complaint was brought alleging that before, during and after the prisoner revolt at Attica in September 1971, the Governor of New York (D) and other officials either committed, conspired to commit, or aided and abetted in the commission of various crimes against prisoners (P). Allegations stated that prisoners (P) were subjected to cruel and inhuman treatment prior to the riot, prisoners (P) were intentionally killed or beaten without provocation during the chaos of the recapturing of the prison after the revolt, and after the recapture, prisoners (P) were maliciously denied medical treatment and prisoners' (P) property was destroyed. The complaint further alleges that the officials appointed by Governor Rockefeller (D) to investigate the crimes related to the inmate takeover failed to investigate and, furthermore, due to Governor Rockefeller's (D) own appointment of the officials, the officials cannot adequately investigate crimes committed by Governor Rockefeller (D) himself. Furthermore, since the special appointment of the officials by Governor Rockefeller (D) usurped the District Attorney's power to investigate, no one is able to investigate or prosecute Governor Rockefeller (D) and the other defendants. The district court dismissed the complaint.

ISSUE: Should the federal judiciary, at the insistence of victims, compel federal and state officials to investigate and prosecute persons who allegedly have violated certain federal and state criminal statutes?

HOLDING AND DECISION: (Mansfield, J.) No. Historically there has been a judicial reluctance to direct federal prosecutions at the insistence of a private party. This reluctance is rooted in the separation of powers doctrine. A system in which the judiciary must act as a supervisor with regard to prosecutorial decisions would be unworkable. Further, it would be difficult, if not impossible, to determine when to compel a prosecution. The plaintiffs in this case have not presented any statutory language arguably creating any mandatory duty to bring the prosecution at issue. Thus, the relief they seek is unavailable. Affirmed.

▶ ANALYSIS

Inmates of Attica stands for the proposition that the judiciary cannot review or supervise the exercise of prosecutorial discretion and that criminal proceedings may not be compelled. In effect, prosecutorial discretion gives prosecutors significant power to affect the law-making process.

Quicknotes

WRIT OF MANDAMUS A court order issued commanding a public or private entity, or an official thereof, to perform a duty required by law.

United States v. Armstrong

Federal government (P) v. Criminal defendant (D)

517 U.S. 456 (1996).

NATURE OF CASE: Review of dismissal of an indictment for possession of crack cocaine and federal firearms offenses.

FACT SUMMARY: After charges were brought against him for violating federal drug laws, Armstrong (D), alleging that he was selected for prosecution because he was black, brought a motion for discovery in support of his selective-prosecution claim or for dismissal of the indictment.

RULE OF LAW
A criminal defendant bringing a selective-prosecution claim must make a credible showing of different treatment of similarly situated persons in order to obtain discovery in support of the claim.

FACTS: Armstrong (D) was arrested for violation of federal drug and firearms laws. Armstrong (D) alleged that he had been selected for prosecution because he was black, and filed a motion for dismissal of the charges or for discovery of Government (P) documents regarding the prosecution of similar defendants. The district court granted the discovery motion and dismissed the indictment when the Government (P) would not comply with discovery. The court of appeals reversed but then, upon hearing the case en banc, affirmed the district court's order of dismissal. The Supreme Court granted certiorari.

ISSUE: Must a criminal defendant bringing a selective-prosecution claim make a credible showing of different treatment of similarly situated persons in order to obtain discovery in support of the claim?

HOLDING AND DECISION: (Rehnquist, C.J.) Yes. A criminal defendant bringing a selective-prosecution claim must make a credible showing of different treatment of similarly situated persons in order to obtain discovery in support of the claim. Under Federal Rule of Civil Procedure 16, which controls discovery in a criminal case, a defendant must show some evidence of disparate treatment—similar to the requirement under equal protection claims. Here, Armstrong (D) did not make such a showing. Thus, the district court's dismissal of the case was improper. Reversed and remanded.

DISSENT: (Stevens, J.) While the defendant did not make a strong enough showing to merit discovery, the district court did not abuse its discretion in requiring some response from the U.S. Attorney's office (P).

ANALYSIS

The Court notes that the test for obtaining discovery for a selective-prosecution claim should be similar to that of an equal protection claim. Recall that to successfully pursue an equal protection claim, the claimant must show both a discriminatory effect and a discriminatory purpose. In order to show a discriminatory effect, the claimant must also show that similarly situated persons (but of a different race or religion) were not prosecuted. From this equal protection language, the Court developed the test in this case.

Wayte v. United States

Criminal defendant (D) v. Federal government (P)

470 U.S. 598 (1985).

NATURE OF CASE: Appeal from reversal of dismissal of federal indictment for draft evasion.

FACT SUMMARY: The United States (P) prosecuted Wayte (D) as part of passive enforcement of legislation requiring young men to register with Selective Service System.

RULE OF LAW

A passive enforcement policy under which the government prosecutes only those who report themselves as having violated the law, or who are reported by others, does not violate either the First or Fifth Amendments.

FACTS: The president by proclamation required certain young men to register with the Selective Service System during the week of July 21, 1980. The Government (P) maintained a file of letters from men, including Wayte (D), who were subject to the registration legislation but explicitly refused to comply with the law. The authors of these letters who were found not to have registered were prosecuted. This policy was adopted pending the implementation of an elaborate system of matching drivers license records and registration records to locate nonregistrants. The Government (P) realized that those prosecuted under this policy were liable to be vocal proponents of nonregistration or persons with religious or moral objections to registering. Among the first to be prosecuted was Wayte (D). When the Government (P) refused to comply with the district court's discovery order, the district court dismissed the indictment on the grounds that the Government (P) had failed to rebut Wayte's (D) prima facie showing of selective prosecution. The court of appeals reversed, and Wayte (D) appealed.

ISSUE: Does a passive enforcement policy under which the government prosecutes only those who report themselves as having violated the law, or who are reported by others, violate either the Fifth or First Amendments?

HOLDING AND DECISION: (Powell, J.) No. A passive enforcement policy under which the government prosecutes only those who report themselves as having violated the law, or who are reported by others, does not violate either the Fifth or First Amendments. Under the Fifth Amendment, the decision to prosecute, even where probable cause is established, may not be deliberately based upon an unjustifiable standard such as race, religion, or other arbitrary classification. No such unjustifiable standard was applied here. The Government (P) did not investigate those who sent letters

criticizing registration unless the letter stated affirmatively that they had refused to comply with the law. Conversely, the Government (P) prosecuted those who reported themselves or were reported by others but who did not publicly protest. The policy therefore had no discriminatory effect against vocal nonregistrants. In addition, no governmental discriminatory intent was established because the Government (P) was only aware that its policy would probably result in the prosecution of vocal objectors. This awareness does not, without more, establish that Wayte (D) was prosecuted because of his protest. As to the First Amendment, when, as here, "speech" and "non-speech" elements are combined in the same course of conduct, a sufficiently important government interest in regulating the non-speech element can justify incidental limitations of First Amendment freedoms. Few interests can be more compelling than a nation's need to ensure its own security. The policy here placed no more limitation than was necessary to ensure registration for the national defense. In addition, passive enforcement was utilized as the only effective interim solution available to carry out the Government's (P) compelling interest. Affirmed.

▶ ANALYSIS

The dissent in *Wayte* argued that the case turned on a technical and comparatively mundane discovery issue. Prior to *Wayte*, the government was not required to turn over files based on a bare allegation of selective prosecution. (*United States v. Cammisano*, 546 F.2d 238 (8th Cir. 1976). *United States v. Berrios*, 501 F.2d 1207 (2d. Cir. 1974), required the defendant to present "some evidence tending to show the existence of the essential elements of the defense and that the documents in the government's possession would . . . be probative of these elements."

Quicknotes

FIFTH AMENDMENT Provides that no person shall be compelled to serve as a witness against himself, or be subject to trial for the same offense twice, or be deprived of life, liberty, or property without due process of law.

FIRST AMENDMENT Prohibits Congress from enacting any law respecting an establishment of religion, prohibiting the free exercise of religion, abridging freedom of speech or the press, the right of peaceful assembly and the right to petition for a redress of grievances.

Brogan v. United States

Individual making false statements (D) v. Federal government (P)

522 U.S. 398 (1998).

NATURE OF CASE: Appeal from criminal conviction for making false statements in violation of a federal statute.

FACT SUMMARY: When James Brogan (D), a union officer, was prosecuted for lying by answering "no" when asked by federal agents whether he had accepted money from a company whose employees were represented by the union, Brogan (D) argued there existed an exception to criminal liability under the federal statute for a false statement that consists of the mere denial of wrongdoing (the so-called "exculpatory no").

🏛 RULE OF LAW
There is no exception to criminal liability under federal statute for a false statement that consists of the mere denial of wrongdoing (the so-called "exculpatory no").

FACTS: A union officer, James Brogan (D), accepted cash payments from a corporation whose employees were represented by the union in violation of federal legislation. When questioned by federal agents as to whether he had received any such payments, he answered "no," thereafter being informed that lying to federal agents in the course of an investigation was a statutory crime. Brogan (D) was indicted both for making the payments and for making a false statement to a federal agency in violation of 18 U.S.C. § 1001 which makes it a crime to make a false statement during a federal investigation. Brogan's (D) conviction on both charges was affirmed by the federal court of appeals, and he appealed.

ISSUE: Is there an exception to criminal liability under federal statute for a false statement that consists of the mere denial of wrongdoing (the so-called "exculpatory no")?

HOLDING AND DECISION: (Scalia, J.) No. There is no exception to criminal liability under federal statute for a false statement that consists of the mere denial of wrongdoing (the so-called "exculpatory no"). By its terms, the statute here at issue (18 U.S.C. § 1001) covers "any" false statement. The word "no" in response to a question assuredly makes a "statement," and Brogan (D) does not contest this his utterance was false or that it was made "knowingly and willfully." In fact, he concedes that under a "literal reading" of the statute he loses. Brogan (D) nevertheless argues that this Court should depart from the literal text that Congress has enacted, and approve the doctrine adopted by many circuits which excludes from

the scope of the statute the "exculpatory no;" in other words, that a simple denial of guilt does not come within the statute. This Court, however, cannot imagine how it could be true that falsely denying guilt in a government investigation does not pervert a governmental function. It is not, and cannot be, our practice to restrict the unqualified language of a statute to the particular evil that Congress was trying to remedy, even assuming that it is possible to identify that evil from something other than the text of the statute itself. Nor does refusal to except the "exculpatory no" violate the "spirit" of the Fifth Amendment. Any dilemma into which the defendant is placed is wholly of the guilty suspect's own making; an innocent person will not find himself in a similar quandary. Affirmed.

CONCURRENCE: (Ginsburg, J.) I do not divine from the Legislature's silence any ratification of the "exculpatory no" doctrine advanced in lower courts. The extensive airing this issue has received, however, may better inform the exercise of Congress's lawmaking authority.

DISSENT: (Stevens, J.) The mere fact that a false denial fits within the unqualified language of the federal statute is not a sufficient reason for rejecting a well-settled interpretation of that statute. It is not at all unusual for this Court to conclude that the literal text of a criminal statute is broader than the coverage intended by Congress.

▶ ANALYSIS

In *Brogan*, the defendant had contended, although unsuccessfully, that refusal to exempt the "exculpatory no" from criminality under federal statute, violated the Fifth Amendment by placing a "cornered suspect" in the "cruel trilemma" of admitting guilt, remaining silent, or falsely denying guilt. Even the honest and contrite guilty person, said the Court, will not regard the third prong of the "trilemma" (the blatant lie) as an available option. "Neither the text nor the spirit" of the Fifth Amendment, noted the Court, confers a "privilege to lie."

■═■

Quicknotes

FIFTH AMENDMENT Provides that no person shall be compelled to serve as a witness against himself, or be subject to trial for the same offense twice, or be deprived of life, liberty, or property without due process of law.

■═■

Costello v. United States

Tax evader (D) v. Federal government (P)

350 U.S. 359 (1956).

NATURE OF CASE: Petition for certiorari after conviction of income tax evasion.

FACT SUMMARY: Three investigating officers were the only witnesses before the grand jury that indicted Costello (D). They had no firsthand knowledge of the transactions upon which their computations were based. Hence, the indict-ment was based solely on hearsay.

RULE OF LAW
An indictment returned by a legally constituted and unbiased grand jury, if valid on its face, is enough to call for trial of the charge on the merits, regardless of the fact that the only evidence before the grand jury was hearsay.

FACTS: At Costello's (D) trial the government called 144 witnesses and introduced 368 exhibits, all of which related to business transactions and expenditures by the Costellos (D). Three government agents, whose investigations had produced the evidence used against Costello (D) at trial, were also called to testify. They were allowed to summarize the evidence already introduced, and to introduce computations showing, if correct, that the Costellos (D) had received far greater income than they had reported. The three agents were the only witnesses before the grand jury. Costello (D) moved to dismiss the indictment on the ground that the only evidence before the grand jury was hearsay since the officers had no firsthand knowledge of the transactions upon which their computations were based. The trial court denied his motion, and the court of appeals affirmed.

ISSUE: May a defendant be required to stand trial and a conviction be sustained when only hearsay evidence was the basis for an indictment returned by a legally constituted and unbiased grand jury?

HOLDING AND DECISION: (Black, J.) Yes. Neither the Fifth Amendment nor any other constitutional provision prescribes the kind of evidence upon which grand juries must act. The grand jury convenes as a body of lay people, free from technical rules. If indictments could be challenged on the ground that there was inadequate or incompetent evidence before the grand jury, a great delay would result before a trial on the merits. An accused could insist on a kind of preliminary trial to determine the adequacy and competency of the evidence before the grand jury. Perhaps most important, such a change would run counter to the whole history of the grand jury institution as a body not hampered by rigid procedural or evidential rules. An indictment returned by a legally constituted and unbiased grand jury, if valid on its face, is enough to call for trial of the charge on the merits. The Fifth Amendment requires nothing more. Costello's (D) conviction is affirmed.

CONCURRENCE: (Burton, J.) In this case, substantial and rationally persuasive evidence apparently was presented to the grand jury. Hence, the indictment should be sustained. However, if it is shown that the grand jury had before it no such evidence upon which to base its indictment, that indict-ment should be quashed.

ANALYSIS

Depending upon its scope, *Costello* may (or may not) reflect the majority position among those states that regularly prosecute by indictment. In many, courts will dismiss an indictment upon a showing that there was no sworn witness or legal documentary evidence before the grand jury. In several, courts have held an indictment is also subject to attack where based solely on the testimony of an incompetent witness. Most indictment states, however, will go no further. An indictment will not be dismissed even if issued solely upon hearsay testimony, and in some jurisdictions indictments regularly are based entirely upon a summary of investigative reports presented by a single officer or the prosecuting attorney.

Quicknotes

GRAND JURY A group summoned to investigate, inform, and accuse persons of crimes when sufficient evidence exists to do so.

United States v. Williams

Federal government (P) v. Criminal defendant (D)

504 U.S. 36 (1992).

NATURE OF CASE: Appeal from grant of motion to quash a grand jury indictment for prosecutorial misconduct.

FACT SUMMARY: A prosecutor (P) attempting to obtain a grand jury indictment failed to inform the panel about potentially exculpatory evidence.

🏛 RULE OF LAW
Prosecutors are not required to present exculpatory evidence at grand jury proceedings.

FACTS: At a grand jury proceeding, the prosecutor (P) failed to inform the panel about potentially exculpatory evidence when trying to get an indictment. Williams (D) then sought to have the indictment quashed on the grounds of prosecutorial misconduct. The court of appeals eventually ruled for Williams (D), and the Government (P) appealed.

ISSUE: Are prosecutors required to present exculpatory evidence at grand jury proceedings?

HOLDING AND DECISION: (Scalia, J.) No. Prosecutors are not required to present exculpatory evidence at grand jury proceedings. Courts have the supervisory power to dismiss indictments due to misconduct before the grand jury. However, this misconduct must amount to a violation of a rule drafted and approved by this Court or by Congress to ensure the integrity of the grand jury. Since the grand jury is an institution separate from the courts, the supervisory power of courts does not extend to compel standards of prosecutorial conduct. Grand juries can investigate merely on the suspicion that the law is being broken and do not require any authorization from the courts. Thus, the operational separateness of the grand jury shows that judicial supervisory powers may only be invoked in limited circumstances. Furthermore, the traditional functioning of the grand jury has always allowed the prosecutor to present only a single side of the case. Imposing a requirement that the prosecutor present exculpatory evidence would be incompatible with the grand jury system. Reversed and remanded.

DISSENT: (Stevens, J.) Although the grand jury has not been assigned to any of the branches of the government by the Constitution, it has always been subject to the control of the courts. The integrity of the grand jury would not be protected by allowing countless forms of prosecutorial misconduct.

▶ ANALYSIS

This decision has come under heavy criticism by commentators. Also, many states have adopted rules that prosecutors must inform the grand jury of any exculpatory evidence that they are aware of. Other states have a lesser requirement, mandating only that substantial exculpatory evidence be presented.

■■■

Quicknotes

EXCULPATORY EVIDENCE A statement or other evidence that tends to excuse, justify, or absolve the defendant from alleged fault or guilt.

GRAND JURY A group summoned to investigate, inform, and accuse persons of crimes when sufficient evidence exists to do so.

■■■

United States v. Velasquez

Federal government (P) v. Joined defendant (D)

772 F.2d 1348 (7th Cir. 1985).

NATURE OF CASE: Appeal from convictions and prison sentences ranging from five to fifteen years.

FACT SUMMARY: Five defendants were charged with cocaine trafficking. In addition, one defendant was charged with heroin violations and four defendants were charged with retaliation and conspiracy to retaliate against two government informants.

RULE OF LAW

The test for misjoinder is what the indictment charges, not what the trial shows.

FACTS: All five defendants were charged with the alleged sale of cocaine in Chicago in May 1982. Estevez, the Government's (P) principal witness, testified that he met with some of the appellants in Miami to plan the trip and pick up the cocaine. "El Toro," a suspected narcotics racketeer, was at the meeting. Estevez and two of the defendants drove to Chicago with the cocaine, met the other defendants, and later went to Rockford with the cocaine. Shortly thereafter, Estevez, fearing he was about to be caught by the FBI, became an informant. The government paid him $20,000 for information. In June 1982, Galvan (D) twice sold heroin to an undercover agent. In October 1982, Galvan (D) and Velasquez (D) kidnapped Estevez and Campana and threatened to kill them for having snitched on "El Toro." The two took Estevez and Campana to the apartment of Gomez (D) who entered later and asked what was going on. He was told to guard Campana, but he later let her go. The cases against Galvan (D) for heroin violation and against Galvan (D) and Velasquez (D) for retaliating against Estevez and Campana were very strong. The evidence of retaliation and cocaine violations was weak against Gomez (D). The cocaine was never found and the only witness was unreliable. Defendants argue that they should not have been indicted and tried together for all of the offenses charged.

ISSUE: Were the acts charged in the indictment "the same series of acts or transactions constituting . . . offenses" under Rule 8?

HOLDING AND DECISION: (Posner, J.) In part. The test for misjoinder is what the indictment charges. There was misjoinder in this case as to the heroin charges against Galvan (D). The indictment does not relate these charges to any of the charges against the other defendants named in the indictment. However with respect to the retaliation and cocaine charges, the indictment does allege, albeit unclear-

ly, that the retaliation was for snitching on the cocaine sale that is the subject of the first group of charges in the indictment. The misjoinder of the heroin charges against Galvan (D) violated Rule 8(b) and compels a new trial of all appellants on all counts unless the violation was a harmless error. The weakness of the evidence of the cocaine violations plus the additional confusion engendered by the trial of the retaliation charges jointly with the cocaine charges makes it clear that the misjoinder of the heroin charges against Galvan (D) was not harmless error as to the cocaine charges. Galvan's (D) heroin conviction and his and Velazquez's (D) convictions for retaliation are affirmed. The court directs acquittal for Gomez (D) on the charge of conspiracy to retaliate. Reversed and remanded as to the judgments of conviction of all defendants on the cocaine charges.

ANALYSIS

The *Velasquez* court found that severance under Rule 14 was appropriate in this case. The misjoinder of Galvan's heroin charges with the appellants' cocaine charges prejudiced the defendants' defense on the cocaine charges. Further, the court found that no reasonable jury would have convicted Gomez of conspiracy to retaliate on the evidence presented, an indication that the jury was confused by the tying together of two unrelated conspiracies.

Quicknotes

MISJOINDER The improper joining of parties or claims in a single lawsuit.

Zafiro v. United States

Codefendant (D) v. Federal government (P)

506 U.S. 534 (1993).

NATURE OF CASE: Appeal of convictions for drug distribution.

FACT SUMMARY: Two defendants accused of distributing drugs contended that they should have been prosecuted separately because they had mutually antagonistic defenses.

🏛 RULE OF LAW
When two defendants have mutually antagonistic defenses, a severance should be granted only if there is a serious risk that a joint trial would prevent the jury from making a reliable judgment.

FACTS: Two men were observed carrying a large box up to a woman's apartment. When two officers approached, they dropped the box and ran into the apartment. The box contained cocaine, and a subsequent search of the apartment revealed other drugs and a large amount of cash. Pursuant to Rule 8, the two men who had been carrying the box, a man who was inside the apartment, and the woman who owned the apartment were joined for trial. The woman sought a severance since she asserted that one of the men was her boyfriend, who stayed at the house occasionally, and she did not know he was dealing drugs. The boyfriend claimed that he was visiting his girlfriend and did not know that she was distributing drugs. The district court denied the severance motion, and all four defendants were convicted. The court of appeals affirmed. The defendants appealed, contending that the severance should have been granted because their defenses were hostile to each other.

ISSUE: Should a severance be automatically granted when two defendants have mutually antagonistic defenses?

HOLDING AND DECISION: (O'Connor, J.) No. When two defendants have mutually antagonistic defenses, a severance should be granted only if there is a serious risk that a joint trial would prevent the jury from making a reliable judgment. Rule 8 of the Federal Rules of Criminal Procedure provides that defendants may be prosecuted together if they are alleged to have participated in the same transactions constituting an offense. Rule 14 permits the court to grant a severance to the defendants if it appears that either side will be prejudiced by joinder. Mutually antagonistic defenses are not automatically prejudicial. The defendant must show that there will actually be prejudice under the circumstances, for instance, if evidence of a codefendant's wrongdoing would erroneously lead a jury to conclude that another defendant was guilty; in such a case, severance should be granted. Rule 14 allows this determination to be made by the trial court using its sound discretion. Jury instructions requiring separate consideration of each defendant's prosecution adequately cure the possibility of prejudice in most cases. The defendants in this case did not show that prejudice resulted from their use of hostile defenses at trial. Therefore, the trial court had discretion to deny severance. Affirmed.

▶ ANALYSIS

The Court also discussed the policy considerations behind joint trials. The Court noted that they were designed to promote economy and efficiency and the avoidance of a multiplicity of trials. The dissent of Justice Stevens points out that the majority opinion seemingly favors joint trials by declaring that severance should only be granted under limited circumstances, rather than simply acknowledging the broad discretion of the trial court.

■=■

CHAPTER 9

Bail, Detention, and the Right to a Speedy Trial

Quick Reference Rules of Law

Stack v. Boyle

Alleged conspiracist (D) v. Government official (P)

342 U.S. 1 (1951).

NATURE OF CASE: Motion to reduce bail as excessive under the Eighth Amendment.

FACT SUMMARY: Petitioners (D) were charged with conspiring to overthrow the federal government by violence or destruction.

RULE OF LAW
Bail must be set as to each individual defendant in an amount reasonably calculated to assure the presence of the accused at trial.

FACTS: Petitioners (D), members of the Communist Party U.S.A., were charged with conspiring to overthrow the federal government by violence or destruction in violation of the Smith Act. Upon arrest, bail was set as to each petitioner in widely varying amounts. On the motion of the Government (P), bail was fixed in the uniform amount of $50,000 for each petitioner (D). The only evidence offered by the Government (P) was a record showing that four persons, apparently unconnected to petitioners (D), had forfeited bail after being convicted under the Smith Act. Petitioners' (D) motions to reduce bail and requests for habeas corpus relief were denied by the district and appellate courts.

ISSUE: Must bail be set as to each individual defendant in an amount reasonably calculated to assure the presence of the accused at trial?

HOLDING AND DECISION: (Vinson, C.J.) Yes. Bail must be set as to each individual defendant in an amount reasonably calculated to assure the presence of the accused at trial. Unless the right to bail is preserved, the presumption of innocence loses its meaning. The standards used in fixing bail are to be applied in each case to each defendant. If there is a need for bail greater than that normally necessary to ensure the presence of any of the petitioners (D) given their circumstances and the seriousness of the charges, the petitioners (D) are constitutionally entitled to a hearing. Petitioners (D) may move for a reduction of bail so that a hearing may be held for the purpose of fixing reasonable bail for each petitioner. Reversed and remanded.

► ANALYSIS

Chief Justice Vinson noted the irony in the district court's readiness to deprive petitioners of their freedom before trial. This arbitrary act, Vinson wrote, "would inject into our own system of government the very principles of totalitarianism which Congress was seeking to guard against in passing the statute under which petitioners have been indicted."

Quicknotes

CONSPIRACY Concerted action by two or more persons to accomplish some unlawful purpose.

EIGHTH AMENDMENT The eighth amendment to the federal constitution prohibiting the imposition of excessive bail, fines and cruel and unusual punishment.

United States v. Salerno

Federal government (P) v. Bail seeker (D)

481 U.S. 739 (1987).

NATURE OF CASE: Appeal of reversal of denial of bail.

FACT SUMMARY: Salerno (D) and Cafaro (D) were denied bail on the grounds that they were dangers to the community.

🏛 RULE OF LAW
The Bail Reform Act of 1984, which allows a federal court to detain an arrestee without bail before trial if the court finds the arrestee dangerous to any other person and the community, is not unconstitutional.

FACTS: Salerno (D) and Cafaro (D), alleged organized-crime leaders, were indicted on a number of serious charges, including conspiracy to commit murder. On a Government (P) motion based on the Bail Reform Act of 1984, the district court held a fully adversarial hearing to determine whether they would be held without bail pending trial. The court denied bail, finding that the Government (P) had established by clear and convincing evidence that no condition of release could secure the safety of the community, since Salerno (D) and Cafaro (D) would likely continue their violent, organized-crime activities if released while awaiting trial. They appealed, arguing that the Act was unconstitutional on its face as a violation of the Due Process Clause of the Fifth Amendment and the Eighth Amendment prohibition against excessive bail. The court of appeals struck down the Act on due process grounds, and the Government (P) appealed.

ISSUE: Is the Bail Reform Act of 1984 unconstitutional on the grounds it allows a federal court to detain an arrestee without bail before trial if the court finds the arrestee dangerous to any other person and the community?

HOLDING AND DECISION: (Rehnquist, C.J.) No. The Bail Reform Act of 1984, which allows a federal court to detain an arrestee without bail before trial if the court finds the arrestee dangerous to any other person and the community, is not unconstitutional. Punishment without trial would violate substantive due process. However, this Act is regulatory, not punitive, since Congress rationally intended regulatory detention to achieve the legitimate goal of protecting the community from dangerous individuals, and the incidents of pretrial detention are not excessive in relation to that goal. Where the arrestee presents a demonstrable, serious danger to the community, the Government's (P) compelling regulatory interest in safety may outweigh the arrestee's right to liberty. The Act also complies with procedural due process requirements by providing for a full-blown adversarial hearing on the issue of detention without ban. Finally, the Eighth Amendment does not require release on bail where Congress has mandated detention on the basis of a compelling interest other than flight; it simply requires that if bail is set that it not be excessive in light of the perceived evil. Reversed.

DISSENT: (Marshall, J.) First, the majority allows the Due Process Clause to be violated by simply redefining punishment as "regulation." Second, a refusal to set bail implicates the Eighth Amendment prohibition against excessive bail since there is no difference between the consequences of setting outrageously high bail and setting no bail at all. Third, the Act is an unconstitutional limitation on the presumption of innocence since it allows individuals under indictment for one crime to be imprisoned by the government for crimes not yet committed. If these same individuals had not been indicted, or had been indicted and acquitted, any imprisonment on the ground that they were "dangerous" would surely be found unconstitutional. Clearly, then, the majority's decision allows an indictment to be used as evidence of criminal activity and as a justification for imprisonment.

DISSENT: (Stevens, J.) There are some circumstances where an individual's dangerousness may justify a brief detention, but in such cases the danger should be serious enough to warrant detention regardless of whether the person has been indicted, convicted, or acquitted of some other offense. Where, as here, an indictment becomes the prerequisite to emergency detention, the detention unconstitutionally infringes upon the presumption of innocence and the prohibition against excessive bail as explained by Justice Marshall.

▶ ANALYSIS

In finding pretrial detention under the Bail Reform Act not excessive, Chief Justice Rehnquist states that the Speedy Trial Act limits the length of pretrial detention. Some courts have required release on bail where pretrial detention has become too lengthy. Other courts have found the length of pretrial detention of up to ten months irrelevant under the Bail Reform Act.

■═■

Continued on next page.

Quicknotes

EIGHTH AMENDMENT The Eighth Amendment to the federal constitution prohibits the imposition of excessive bail, fines, and cruel and unusual punishment.

FOURTEENTH AMENDMENT DUE PROCESS CLAUSE Provides that protections mandated by the U.S. Constitution and observed by the federal government are equally applicable, and therefore must be observed by the States.

■▬■

Barker v. Wingo

Convicted murderer (D) v. Government official (P)

407 U.S. 514 (1972).

NATURE OF CASE: Petition for certiorari of a murder conviction.

FACT SUMMARY: Although Barker (D) made no objections during the first four years of a five-year delay between his arrest and conviction for murder, he subsequently claimed that his right to a speedy trial had been violated.

🏛 RULE OF LAW
The determination of whether a defendant has been deprived of his Sixth Amendment right to a speedy trial must be made on a case-by-case basis by balancing the following four factors: (1) length of delay, (2) reason for delay, (3) the defendant's assertion of his right, and (4) prejudice to the defendant.

FACTS: On July 20, 1958, an elderly couple was murdered. Shortly afterwards, Silas Manning and Willie Barker (D) were arrested as suspects. On September 15 they were indicted, counsel was appointed on September 17, and Barker's (D) trial was set for October 21. However, Barker (D) was not brought to trial for more than five years after his arrest due to numerous continuances by the prosecution. Initially the continuances were for the purpose of first convicting Manning, against whom the Commonwealth had a stronger case, to assure his testimony at Barker's (D) trial (i.e., to eliminate problems of self-incrimination). However, Manning was not convicted until 1962. Afterward, Barker's (D) trial was delayed another seven months due to the illness of the chief investigating officer in the case. During these continuances, Barker (D) was free except for ten months in jail, and he made no objections during the first four years of delay. However, Barker (D) objected to the last few continuances, and, at his trial, he moved for dismissal on the basis that his Sixth Amendment right to a speedy trial had been violated. This motion was denied and Barker (D) was convicted of murder. Upon appeal to the Kentucky Court of Appeals, the conviction was affirmed. Barker (D) then petitioned for habeas corpus in the U.S. district court. Upon denial of that petition, he appealed to the Sixth Circuit Court of Appeals. Upon affirmance of his conviction, Barker (D) brought a petition for certiorari.

ISSUE: Is a delay of five years between the arrest and trial of a defendant a violation per se of his Sixth Amendment right to a speedy trial?

HOLDING AND DECISION: (Powell, J.) No. The determination of whether a defendant has been deprived of his Sixth Amendment right to a speedy trial must be made on a case-by-case basis by balancing the following four factors: (1) length of delay, (2) reason for delay, (3) the defendant's assertion of his right, and (4) prejudice to the defendant. Since the deprivation of the right to a speedy trial does not per se prejudice the ability of an accused to defend himself, it is impossible to state "with precision" when the right has been denied. Each factor, therefore, must be separately analyzed. First, it is true that a long delay before trial is more likely to be justified for a serious, complex crime (e.g., murder) than for a simple one. Here, however, the delay of over five years was extreme by any standard. Second, it is true that a delay in bringing an accused to trial may be justified by a showing of some strong reason for it. Here, however, there was a strong reason for delay (i.e., illness of the chief investigator) for only seven months of the five-year delay. Although some additional delay might also have been necessary to acquire Manning as a witness, over four years was clearly unreasonable. Third, it is true that failure to assert the right to a speedy trial will not constitute a waiver of that right, unless it is found to be an "intentional relinquishment or abandonment of a known right." Here, however, it is obvious that Barker (D) did not want a trial at all, hoping, rather, that the delays would ultimately result in dismissal of the charges against him. Fourth, it is true that the prejudice which results from a delay of a defendant's trial must be evaluated in the light of those interests which a speedy trial was designed to protect (i.e., prevention of "oppressive pretrial incarceration," minimization of anxiety and concern of the accused, and limitation on the possibility that the defense will be "impaired"). Here, however, prejudice was minimal. Although Barker (D) was prejudiced to some extent by spending some time in jail and by living for years under "a cloud of suspicion," none of his witnesses died or became unavailable. In conclusion, the facts that Barker (D) did not want a trial and was not prejudiced by the delay outweigh the unjustified length of delay. Judgment affirmed.

Continued on next page.

▶ *ANALYSIS*

This case illustrates the discretion available (through the balancing test) to the courts in determining when the right to a speedy trial has been violated, and the emphasis on the desire of an accused to have a speedy trial. Note that an accused "waives" the right to a speedy trial if he flees the state after arraignment or requests postponement of his trial. Note, also, that the right to a speedy trial attaches only after a person is accused (i.e., indicted or arrested), so that it is not violated by police delay in filing charges. However, if such a delay was purposeful, due process requires dismissal of the charges.

■■■■

Quicknotes

SIXTH AMENDMENT Provides the right to a speedy and public trial by impartial jury, the right to be informed of the accusation, the right to confront witnesses, and the right to have the assistance of counsel in all criminal prosecutions.

■■■■

United States v. Lovasco

Federal government (P) v. Criminal indictee (D)

431 U.S. 783 (1977).

NATURE OF CASE: Appeal from dismissal of a criminal indictment.

FACT SUMMARY: The district court dismissed the criminal indictment against Lovasco (D) due to the delay between the commission of the offense and the initiation of prosecution.

🏛 RULE OF LAW
To prosecute a criminal defendant following investigative delay does not deprive him of due process, even if his defense might have been somewhat prejudiced by the lapse of time.

FACTS: Although the offenses of possessing firearms stolen from the U.S. mail and dealing in firearms without a license allegedly occurred between July 25 and August 31, 1973, Lovasco (D) was not indicted for those crimes until March 6, 1975. The initial report noted that he told Government (P) agents just one month after the alleged commission of the crimes that he had possessed and sold five of the stolen guns. By that time, there was also strong evidence linking him to the remaining three weapons. However, the agents were unable to confirm or refute his claim that he had found the guns in his car when he returned to it after visiting his son, a mail handler, at work. Little additional information was uncovered in the 17 months that followed before initiation of prosecution. Evidence showed that two witnesses whom Lovasco (D) claimed would have helped his defense had died, one nine months and the other more than a year after the initial investigative report on the crimes was completed. Thus, the district court granted Lovasco's (D) motion to dismiss the indictment on the ground that the unreasonable and unnecessary delay in initiating prosecution had prejudiced his defense and thus violated his due process rights. The court of appeals affirmed.

ISSUE: Does it violate the Due Process Clause to prosecute a criminal defendant following investigative delay, even if his defense is somewhat prejudiced by the lapse of time?

HOLDING AND DECISION: (Marshall, J.) No. Even if his defense is somewhat prejudiced by the lapse of time between commission of the crimes and initiation of prosecution, prosecuting a defendant following investigative delay does not deprive him of due process. Proof of actual prejudice is a necessary prerequisite to and makes a due process claim concrete and ripe for adjudication, but it does not make the claim automatically valid. The determining question is whether com-pelling a particular defendant to stand trial after delay in a particular case violates those "fundamental conceptions of justice which lie at the base of our civil and political institutions." It does not in cases like this. Reversed.

DISSENT: (Stevens, J.) The judgment of the court of appeals should be affirmed. Otherwise, the Constitution imposes no constraints on the prosecutor's power to postpone the filing of formal charges until it suits his convenience.

▶ ANALYSIS

The Court is careful not to say that prejudicial preaccusation delay could never be a due process violation. This may prove most important in the future, since the Sixth Amendment right to a speedy trial has been found inapplicable to preindictment delays.

■=■

Quicknotes

DUE PROCESS CLAUSE Clauses found in the Fifth and Fourteenth Amendments to the United States Constitution providing that no person shall be deprived of "life, liberty, or property, without due process of law."

SIXTH AMENDMENT Provides the right to a speedy and public trial by impartial jury, the right to be informed of the accusation, the right to confront witnesses, and the right to have the assistance of counsel in all criminal prosecutions.

■=■

Doggett v. United States

Criminal defendant (D) v. Federal government (P)

505 U.S. 647 (1992).

NATURE OF CASE: Appeal from conviction for cocaine distribution.

FACT SUMMARY: Doggett (D) was indicted in 1980 for drug offenses but not brought to trial until 1988 due to the government's lack of diligence in tracking him.

RULE OF LAW

An excessive delay between indictment and trial raises a presumption of prejudice to the defendant if the delay was caused by the government's negligence.

FACTS: Doggett (D) was indicted for drug offenses in 1980. The Drug Enforcement Agency (DEA) sought to arrest him, but he had left the country. The DEA found out that Doggett (D) was under arrest in Panama in 1981. The Government (P) did not seek extradiction but only asked Panama to expel him when it was through with his proceedings. Doggett (D) was let go from Panama in 1982 and went to Colombia briefly before returning to the United States, apparently unaware of the outstanding indictment. He settled in Virginia, got a job, married, and lived openly under his own name. Although the DEA found out in 1985 that Doggett (D) had left Panama in 1982, it made no attempt to find him until 1988, when agents ran a credit check on people subject to outstanding warrants. Within minutes they learned where Doggett (D) lived and worked, and he was arrested. Doggett (D) entered a conditional plea of guilty to preserve his claim that his right to a speedy trial had been violated. The court of appeals affirmed his conviction, and Doggett (D) appealed.

ISSUE: Does an excessive delay between indictment and trial raise a presumption of prejudice to the defendant if the delay was caused by the government's negligence?

HOLDING AND DECISION: (Souter, J.) Yes. An excessive delay between indictment and trial raises a presumption of prejudice to the defendant if the delay was caused by the government's negligence. The Sixth Amendment guarantees that the accused is entitled to a speedy trial in all criminal prosecutions. Precedent shows that there are a few critical factors that must be looked at: (1) the length of the delay; (2) whether the delay is due to the government or the defendant; (3) whether the defendant asserted his right to a speedy trial; and (4) the prejudice suffered by the defendant. In the present case, the delay of eight years between indictment and arrest was an uncommonly lengthy delay. The Government's

(P) claim of diligence in finding Doggett (D) is contrary to the evidence. For six years, the Government (P) made no serious effort to find him, which may have reflected his relative unimportance. There was no evidence that Doggett (D) was aware of the indictment, so it was impossible for him to assert his speedy trial rights prior to his arrest. The final factor is prejudice suffered by Doggett (D) due to the delay. Although Doggett (D) was unable to show precisely how he was prejudiced, the unreasonable delay in this case raises a presumption of prejudice. The presumption arises because it is difficult to prove that time has eroded exculpatory evidence. This presumed prejudice combined with the Government's (P) negligence in causing the delay is enough to demonstrate that Doggett's (D) right to a speedy trial was violated. Conviction reversed.

DISSENT: (Thomas, J.) The purpose of the Sixth Amendment right to a speedy trial was to ensure fairness to the defendant. Absent any showing that the delay harmed Doggett (D), the speedy trial right is simply not implicated.

► ANALYSIS

Both the majority and the dissent pointed out that the usual harm cited by defendants by a delay is anxiety and concern and pretrial incarceration. Justice Thomas went so far as to advocate that when the defendant is unaware of the charges (as in the case of Doggett (D)), there can be no violation. However, the majority is certainly correct in finding that the government should not be encouraged to neglect prosecutions.

Quicknotes

SIXTH AMENDMENT Provides the right to a speedy and public trial by impartial jury, the right to be informed of the accusation, the right to confront witnesses, and the right to have the assistance of counsel in all criminal prosecutions.

CHAPTER 10

Guilty Please and Plea Bargaining

Quick Reference Rules of Law

United States v. Broce

Federal government (P) v. Criminal defendant (D)

488 U.S. 563 (1989).

NATURE OF CASE: Review of a double jeopardy challenge to a conviction.

FACT SUMMARY: Defendants were convicted of two separate counts of conspiracy after entering guilty pleas.

🏛 RULE OF LAW
A valid guilty plea and conviction should not be set aside where defendants fail to consciously waive a double jeopardy defense.

FACTS: Broce (D) and a construction company Broce (D) owned were charged with two conspiracies to rig bids and suppress competition in violation of the Sherman Antitrust Act. Broce (D) and his company (D) pleaded guilty to both charges. Defendants did not challenge either the adequacy of counsel's advice or the sufficiency of the plea colloquy. In a separate litigation that took place at about the same time, another local construction company and its head, Robert Beachner, were charged with participation in another bid-rigging conspiracy. Beachner and his company took the case to trial and were acquitted. The government then brought charges against Beachner in other bid-rigging conspiracies. Beachner moved to dismiss these charges on the basis that they were part of the same conspiracy that the government had charged earlier and for which Beachner had been acquitted. He maintained that the new charges thus violated the Double Jeopardy Clause. Beachner's double jeopardy challenge was successful and his motion to dismiss granted. Broce (D) raised the same argument in connection with his guilty plea. The district court found that Broce (D) did not raise grounds sufficient to justify setting aside an otherwise valid guilty plea.

ISSUE: Should an otherwise valid guilty plea and conviction be set aside where defendants did not consciously waive a double jeopardy defense?

HOLDING AND DECISION: (Kennedy, J.) No. Conscious waiver is not necessary with respect to each potential defense relinquished by a plea of guilty. Relinquishment does not derive from the defendant's subjective understanding of the range of defenses but from the admissions necessarily made upon entry of a voluntary plea of guilty. Defendants, as here, are not entitled to collateral relief where they have not challenged the voluntary and intelligent character of their pleas. The government has a substantial interest in the finality of a guilty plea.

▶ ANALYSIS

In dicta, the *Broce* court suggests that by pleading guilty, defendants lose all claims other than those that can be resolved with further fact-finding.

Quicknotes

DOUBLE JEOPARDY A prohibition against a second prosecution for the same offense after an acquittal or conviction for that offense in a prior proceeding or against multiple punishments for the same offense.

North Carolina v. Alford

State (P) v. Criminal defendant (D)

400 U.S. 25 (1970).

NATURE OF CASE: Appeal from a conviction for second-degree murder.

FACT SUMMARY: Alford (D), although still claiming his innocence, pleaded guilty and was convicted of second-degree murder.

RULE OF LAW
An assertion of innocence by a defendant does not, of itself, render a plea of guilty invalid.

FACTS: Faced with strong evidence of guilt and no substantial evidentiary support for the claim of innocence, Alford's (D) attorney recommended that he plead guilty. The prosecutor agreed to accept a plea of guilty to a charge of second-degree murder, and Alford (D) pleaded guilty to the reduced charge. Alford (D), however, maintained that he had not committed the murder but that he was pleading guilty because he faced the threat of the death penalty if he did not do so. The court sentenced Alford (D) to the maximum penalty allowed, and Alford (D) sought post-conviction relief in state court, which was refused. After two unsuccessful petitions for a writ of habeas corpus, the court of appeals reversed the conviction on the ground that Alford's (D) guilty plea was made involuntarily, and the state appealed.

ISSUE: Does a defendant's assertion of innocence negate any admission of guilt and render his guilty plea invalid?

HOLDING AND DECISION: (White, J.) No. The constitution does not bar imposition of a prison sentence upon an accused who is unwilling expressly to admit his guilt but who, faced with grim alternatives, is willing to waive his trial and accept the sentence. The standard remains whether the plea represents a voluntary and intelligent choice among the alternative courses of action open to the defendant. Here, confronted with the choice between a trial for first-degree murder, on the one hand, and a plea of guilty to second-degree murder, on the other, Alford (D) quite reasonably chose the latter and thereby limited the maximum penalty to a 30-year term. That he would not have pleaded except for the opportunity to limit the possible penalty does not necessarily demonstrate that the plea of guilty was not the product of a free and rational choice, especially where the defendant was represented by competent counsel whose advice was that the plea would be to the defendant's advantage. Vacated and remanded.

DISSENT: (Brennan, J.) Without reaching the question whether due process permits the entry of judgment upon a plea of guilty accompanied by a contemporaneous denial of acts constituting the crime, at the very least such a denial of guilt is also a relevant factor in determining whether the plea was voluntarily and intelligently made. It is sufficient in my view to state that the facts set out in the majority opinion demonstrate that Alford (D) was "so gripped by fear of the death penalty" that his decision to plead guilty was not voluntary but was "the product of duress as much so as choice reflecting physical restraint."

ANALYSIS

The problem with Alford's assertion of innocence here is that it was not in accord with his actions. According to confirmed testimony, Alford (D) left his home with his gun stating his intention to kill and he later declared that he had carried out his intention.

Quicknotes

HABEAS CORPUS A proceeding in which a defendant brings a writ to compel a judicial determination of whether he is lawfully being held in custody.

Hill v. Lockhart

Convicted murderer (P) v. Government official (D)

474 U.S. 52 (1985).

NATURE OF CASE: Appeal from denial of writ of habeas corpus relief.

FACT SUMMARY: Without a hearing, the district court denied writ of habeas corpus relief in an ineffective assistance of counsel claim following a guilty plea, and the court of appeals affirmed.

🏛 RULE OF LAW
A defendant must demonstrate prejudice in addition to unreasonable error to enter a valid ineffective assistance of counsel challenge to a guilty plea.

FACTS: Petitioner William Lloyd Hill pleaded guilty in Arkansas trial court to charges of first-degree murder and theft of property. More than two years later, Hill (P) sought federal habeas relief on the ground that his court-appointed attorney failed to advise him that, as a second offender, he was required to serve one-half of his sentence before becoming eligible for parole. The district court denied habeas relief without a hearing, and the court of appeals affirmed.

ISSUE: Must a defendant demonstrate prejudice, in addition to unreasonable error, to enter a valid ineffective assistance of counsel claim related to a guilty plea?

HOLDING AND DECISION: (Rehnquist, J.) Yes. Applying the two-part Strickland standard will serve the fundamental interest of finality of guilty pleas. The prejudice requirement should focus on whether the ineffective assistance of counsel affected the outcome of the plea process. In this case, the alleged error of counsel was erroneous advice as to the eligibility for parole under the sentence agreed to in the plea bargain. Petitioner, however, did not demonstrate that had he been informed of his parole eligibility date, he would have pleaded not guilty and insisted on going to trial. Further, petitioner failed to demonstrate any special circumstances to support his contention that he placed particular emphasis on his parole eligibility in determining whether or not to plead guilty. The judgment of the court of appeals is affirmed.

▶ ANALYSIS

The relevant question under the Strickland prejudice standard is whether there was a reasonable probability that, but for counsel's errors, the outcome would have been different.

Brady v. United States

Convicted kidnapper (D) v. Federal government (P)

397 U.S. 742 (1970).

NATURE OF CASE: Petition for collateral relief attacking conviction of kidnapping.

FACT SUMMARY: Brady (D) claimed that rather than risk trial, and a possible death sentence, he pled guilty.

🏛 RULE OF LAW
Although a federal penal statute that permits imposition of the death sentence only upon a jury's recommendation is unconstitutional because it makes the risk of death the price of a jury trial, not every guilty plea entered under the act is invalidated simply upon an assertion that the defendant pled guilty from a fear of death.

FACTS: In 1959, Brady (D) was charged with kidnapping in violation of 18 U.S.C. § 1201(a). The section provided for a maximum penalty of death upon conviction if the jury should so recommend. At first, Brady (D) elected to plead not guilty and made no serious attempt to waive a jury trial. Upon learning that a codefendant would be available to testify against him, Brady (D) changed his plea to guilty. His plea was accepted after the trial judge questioned Brady (D) as to its voluntariness. In 1967, Brady petitioned for collateral postconviction relief, claiming that § 1201(a) operated to coerce his confession. In 1968, the Supreme Court, in *United States v. Jackson*, 390 U.S. 570 (1968), held that § 1201(a) was unconstitutional in that it "needlessly penalize(d)" the assertion of the Sixth Amendment right to jury trial and the Fifth Amendment right not to plead guilty.

ISSUE: Does the decision in *United States v. Jackson* require the invalidation of every plea of guilty entered under 18 U.S.C. § 1201(a), at least when the fear of death is shown to have been a factor in the plea?

HOLDING AND DECISION: (White, J.) No. Although Jackson prohibited the imposition of death under 18 U.S.C. § 1201(a), it did not fashion a new standard to supplant the test that guilty pleas are valid if both "voluntary" and "intelligent." Even assuming that Brady (D) would not have pleaded guilty but for the death penalty provision, this does not prove that the entering of the plea was an involuntary act. There is no claim here that Brady's (D) plea was induced by actual or threatened physical harm or by mental coercion or that he did not rationally weigh the advantages of not going to trial. There is nothing here to differentiate Brady (D) from the defendant who is advised to plead guilty out of a desire to get more lenient treatment from the judge or to get favorable plea bargaining. Such plea inducements conform with accepted notions of conserving judicial time and resources and with commencing with the rehabilitative goals of the criminal justice system. A contrary holding would require government to forbid guilty pleas altogether. Brady's (D) plea was also intelligently made. Although § 1201(a) was later invalidated, a defendant is not entitled to withdraw his plea because he discovers the statute is unconstitutional long after his plea has been accepted simply because he miscalculated. The truth or reliability of Brady's (D) plea is not impugned by Jackson.

▶ *ANALYSIS*

While the court was not inclined to expand the scope of the voluntariness standard, it indicated, in *Boykin v. Alabama*, 395 U.S. 238 (1969), a willingness to provide for more controls over the acceptance, by the trial court, of a "voluntary" plea. The Court held that a guilty plea is not presumed voluntary where the judge does not question the defendant concerning his plea and the defendant does not address the court, and the trial judge must employ the great care in canvassing the plea with the accused to make sure he completely understands of what the plea connotes and its consequences.

Quicknotes

18 U.S.C. § 1201 (A) Provides that discretion for assigning the death penalty rest with the jury; later, this section was invalidated.

COERCED CONFESSION A statement made by a person charged with the commission of a criminal offense, acknowledging his guilt in respect to the charged offense, that was made when the confessor's free will was overcome as a result of threats, promises, or undue influence, and which is inadmissible at trial.

Bordenkircher v. Hayes

Government official (P) v. Check forger (D)

434 U.S. 357 (1978).

NATURE OF CASE: Appeal from a criminal conviction and penalty enhancement.

FACT SUMMARY: The prosecutor informed Hayes (D) that he would seek an indictment under the Kentucky Habitual Criminal Act if he did not plead guilty to the charge of uttering a forged instrument; Hayes (D) pled innocent, a jury convicted him, and his sentence was enhanced when the prosecutor initiated the Habitual Criminal indictment.

🏛 RULE OF LAW
A prosecutor can attempt to gain a defendant's assent to a plea bargain by informing the defendant that more severe charges will be brought if no bargain is struck.

FACTS: Hayes (D), who was charged with uttering a forged instrument (for $88.30), faced a sentence of two to ten years if convicted. The prosecutor offered a five-year sentence in return for a guilty plea and told Hayes (D) that refusal to take the "bargain" would result in his seeking an additional indictment under the Kentucky Habitual Criminal Act, which makes a life sentence mandatory if there are two prior felony convictions. When Hayes (D) declined the plea bargain, he was subjected to the additional indictment and sentenced to life imprisonment under the Habitual Criminal Act, after having been found guilty of the uttering charge. The two previous felonies in which Hayes (D) was involved had never resulted in his imprisonment; one was a rape charge reduced to a plea of detaining a female, and the other was a robbery conviction resulting in five years in a reformatory. Finding the prosecutor to have acted vindictively in securing the second indictment, the court of appeals reversed Hayes's (D) conviction for violation of due process of law.

ISSUE: Is it constitutionally permissible for a prosecutor to try to influence a defendant to accept a plea bargain by informing him that more severe charges will be brought if it is refused?

HOLDING AND DECISION: (Stewart, J.) Yes. As the constitutionality and utility of plea bargaining have been recognized, there is no bar to the prosecutor's use of the possibility of more severe charges being brought for purposes of persuading a defendant to accept a plea bargain. As long as the defendant is advised that the bringing of additional charges will accompany his refusal to bargain, the situation becomes similar to that where the prosecutor offers to drop a charge as part of the plea bargain. If plea bargaining is a recognized process, neither can be forbidden simply because the charging decision is influenced by what a prosecutor hopes to gain in plea bargaining negotiations. In accepting plea bargaining, it is implicit that there is acceptance of the notion that the prosecutor's interest is to persuade the defendant not to exercise his right to plead not guilty. As long as the prosecutor has probable cause to believe the accused committed the offense, and his discretion is exercised in accordance with justifiable standards, there is no due process violation. Reversed.

DISSENT: (Powell, J.) Discretion used to deter the exercise of constitutional rights is not constitutionally exercised. The prosecutor's initial failure to charge indicates his own appreciation of the unreasonableness of placing Hayes (D) in jeopardy of life imprisonment when many murderers and rapists face lighter sentences.

▎*ANALYSIS*

The case in which the Court first recognized plea bargaining as a legitimate practice was *Brady v. United States*. While the majority here suggests that such an acceptance implies sanctioning of prosecutorial use of charging powers to influence a defendant to plead guilty, the *Brady* decision specifically states that it makes no reference to such use by the prosecutor or a similar use by the judge of his sentencing power.

Quicknotes

PLEA BARGAIN An agreement between a prosecutor and a criminal defendant that is submitted to the court for approval, generally involves the defendant's pleading guilty to a lesser charge or count in exchange for a more lenient sentence.

United States v. Pollard

Federal government (D) v. Espionage convict (P)

959 F.2d 1011 (D.C. Cir. 1992).

NATURE OF CASE: Appeal from the dismissal of a writ of habeas corpus claim.

FACT SUMMARY: The district court dismissed without a hearing petitioner's motion to withdraw his guilty plea.

🏛 RULE OF LAW
Plea wiring does not offend due process or the privilege against compulsory self-incrimination.

FACTS: From June 1984 through November 1985, Jonathan Pollard (P), an Intelligence Research Specialist with the United States Navy, removed large amounts of highly classified U.S. intelligence information from his office, copied it, and delivered it to agents of the Israeli government. Initially Pollard (P) was not paid, but during the last twelve months of this period, he received between $1,500.00 and $2,500.00 per month from Israeli handlers. One year after the regular deliveries began, Pollard (P) was questioned by the FBI and Naval Investigative Service about the removal of classified information from his office. During this interview, he received permission to call his wife twice. During these conversations, he used "cactus," a prearranged code word that directed Mrs. Pollard to remove a suitcase full of classified information from the Pollards' apartment. Mrs. Pollard performed this task and contacted the Israeli handlers to tell them Pollard (P) was in trouble. Pollard lied during the interviews and stalled for time. Pollard (P) pleaded guilty to espionage on June 4, 1986. Three years after sentencing, Pollard (P) sought to attack his sentence collaterally by filing a habeas petition, claiming that the government obtained his guilty plea improperly by linking his wife's plea to his own. The district court dismissed Pollard's (P) motion without a hearing.

ISSUE: Is plea wiring so coercive as to risk inducing false guilty pleas?

HOLDING AND DECISION: (Silberman, J.) No. Plea wiring is the practice of linking pleas during plea bargaining and offering adverse or lenient treatment to some person other than the accused. This practice is not coercive. Only physical harm, threats of harassment, misrepresentation, or "promises that are by their nature improper as having no proper relationship to the prosecutor's business" render a guilty plea legally involuntary. In this case, Pollard (P) had several opportunities to confess any misgivings during the plea colloquy, but he never gave the slightest hint that his plea was involuntary. Further, the Government (P) had probable cause to arrest and prosecute both Pollard (P) and his wife and did not conduct the plea negotiations in bad faith. Thus, the guilty plea here is not constitutionally infirm.

▶ ANALYSIS

Under Pollard, prosecutors may link the fates of both spouses in the prosecution of either spouse where both spouses are charged with criminal activity.

◼▬◼

Quicknotes

PLEA BARGAIN An agreement between a prosecutor and a criminal defendant that is submitted to the court for approval, generally involves the defendant's pleading guilty to a lesser charge or count in exchange for a more lenient sentence.

◼▬◼

Newton v. Rumery

Municipality (D) Civil litigant (P)

480 U.S. 386 (1987).

NATURE OF CASE: Appeal from a failure to dismiss a 42 U.S.C. §1983 lawsuit.

FACT SUMMARY: Although Rumery (P) entered into a "release-dismissal" agreement with the town of Newton (D) to forego a §1983 lawsuit against the town in exchange for the town's not bringing criminal charges against him, Rumery (P) nevertheless sued the town on the grounds the agreement was unenforceable as violating public policy.

🏛 **RULE OF LAW**
A court may properly enforce an agreement in which a criminal defendant releases his right to file an action under 42 U.S.C. §1983 in return for a prosecutor's dismissal of pending criminal charges.

FACTS: After investigating felonious sexual assault charges against David Champy, the chief of police of the town of Newton (D), accused Rumery (P), a friend of Champy, of witness tampering in the Champy case. Rumery's (P) defense attorney and the deputy district attorney, after discussions, reached a written agreement under which the prosecutor would dismiss the charges against Rumery (P) if Rumery (P) would agree not to sue the town under 42 U.S.C. §1983 (a so-called "release-dismissal" agreement). The agreement was drafted by the defense attorney and signed by all parties. The criminal charges were accordingly dropped. Notwithstanding the agreement, ten months later Rumery (P) filed a §1983 action against the town of Newton (D), alleging the town's violation of his constitutional rights. Rejecting Rumery's (P) argument that the agreement was unenforceable as violating public policy, the federal district court dismissed Rumery's (P) suit. The federal court of appeals reversed, and the town of Newton (D) appealed.

ISSUE: May a court properly enforce an agreement in which a criminal defendant releases his right to file an action under 42 U.S.C. §1983 in return for a prosecutor's dismissal of pending criminal charges?

HOLDING AND DECISION: (Powell, J.) Yes. A court may properly enforce an agreement in which a criminal defendant releases his right to file an action under 42 U.S.C. §1983 in return for a prosecutor's dismissal of pending criminal charges. While it is true that some release-dismissal agreements may not be the product of an informed and voluntary decision, such possibility does not justify invalidating all such

agreements. In other contexts criminal defendants are required to make difficult choices that effectively waive constitutional rights. For example, it is well settled that plea bargaining does not violate the Constitution even though a guilty plea waives important constitutional rights. We see no reason to believe that release-dismissal agreements pose a more coercive choice than other situations we have accepted. In many cases a defendant's choice to enter into a release-dismissal agreement will reflect a highly rational judgment that the certain benefits of escaping criminal prosecution exceed the speculative benefits of prevailing in a civil action. Here, Rumery's (P) voluntary action to enter this agreement exemplifies such a judgment. Rumery (P) is a sophisticated businessman. He was not in jail and was represented by an experienced criminal lawyer, who drafted the agreement. Rumery (P) considered the agreement for three days before signing it. The benefits of the agreement to Rumery (P) are obvious: he gained immunity from criminal prosecution in consideration of abandoning a civil suit that he may well have lost. While availability of such agreements may, in particular cases, threaten important public interests, a per se rule of invalidity fails to credit other relevant public interests and improperly assumes prosecutorial misconduct. Reversed.

CONCURRENCE: (O'Connor, J.) It is the burden of those relying upon release-dismissal agreements to establish that the agreement is neither involuntary nor the product of an abuse of criminal process. Many factors may bear on this question.

DISSENT: (Stevens, J.) The deliberate and rational character of Rumery's (P) decision is not a sufficient reason for concluding that the agreement is enforceable. Not only is a person in Rumery's (P) position presumptively innocent as a matter of law; as a factual matter the prosecutor's interest in obtaining a covenant not to sue will be strongest in those cases in which he or she realizes that the defendant was innocent and was wrongfully accused.

▶ **ANALYSIS**

In *Newton*, the Supreme Court made clear its viewpoint that simply because a prosecutor may have the opportunity to seize an occasion for wrongdoing and act improperly, does not compel an assumption that all—or even a significant

Continued on next page.

number of—release-dismissal agreements stem from prosecutors abandoning the independence of judgment required
by their public trust. Tradition and experience, said the Court,
justified its belief that the majority of prosecutors would be
faithful to their duty.

■■

Quicknotes

PROSECUTORIAL IMMUNITY Statutory protection afforded to a
witness against prosecution as a result of his testimony.

■■

United States v. Mezzanatto

Federal government (P) v. Criminal defendant (D)

513 U.S. 196 (1995).

NATURE OF CASE: Appeal on evidentiary grounds from the reversal of a conviction.

FACT SUMMARY: Holding that respondent's agreement to allow admission of his plea statements for purposes of impeachment was unenforceable, a panel of the Ninth Circuit reversed respondent's conviction.

🏛 **RULE OF LAW**
The exclusionary provisions of the plea statement rules may be waived by the defendant.

FACTS: Mezzanato (D) was arrested and charged with possession of methamphetamine with intent to distribute after an undercover police officer purchased a pound of the substance from him. During plea negotiations, Mezzanatto (D) indicated that he wanted to cooperate with the Government (P). The prosecutor informed the respondent that such cooperation depended on his agreeing to allow the Government (P) to use any statements made during the negotiations to impeach contradictory testimony he might give at trial. After conferring with counsel, Mezzanato (D) agreed. Mezzanato (D) testified at trial and the prosecutor cross-examined him about the inconsistent statements he had made at the plea agreement meeting. Respondent denied making the earlier statements, and the prosecutor countered with the testimony of one of the officers present at the earlier plea meeting. The jury found Mezzanato (D) guilty and the district court sentenced him to 170 months in prison. A panel of the Ninth Circuit reversed holding that respondent's agreement to allow admission of his plea statements for purposes of impeachment was unenforceable.

ISSUE: May the exclusionary provisions of the plea statement rules be waived by the defendant?

HOLDING AND DECISION: (Thomas, J.) Yes. The Ninth Circuit assumes from Congressional silence that Congress intended to preclude waiver agreements, such as Mezzanato's (D). This decision was in error. A criminal defendant may knowingly and voluntarily waive many of the most fundamental protections afforded by the Constitution. Additionally, absent an affirmative indication of congressional intent to preclude waiver, this Court has presumed that statutory provisions are subject to waiver by voluntary agreement. In this case, respondent conferred with counsel and accepted the prosecutor's proposed waiver. There is no per se prohibition of waiver of the plea statement rules. Reversed.

CONCURRENCE: (Ginsburg, J.) A waiver may inhibit plea bargaining, contrary to the majority's premise that it will always promote plea bargaining.

DISSENT: (Souter, J.) The majority's decision may place restrictions on the candor of plea discussions, thus inhibiting compromise.

▶ *ANALYSIS*

Under *Mezzanatto*, defendants may waive the exclusion of statements made in plea discussions.

■■■■

Quicknotes

PLEA BARGAIN An agreement between a prosecutor and a criminal defendant that is submitted to the court for approval, generally involves the defendant's pleading guilty to a lesser charge or count in exchange for a more lenient sentence.

■■■■

Santobello v. New York

Convicted felon (D) v. State (P)

404 U.S. 257 (1971).

NATURE OF CASE: Appeal from a felony conviction and one-year prison sentence.

FACT SUMMARY: Santobello (D) challenged his conviction and sentence based on the breach of a commitment by the prosecutor made in the course of plea bargaining.

🏛 RULE OF LAW
When the state fails to keep a commitment concerning the sentence recommendation on a guilty plea, a new trial is required.

FACTS: Indicted on two felony counts, Santobello (D) negotiated with the assistant district attorney and agreed to plead guilty to a lesser included offense, provided the prosecutor agreed to make no recommendation as to the sentence. Following procedural delays between Santobello's (D) conviction and the imposition of sentence, during which time both defense counsel and prosecutor were replaced, the new prosecutor at the sentence hearing requested the maximum sentence of one year. The trial judge imposed the maximum sentence and Santobello (D) appealed. His conviction was affirmed in the state courts.

ISSUE: Does the state's failure to keep a commitment concerning the sentence recommended on a guilty plea require a new trial?

HOLDING AND DECISION: (Burger, C.J.) Yes. The state's failure to keep a commitment concerning the sentence recommended on a guilty plea requires a new trial. The disposition of criminal charges by agreement between the prosecutor and the accused, sometimes loosely called "plea bargaining," is an essential component of the administration of justice. Properly administered, it is to be encouraged. It leads to prompt and largely final disposition of most criminal cases. However, these considerations presuppose fairness in securing agreement between an accused and a prosecutor. When a plea rests in any significant degree on a promise or agreement of the prosecutor, so that it can be said to be part of the inducement or consideration, such promise must be fulfilled. Here, on the record, Santobello (D) "bargained" and negotiated for a particular plea in order to secure dismissal of more serious charges but also on condition that no sentence recommendation would be made by the prosecutor. That a breach of agreement was inadvertent does not lessen its impact. The interests of justice and appropriate recognition of the duties of the prosecution in relation to promises made in the negotiation of pleas of guilty will be best served by remanding the case to the state courts for further consideration. Judgment vacated and case remanded for reconsideration.

CONCURRENCE: (Douglas, J.) When the "plea bargain" is not kept by the prosecutor, the sentence must be vacated and the state court will decide in light of the circumstances of each case whether due process requires (a) that there be specific performance of the plea bargain or (b) that the defendant be given the option to go to trial on the original charges.

CONCURRENCE AND DISSENT IN PART: Marshall, J.) The petitioner must be permitted to withdraw his guilty plea. This is the relief petitioner requested and, on the facts set out by the majority, it is the form of relief to which he is entitled.

▶ ANALYSIS

The Court here, in not only the majority but also the concurring and dissenting opinions, affirmed both the constitutionality and viability of modern plea bargaining. What is noteworthy here is that the Court, per Douglas, applied the common law principles of contract law, rather than criminal law, in fashioning the "remedies" available to the defendant when the prosecutor "breaches" his commitment (i.e., specific performance of the bargain, or rescission of the entire agreement, including the guilty plea).

■≡■

Quicknotes

PLEA BARGAIN An agreement between a prosecutor and a criminal defendant that is submitted to the court for approval, generally involves the defendant's pleading guilty to a lesser charge or count in exchange for a more lenient sentence.

■≡■

Mabry v. Johnson

Parties not identified.

467 U.S. 504 (1984).

NATURE OF CASE: Appeal from dismissal of a writ of habeas corpus petition.

FACT SUMMARY: The district court dismissed the writ of habeas corpus petition, finding that respondent understood the consequences of his guilty plea.

RULE OF LAW

When a plea rests upon a prosecutor's promise, such that the promise is part of the inducement or consideration, such a promise must be fulfilled.

FACTS: In the evening of May 22, 1970, three members of a family returned home to find a burglary in progress. Shots were exchanged resulting in the daughter's death and the wounding of the father and the respondent, one of the burglars. Respondent was tried and convicted on three charges: burglary, assault, and murder. The murder conviction was set aside by the Arkansas Supreme Court. Plea negotiations ensued. At the time of negotiations, respondent was serving concurrent 21- and 12-year sentences on the burglary and assault convictions. A deputy prosecutor proposed to respondent's attorney that, in exchange for a guilty plea to the charge of accessory after a felony murder, the prosecutor would recommend a sentence of 21 years to be served concurrently with respondent's burglary and assault charges. Counsel communicated the offer to respondent, who accepted. The prosecutor then told counsel that he had made a mistake and withdrew the offer. Instead the prosecutor offered to recommend a sentence of 21 years to be served consecutively with respondent's other sentences. Respondent rejected the offer and elected to stand trial. The judge declared a mistrial on the second day of trial and plea negotiations resumed. Respondent eventually accepted the prosecutor's second offer. After exhausting his state remedies, respondent filed a habeas petition. The district court dismissed the petition.

ISSUE: Does a defendant's acceptance of a prosecutor's proposed plea bargain create a constitutional right to have the bargain specifically enforced?

HOLDING AND DECISION: (Stevens, J.) No. A guilty plea may be constitutionally challenged under the due process clause only when the defendant was not fully apprised of its consequences. In this case, respondent's plea was not induced by the prosecutor's withdrawn offer. Respondent thus was not deprived of his liberty in any fundamentally unfair way. Respondent was fully aware of the likely consequences of his guilty plea.

▶ ANALYSIS

Mabry makes clear that plea bargaining will not be analyzed under the ordinary rules of contract law.

Quicknotes

PLEA BARGAIN An agreement between a prosecutor and a criminal defendant that is submitted to the court for approval, generally involves the defendant's pleading guilty to a lesser charge or count in exchange for a more lenient sentence.

Ricketts v. Adamson

Government official (P) v. Convicted murderer (D)

483 U.S. 1 (1987).

NATURE OF CASE: Review of an en banc issuance of a writ of habeas corpus.

FACT SUMMARY: Holding that the State violated respon-dent's rights under the Double Jeopardy Clause, the court of appeals, en banc, directed the issuance of a writ of habeas corpus.

🏛 RULE OF LAW
Where a plea agreement eliminates the double jeopardy defense in the event of defendant's breach and defendant understands and knowingly agrees to these terms, defendant may be retried on the same offense.

FACTS: Respondent entered into a plea agreement whereby he agreed to plead guilty to a charge of second-degree murder and to testify against two other individuals—Max Dunlap and James Robison—allegedly involved in the murder of a reporter. The parties agreed that respondent would receive a prison sentence of 48–49 years with a total incarceration time of 20 years and 2 months. In January 1977 the state trial court accepted the plea and the sentence. Respondent testified against Dunlap and Robison, and they were convicted of first-degree murder. Thereafter, respondent was sentenced, but imposition of the sentence was withheld. In February of 1980, the Arizona Supreme Court reversed the convictions of Dunlap and Robison. The prosecutor sought respondent's co-operation in the retrial of Dunlap and Robison. Respondent, believing his obligation under the plea agreement had terminated when he was sentenced, agreed to testify only if certain additional conditions were met. The State informed respondent that he was in violation of the plea agreement, but the trial court refused to compel respondent to answer questions. The Arizona Supreme Court declined to accept jurisdiction of the State's petition for special action to review the trial judge's decision. On May 8, 1980, the State filed a new information charging respondent with first-degree murder. Respondent moved to quash on double jeopardy grounds, but his motion was denied. After several further rulings, respondent offered to testify at the retrials, but his offer was rejected. Respondent was convicted of first-degree murder and sentenced to death. The judgment was affirmed on direct appeal. Respondent then sought federal habeas corpus relief. The district court dismissed the petition a court of appeals panel affirmed. The court of appeals en banc held that the State had violated respondent's rights under the Double Jeopardy Clause and directed the issuance of the writ.

ISSUE: Did respondent's breach of the plea agreement remove the bar of double jeopardy on the first-degree murder charge?

HOLDING AND DECISION: (White, J.) Yes. The plea agreement in this case specifically provided that if respondent refused to testify, the entire plea agreement would be null and void. The agreement provided that, in the event the agreement became null and void, the parties would be returned to the status quo ante. Thus, the respondent would have no double jeopardy defense to assert if he violated the plea agreement. The respondent understood these provisions of the plea agreement and the consequences of breach. Reversed.

DISSENT: (Brennan, J.) The majority errs in failing to examine whether there was a breach of the plea agreement. The agree-ment does not contain an explicit waiver of the double jeopardy protection. Respondent's interpretation of the agreement was reasonable as the agreement made no reference to any obligations during a potential retrial.

▶ ANALYSIS
On remand, the Ninth Circuit decided that Adamson's death sentence was unconstitutionally arbitrary and thus a violation of due process.

■══■

Quicknotes

DOUBLE JEOPARDY A prohibition against a second prosecution for the same offense after an acquittal or conviction for that offense in a prior proceeding or against multiple punishments for the same offense

PLEA BARGAIN An agreement between a prosecutor and a criminal defendant that is submitted to the court for approval, generally involves the defendant's pleading guilty to a lesser charge or count in exchange for a more lenient sentence.

■══■

Discovery and Disclosure

Quick Reference Rules of Law

Kyles v. Whitley

Convicted murderer (D) v. Government official (P)

514 U.S. 419 (1995).

NATURE OF CASE: Petition for writ of habeas corpus after murder and death sentence were affirmed on direct appeal.

FACT SUMMARY: After Kyles's conviction for first-degree murder, it was revealed that the State failed to provide Kyles with certain evidence that was favorable to his case.

🏛 RULE OF LAW
The test for materiality of nondisclosed evidence is whether there is a "reasonable probability" that if the evidence had been revealed, the result would have been different.

FACTS: Kyles was convicted of the first-degree murder of Dolores Dye in a supermarket parking lot. After his sentence was affirmed on direct appeal, it was revealed that the State (P) failed to reveal certain evidence to him that was favorable to his defense. The undisclosed evidence included: inconsistent eyewitness statements; numerous statements made by a police informant; and a list of license plates from cars parked at the crime scene, which did not include Kyles's car. Kyles's first trial resulted in a hung jury; he was tried again, and convicted of first-degree murder and sentenced to death. Prior to Kyles's first trial, his attorneys filed a motion for disclosure of exculpatory evidence. The prosecution responded that there was no such evidence. Petitioner's request for federal habeas corpus relief was denied by the district and appellate courts.

ISSUE: Where the state fails to disclose evidence that may be exculpatory, is the nondisclosed evidence material only where it is likely to create reasonable doubt?

HOLDING AND DECISION: (Souter, J.). No. Favorable evidence is material and constitutional error results from its suppression where there is a "reasonable probability" that, had the evidence been disclosed, the result of the proceeding would have been different. The primary question is not whether the defendant would have likely received a different verdict, but whether he received a fair trial. Materiality is not the same as sufficiency. A defendant is not required to prove that after discounting the inculpatory evidence in light of the undisclosed evidence there was not enough to convict. Requiring a "reasonable probability" that the results of the proceeding would have been different obviates the need for a harmless error review. The materiality review considers the suppressed evidence collectively and not item-by-item. Here, the disclosure of the suppressed evidence would have made a different result reasonably probable; thus due process was violated. Reversed and remanded.

DISSENT: (Scalia, J.) The true test of materiality is whether, in light of all the evidence, including the nondisclosed evidence, a jury would have a reasonable doubt about the petitioner's guilt. Here, even with all the evidence, the jury could still have found the defendant guilty because of other evidence that was not discounted by the nondisclosed evidence. Therefore, the nondisclosed evidence was not material.

▶ ANALYSIS

The development of the prosecution's affirmative duty to disclose exculpatory evidence is associated with *Brady v. Maryland*, 363 U.S. 83 (1963). Under *Brady*, "the suppression by the prosecution of evidence favorable to an accused upon request violates the due process where the evidence is material either to guilt or to punishment, irrespective of the good faith or bad faith of the prosecution." Materiality is but one aspect of a *Brady* claim.

■=■

Quicknotes

MATERIALITY Importance; the degree of relevance or necessity to the particular matter.

■=■

Williams v. Florida

Convicted robber (D) v. State (P)

399 U.S. 78 (1970).

NATURE OF CASE: Appeal from conviction of robbery.

FACT SUMMARY: Florida law requires that a defendant submit to a limited form of pretrial discovery by the state whenever he intends to rely at trial on the defense of alibi.

RULE OF LAW

The constitutional privilege against self-incrimination is not violated by a requirement that the defendant give notice of an alibi defense and disclose his alibi witnesses.

FACTS: Williams (D) was charged with robbery. Prior to his trial, Williams (D) sought a protective order to be excused from complying with a Florida law that requires a defendant, on written demand of the prosecution, to give notice in advance of trial if the defendant intends to claim an alibi and to furnish the prosecution with information as to the place he claims to have been and with the names and addresses of the alibi witnesses he intends to use. Williams (D) wanted to declare his intent to use an alibi but objected to further disclosure on the ground that the rule would compel him to be a witness against himself in violation of the Fifth and Fourteenth Amendments. The rule also obligated the state to notify a defendant of any rebuttal witnesses to the alibi defense the state intended to call. Failure to comply, by either side, resulted in the exclusion of the defendant's alibi evidence or the state's rebuttal evidence. When Williams's (D) motion for the protective order was denied, he complied with the rule. On the morning of his trial, the State (P) interviewed a Mrs. Scotty, Williams's (D) chief alibi witness. At trial, Mrs. Scotty gave testimony that contradicted her pretrial statements. The State (P) also furnished a rebuttal witness. Williams (D) was convicted, and his conviction was affirmed on appeal.

ISSUE: Is a notice-of-alibi rule violative of the Fifth and Four-teenth Amendments by compelling a defendant to be a witness against himself?

HOLDING AND DECISION: (White, J.) No. The rule is fair to both the defendant and state in permitting liberal discovery. The state has a legitimate interest in protecting itself against eleventh-hour defenses: although based on an adversary system, a trial is not yet a poker game in which players may conceal their cards at will. No pretrial statements of Mrs. Scotty were introduced at trial; her pretrial testimony was only used to find rebuttal witnesses. A defendant is always in a dilemma whether to remain silent or present a defense that may prove disastrous. Nothing in the rule obligates the defendant to rely on an alibi or prevents him from abandoning it as a defense. The rule only requires that a defendant accelerate the timing of his disclosure of information he would have revealed at trial anyway. A defendant is not entitled to await the end of the prosecution's case against him before announcing the nature of his defense anymore than he can await the jury's verdict on the state's case before deciding to take the stand himself. Absent the rule, the prosecution would be entitled to a continuance at trial on the grounds of surprise; the rule thus serves to prevent a disrupted trial. Affirmed.

CONCURRENCE: (Burger, C.J.) The rule serves an added function of disposing of many cases before trial. If the prosecutor interviews the defendant's alibi witnesses and finds them to be reliable and unimpeachable, he might be strongly inclined to dismiss charges against the defendant. On the other hand, a defendant who knows that his alibi defense will be thoroughly investigated by the prosecution before trial may well be induced to change his plea.

DISSENT: (Black, J.) Before trial, defense counsel can only guess at what the state's case might be. The rule thus compels defendants with any thoughts at all of pleading alibi to be forced to disclose their intentions so as to preserve the possibility of later raising the defense—the decision goes to more than just "timing." Pretrial disclosure will adversely affect the defendant who then decides to forego raising an alibi defense. His alibi witnesses will still help the prosecution to new leads or evidence. The rule is a clear violation of the Fifth Amendment because it requires a defendant to give information to the state that may destroy him. The majority's decision opens the way to compel complete pretrial discovery of a defendant's case, and any defenses he might raise.

ANALYSIS

At the time *Williams* was decided, fifteen states other than Florida had notice-of-alibi requirements of varying kinds. One such rule, in *Wardins v. Oregon*, 412 U.S. 470 (1973), was struck down because it failed to provide reciprocal discovery rights to the defendant. The Court found this omission vio-

Continued on next page.

lative of the Due Process Clause of the Fourteenth Amendment. Because exclusion of the testimony of alibi witnesses is a drastic sanction for failure on the defendant's part to comply with the rule's disclosure requirements, other sanctions have been suggested. These include: (1) granting a continuance to the prosecution; (2) allowing the prosecution or court to comment on the defendant's failure to the jury; (3) placing the defense counsel in contempt when the failure was not in "good faith."

■■■■

Quicknotes

FOURTEENTH AMENDMENT DUE PROCESS CLAUSE Provides that protections mandated by the U.S. Constitution and observed by the federal government are equally applicable, and therefore must be observed by the States.

PRIVILEGE AGAINST SELF-INCRIMINATION A privilege guaranteed by the Fifth Amendment to the federal Constitution in a criminal proceeding for communications made by an accused and protecting an accused or witness from having to give testimony that may incriminate himself.

■■■■

Taylor v. Illinois

Convicted attempted murderer (D) v. State (P)

484 U.S. 400 (1988).

NATURE OF CASE: Appeal of criminal conviction.

FACT SUMMARY: Illinois (P) requires pretrial disclosure of all defense witnesses, but Taylor (D), who claimed that an exculpatory witness was not on the list because he could not be located before trial, was not allowed by the trial judge to call the witness to testify.

🏛 RULE OF LAW
When the defense intentionally omits a witness from a required pretrial witness list to gain a tactical advantage, the trial judge may refuse to let the witness testify.

FACTS: Illinois (P) law requires the defense to provide a pretrial list of all witnesses it intends to call. During his trial, Taylor's (D) defense counsel wished to call a witness who was not on the pretrial list. Taylor (D) claimed that the witness could not be located before trial, but the witness admitted at a hearing that defense counsel had visited him the week before trial. The trial judge, concluding that the witness was not credible and that the evidence might be manufactured, did not allow the witness to testify. Taylor (D) appealed, arguing that the Sixth Amendment Compulsory Process Clause bars a judge from precluding the testimony of a surprise witness.

ISSUE: When the defense intentionally omits a witness from a required pretrial witness list to gain a tactical advantage, may the trial judge refuse to let the witness testify?

HOLDING AND DECISION: (Stevens, J.) Yes. When the defense intentionally omits a witness from a required pretrial witness list to gain a tactical advantage, the trial judge may refuse to let the witness testify. The Compulsory Process Clause mandates not only that a defendant may compel the presence of a witness, but also that the trier of fact must hear the witness. However, when the defendant fails to comply with discovery rules, the defendant's rights must be weighed against the public interest in excluding unreliable or perjured testimony, in avoiding prejudice to the prosecution, and in enforcing rules for the fair and efficient functioning of the adversary process. While there are less drastic sanctions available (granting a continuance or mistrial or disciplining the defendant or defense counsel, for example), in the event a discovery violation is willful only the severest sanction—witness preclusion—may be strong enough to combat the defendant's powerful incentive to present perjured testimony.

Finally, unless defense counsel is constitutionally ineffective, the adversary process requires a client to be held responsible for the actions of his attorney. Accordingly, there was no error committed by not allowing Taylor's (D) omitted witness to testify at trial. Affirmed.

DISSENT: (Brennan, J.) Where the defendant is not personally responsible for the discovery violation, alternative sanctions are adequate and avoid the arbitrary and disproportionate sanction of witness preclusion. Unless the defendant is responsible, the Compulsory Process Clause should require a per se rule against discovery sanctions that exclude criminal defense evidence.

▶ ANALYSIS

Under *Wardius v. Oregon*, 412 U.S. 470 (1973), where discovery rules place a particular burden on the defense, due process requires that the defense must have reciprocal discovery rights against the prosecution. Federal Rule of Criminal Procedure 16 provides defendants with a number of discovery and inspection rights, essentially providing the prosecution with reciprocal rights where the defense has chosen to exercise its rights first. The Federal Rules do not require either party to provide a pretrial list of all witnesses, but federal judges have discretion to order the government to provide a witness list.

■=■

CHAPTER 12

The Jury and the Criminal Trial

Quick Reference Rules of Law

Ballew v. Georgia

Criminal defendant (D) v. State (P)

435 U.S. 223 (1978).

NATURE OF CASE: Appeal from a conviction for distributing obscene materials.

FACT SUMMARY: Ballew (D) appealed his conviction for distributing obscene materials on the ground that it was unconstitutional to be tried by a jury consisting of only five persons.

RULE OF LAW
It is a denial of the accused's right to trial by jury, guaranteed by the Sixth and Fourteenth Amendments, to try him by a jury consisting of fewer than six persons.

FACTS: Georgia law permitted misdemeanor juries to consist of five persons. Ballew (D) was convicted of the misdemeanor of distributing obscene materials by such a jury. He appealed his conviction, charging that the size of the jury had deprived him of his right to trial by jury as guaranteed by the Sixth and Fourteenth Amendments. The court of appeals affirmed his conviction.

ISSUE: Can a criminal defendant be tried by a jury of fewer than six persons?

HOLDING AND DECISION: (Blackmun, J.) No. It is a denial of a criminal defendant's right to trial by jury, as guaranteed by the Sixth and Fourteenth Amendments, to be tried by a jury consisting of fewer than six persons. Studies raise significant questions about the wisdom and constitutionality of a reduction of jury size below six. Any further reduction promotes inaccurate and possibly biased decision-making, causes untoward differences in verdicts, and prevents juries from truly representing their communities. This seriously impairs the purpose and function of the jury in a criminal trial. Whatever saving is produced by reducing jury size from six to five simply is not significant and does not constitute a significant state interest to justify such reduction. Reversed and remanded.

CONCURRENCE: (Brennan, J.) Criminal juries must contain more than five persons, but Ballew (D) should not be subjected to retrial because the obscenity statute under which the charge was made is unconstitutional.

CONCURRENCE: (Powell, J.) The wisdom and necessity of such heavy reliance on numerology derived from statistical studies not subject to the traditional testing mechanisms of the adversary process is debatable. Every feature of jury trial practice does not have to be the same in both federal and state courts.

ANALYSIS

The Court had held six-member juries in criminal cases constitutional in *Williams v. Florida*, 399 U.S. 78 (1970). It noted common law juries contained 12 members by historical accident and held a jury need only be of sufficient size to promote group deliberation, insulate members from outside intimidation, and provide a representative cross section of the community.

Quicknotes

FOURTEENTH AMENDMENT Declares that no state shall make or enforce any law that shall abridge the privileges and immunities of citizens of the United States. No state shall deny to any person within its jurisdiction the equal protection of the laws.

SIXTH AMENDMENT Provides the right to a speedy and public trial by impartial jury, the right to be informed of the accusation, the right to confront witnesses, and the right to have the assistance of counsel in all criminal prosecutions.

Duren v. Missouri

Criminal defendant (D) v. State (P)

439 U.S. 357 (1979).

NATURE OF CASE: Appeal from the denial of pretrial and post-conviction motions to quash the petit jury panel.

FACT SUMMARY: Duren (D) was indicted for first-degree murder and first-degree robbery. In pretrial and post-conviction motions, Duren (D) claimed that he was denied a jury chosen from a fair cross section of the community because the particular provisions of Missouri law allowed women who requested an automatic exemption to be exempted from jury duty.

> ## RULE OF LAW
> Where women are systematically underrepresented in the final pool of jurors due to laws relating to jury selection, a defendant's constitutional right to a jury by a fair cross section is violated.

FACTS: Duren (D) established that the Missouri law that granted an automatic exemption to women resulted in a jury panel for his trial that was comprised of 53 people, only 5 of whom were female despite the 1970 census that showed that women comprised 54 percent of the population of Jackson County in Missouri. The State (P) did not dispute Duren's (D) statistics. The Missouri Supreme Court held that the number of potential female jurors more than satisfied constitutional standards. During oral argument, the State (P) argued that the state interest advanced by the law was to safeguard the important role women held in family and home life.

ISSUE: Are jury venires that average less than 15 percent females and from which females are systematically excluded a violation of the Constitution's fair cross-section requirement?

HOLDING AND DECISION: (White, J.) Yes. The systematic exclusion of females violates the Constitution's fair cross-section requirement under the Sixth and Fourteenth Amendments. The fair cross-section inquiry established in *Taylor v. Louisiana*, 419 U.S. 522 (1975), requires a defendant to show: (1) that the alleged excluded group is a "distinctive" group in the community, (2) that the representation of that group in the venires from which a jury is selected is unfair and unreasonable in relation to the number of that group in the community, and (3) that the underrepresentation is due to a systematic exclusion of that group in the jury selection process. If all three requirements are met, the defendant has established a prima facie showing of a violation. Duren (P)

met all three requirements because women made up 54 percent of the population of Jackson County and the large discrepancy between men and women, which occurred every week for a period of a year, was inherent in the jury selection process. Significantly the final percentage of females available at the venire stage of jury selection was only 14.5 percent where the percentage of women summoned was 26.7 percent. The State's (P) argument that women should be exempted more easily than men due to their home and family roles is an insufficient justification for the disproportionate exclusion of women from jury venires because this policy has resulted in a prima facie violation of the fair cross-section requirement of the Constitution.

DISSENT: (Rehnquist, J.) The State (P) has adequately demonstrated its justification for the underrepresentation of women. Local state officials are better equipped to determine who should or should not be allowed exemptions from jury service, depending on the particulars of that locale. In less populated areas, for instance, serving on a jury may impose substantial burdens on females without necessarily resulting in a higher percentage of females on the jury panel.

▶ ANALYSIS

The importance of having a fair cross section of the community represented in jury venires became an issue due to prior cases where certain racial groups and women were excluded from jury service. The Court's decision in *Duren* extends prior rulings to ensure that juries are representative of the communities in which they serve. The Court applied the right to an impartial trial (Sixth Amendment) and to equal protection under the law (Fourteenth Amendment) to jury selection.

Quicknotes

FOURTEENTH AMENDMENT Declares that no state shall make or enforce any law that shall abridge the privileges and immunities of citizens of the United States. No state shall deny to any person within its jurisdiction the equal protection of the laws.

SIXTH AMENDMENT Provides the right to a speedy and public trial by impartial jury, the right to be informed of the accusation, the right to confront witnesses, and the right to have the assistance of counsel in all criminal prosecutions.

Batson v. Kentucky

Criminal defendant (D) v. State (P)

476 U.S. 79 (1986).

NATURE OF CASE: Appeal of conviction for burglary and receiving stolen goods.

FACT SUMMARY: After the Kentucky (P) prosecutor used peremptory challenges to strike all African-American jurors, Batson (D), an African-American, unsuccessfully moved to dismiss the jury on grounds he was denied equal protection.

RULE OF LAW

To establish an equal protection violation for a state's use of peremptory challenges to exclude members of his race from a petit jury, a defendant must make out a prima facie case by showing: (1) he is a member of a cognizable racial group and (2) either that members of his race have not been summoned for jury duty in that jurisdiction for an extended period of time or that the circumstances of his case raise an inference of purposeful discrimination.

FACTS: At Batson's (D) trial for burglary and receiving stolen goods, the Kentucky (P) prosecutor used peremptory challenges to remove all four African-Americans from the jury. Batson (D), an African-American, moved to dismiss the jury before it was sworn in, arguing that the State's (P) use of its peremptory challenges violated Batson's (D) Sixth Amendment right to a jury drawn from a fair cross section of the community and his Fourteenth Amendment right to equal protection. The trial judge denied the motion, stating that peremptory challenges could be used to strike anyone. Batson (D) was convicted, and he appealed.

ISSUE: To establish an equal protection violation for a state's use of peremptory challenges to exclude members of his race from a petit jury, must a defendant make out a prima facie case by showing: (1) he is a member of a cognizable racial group and (2) either that members of his race have not been summoned for jury duty in that jurisdiction for an extended period of time or that the circumstances of his case raise an inference of purposeful discrimination?

HOLDING AND DECISION: (Powell, J.) Yes. To establish an equal protection violation for a state's use of peremptory challenges to exclude members of his race from a petit jury, a defendant must make out a prima facie case by showing: (1) he is a member of a cognizable racial group and (2) either that members of his race have not been summoned for jury duty in that jurisdiction for an extended period of time or that the circumstances of his case raise an inference of purposeful discrimination. Once a prima facie case has been established, the State must provide a neutral explanation for the exercise of its peremptory challenges or else the defendant's conviction will be overturned. Whether a defendant has made out a prima facie showing based solely on evidence from his own case involves consideration of all relevant circumstances, for example, any "pattern" of strikes against jurors of the defendant's race and any questions and statements made by the prosecutor during voir dire. Once the burden shifts to the state to rebut a prima facie case, the prosecutor's explanation need not rise to the level of justifying a challenge for cause, but a statement that jurors will be partial to members of their own race or a simple denial of discriminatory intent will not suffice. African-Americans have an equal right to participation on juries, and their discriminatory exclusion impedes the pursuit of equal justice for defendants, excluded jurors, and the entire community. Thus, the Equal Protection Clause extends beyond selection of the jury venire to the petit jury and to the prosecutor's peremptory challenges. While peremptory challenges are important in our judicial system, they are often used to discriminate against African-Americans, and so a requirement that trial judges be sensitive to the discriminatory use of peremptory challenges strikes a balance between the continued use of peremptory challenges and equal protection. Reversed and remanded.

CONCURRENCE: (Marshall, J.) Peremptory challenges should be completely eliminated because their use cannot be reconciled with the requirements of equal protection. The discriminatory use of peremptory challenges will not be ended by this decision. Defendants cannot attack challenges unless their use is so flagrant as to establish a prima facie case. Even if a prima facie case can be made out, a prosecutor may easily fabricate non-discriminatory motives, or his "neutral" determination that a juror is, for example, "sullen" or "distant" may be based on unconscious racism. The trial judge will have a difficult time determining the prosecutor's motives, and the judge's decision may be based on his own conscious or unconscious racism.

DISSENT: (Rehnquist, J.) The use of peremptory challenges to strike minorities from juries does not violate equal protection so long as challenges are also used to exclude jurors of all races and nationalities.

Continued on next page.

▶ *ANALYSIS*

Justice Powell's opinion explicitly left open the issue of whether a criminal defendant can use race-based peremptory challenges. In *Edmonson v. Leesville Concrete Co.*, 500 U.S. 614, (1991), the Supreme Court extended the bar against discriminatory peremptory challenges to civil cases involving private litigants. The Court found state action in the discrimination, a prerequisite for Equal Protection Clause analysis, since it is the state which empowers the jury and discharges a juror upon the use of a peremptory challenge. This reasoning would seem to extend to the use of peremptory challenges by criminal defendants.

■■■

Quicknotes

EQUAL PROTECTION CLAUSE A constitutional provision that each person be guaranteed the same protection of the laws enjoyed by other persons in like circumstances.

■■■

Mu'Min v. Virginia

Convicted murderer (D) v. State (P)

500 U.S. 415 (1991).

NATURE OF CASE: Appeal of conviction for murder.

FACT SUMMARY: During voir dire, eight of twelve jurors professed prior knowledge of Mu'Min's (D) case, but the trial judge refused to ask about the content of their knowledge or to excuse them from the jury, finding it sufficient that all jurors stated that they could be impartial.

> 🏛 **RULE OF LAW**
> The Sixth Amendment does not require a judge to question prospective jurors on the content of their prior knowledge of the case, so long as the jurors believably state that they can be impartial.

FACTS: Mu'Min's (D) murder case generated substantial pretrial publicity, including accounts of details of the murder, his prior criminal record (which included a murder conviction), and indications that he had confessed. Sixteen of twenty-six venirepersons stated that they had read or heard about the case. Despite defense requests, the trial judge refused to ask prospective jurors during voir dire about the source or content of their knowledge, asking only questions to determine whether they could be impartial. The judge denied Mu'Min's (D) motion to remove for cause all jurors who had been exposed to pretrial publicity, but he excused two jurors who could not say they could ignore their prior knowledge. Of the twelve jurors who ultimately heard Mu'Min's (D) case, eight had some prior knowledge, though none had indicated a prior opinion or any bias. Mu'Min (D) was convicted and sentenced to death, and he appealed, arguing that the judge's refusal to question prospective jurors as to the content of their prior knowledge or to excuse them from the jury violated his Sixth Amendment right to an impartial jury and Fourteenth Amendment right to due process.

ISSUE: Does the Sixth Amendment require a judge to question prospective jurors on the content of their prior knowledge about the case, even when the jurors believably state that they can be impartial?

HOLDING AND DECISION: (Rehnquist, C.J.) No. The Sixth Amendment does not require a judge to question prospective jurors on the content of their prior knowledge about the case, so long as the jurors believably state that they can be impartial. The Constitution mandates only that a juror be impartial, not that a juror be ignorant of the case. The trial judge has wide discretion in conducting voir dire, since he is in the best position to evaluate the biases of his own community, and the examination conducted in this case was sufficient to uncover impartiality. Whenever a venireperson indicated prior knowledge about the case, he was further questioned to determine whether he could be impartial, and two jurors who indicated an inability to put aside their prior knowledge were excused. In the exceptional case where pretrial publicity has so prejudiced the community that jurors' claims of impartiality cannot be believed, the judge must question the jurors more extensively to determine whether they can be impartial. This is not such a case. Affirmed.

CONCURRENCE: (O'Connor, J.) The trial judge could have done more by way of asking individual jurors what they remembered reading about the case. Context questions, however, are not so indispensable that it violates the Sixth Amendment for a trial judge to evaluate a juror's credibility instead by reference to the full range of potentially prejudicial information that has been reported.

DISSENT: (Marshall, J.) Once a prospective juror admits to prior knowledge of a case, content questioning must be a part of voir dire because it is necessary to determine whether the type and extent of prior knowledge would disqualify the juror as a matter of law, to give depth to the trial court's finding of impartiality, and to accurately assess whether a prospective juror's profession of impartiality is believable.

DISSENT: (Kennedy, J.) When a juror admits exposure to pretrial publicity about a case, the court must conduct a colloquy with that individual juror to assess the juror's ability to be impartial. Findings of impartiality must be based on something more than the mere silence of the individual in response to questions asked en masse. The voir dire in this case was inadequate for an informed ruling that the jurors were qualified to sit. Evaluating impartiality by asking about a juror's exposure or by explaining the trial process and then assessing a juror's commitment to follow the law and instructions would have been enough. Moreover, the questions the trial judge asked in this case would have sufficed if he had asked them of individual jurors and received meaningful responses.

Continued on next page.

▶ *ANALYSIS*

A trial judge is required to examine jurors concerning racial bias where there are substantial indications of racial bias, a standard similar to that where pretrial publicity is at issue. In *Turner v. Murray*, 476 U.S. 28 (1986), the Supreme Court required examinations on racial bias where an African-American man was accused of murdering a white. Other situations where some courts have required extra voir dire examination include the following: juror has a relationship to law enforcement or to the victim, juror has suffered a similar harm as the victim, juror has done prior jury service, and juror may have a particular moral repulsion to the crime charged.

■≡■

Quicknotes

SIXTH AMENDMENT Provides the right to a speedy and public trial by impartial jury, the right to be informed of the accusation, the right to confront witnesses, and the right to have the assistance of counsel in all criminal prosecutions.

■≡■

Darden v. Wainwright

Convicted murderer (D) v. Government official (P)

477 U.S. 168 (1986).

NATURE OF CASE: Appeal of denial of habeas corpus.

FACT SUMMARY: At the guilt phase of a murder trial, the prosecution made improper closing statements concerning the crime.

🏛 RULE OF LAW
Improper closing statements by counsel will void a conviction only if they make the trial so unfair as to violate due process.

FACTS: Darden (D) was charged with a particularly vicious series of crimes, including murder. At his trial, counsel for the prosecution made various improper closing arguments, which appealed to passion rather than facts, although evidence was not misstated, and no comments were made about the exercise of rights. Darden (D) was sentenced to death. This was affirmed on appeal, and the court of appeals denied habeas corpus. Darden (D) appealed.

ISSUE: Will improper closing statements by counsel void a conviction only if they make the trial so unfair as to violate due process?

HOLDING AND DECISION: (Powell, J.) Yes. Improper closing statements by counsel will void a conviction only if they make the trial so unfair as to violate due process. It is not enough to void a conviction that remarks by counsel are improper or incorrect. The relevant question is whether the remarks made the trial so unfair as to violate due process. Here, the remarks, while appealing to the passion of the jurors, did not misstate the evidence, and did not comment on the exercise of constitutional rights. The trial still was fundamentally fair. Affirmed.

DISSENT: (Blackmun, J.) The prosecution in this case offered personal opinions as to guilt, injected broader issues into the trial, and used arguments designed to inflame the passions of the jury. The result of all this was an unfair trial.

▶ ANALYSIS

The dissent did not appear to question the standard of review used by the Court. Due process would appear to be the standard the dissent proposed. However, the dissent disagreed with the Court's conclusion that the trial was not fundamentally unfair.

Quicknotes

PROCEDURAL DUE PROCESS The constitutional mandate that if the state or federal government acts so as to deny a citizen of a life, liberty or property interest the individual is first entitled to notice and the right to be heard.

Portuondo v. Agard

Government official (P) v. Criminal defendant (D)

529 U.S. 61 (2000).

NATURE OF CASE: Petition for a writ of habeas corpus in federal court.

FACT SUMMARY: Agard (D) stood trial for sodomy, assault, and weapons charges. The victim and her friend were the main witnesses for the State (P). The prosecutor suggested on summation that Agard (D), by being present during the trial, was able to hear all other witnesses and then himself testify according to the evidence already presented. Defense objected to this characterization but Agard (D) was subsequently convicted on some of the charges. Agard (D) then filed for a writ of habeas corpus, claiming that the prosecutor had violated his rights under the Fifth and Sixth Amendments to be present at trial and confront his accusers and under the Fourteenth Amendment to have due process.

⚖ RULE OF LAW
A prosecutor may suggest on summation that a defendant's presence in the courtroom during trial, where the defendant hears all previous witnesses against him, may allow that defendant to tailor his testimony if he takes the stand.

FACTS: Agard (D) was on trial for nineteen sodomy and assault charges and three weapons charges that hinged on the credibility of the involved parties. The alleged victim and her friend testified that Agard (D) had committed physical assault, rape, and sodomy against the victim. Agard (D) alleged that the sexual encounter was consensual, but he had struck the victim once in the face. On summation, the prosecutor suggested that Agard (D) had a "big advantage" by being able to hear the other witnesses and then possibly tailor his testimony to fit that evidence. Defense counsel objected. Agard (D) was convicted of one count of anal sodomy and two counts of third-degree possession of a weapon. The district court declined to grant habeas relief, but the Second Circuit reversed.

ISSUE: Is it constitutional for a prosecutor, on summation, to point out to the jury the fact that the defendant, by being present throughout the trial, had the opportunity to hear all of the other witnesses' testimony and could, therefore, alter his testimony accordingly?

HOLDING AND DECISION: (Scalia, J.) Yes. Defendants who testify should be treated no differently than other witnesses. When a witness has the opportunity to hear previous testimony and then tailor his testimony accord-

ingly, there is a threat to the integrity of the trial. A prosecutor calling the jury's attention to this fact does not prejudice the defendant-witness because jury members have seen during the trial that the defendant was present and could, therefore, deduce for themselves that the defendant might alter his testimony to suit that evidence. This case is distinguishable from the Court's previous ruling in *Griffin v. California*, 380 U.S. 609 (1965). In *Griffin*, the comments involved the defendant's refusal to testify and suggested that such a refusal was evidence of guilt, which unconstitutionally infringed on the defendant's right to remain silent. In *Griffin*, then, the Court prohibited the prosecutor from urging the jury to do something the jury was not permitted to do—take the fact that a defendant had evoked his right against self-incrimination and to use that right as evidence against him. In this case, the prosecutor simply highlighted what the jury was already able to perceive—that Agard (D) had been listening to the previous witnesses. The comments were, therefore, concerned with Agard's (D) credibility as a witness and did not violate his due process rights. Reversed.

CONCURRENCE: (Stevens, J.) The Court has implicitly condoned the prosecutor's tactics when the Court should have discouraged them.

DISSENT: (Ginsburg, J.) The Court has transformed a defendant's right to be present at trial from a Sixth Amendment right into a burden on his credibility. The fact that Agard's (D) testimony was coherent might be because he was telling the truth, but his veracity has been questioned because he has a constitutional right to be present during the trial. New York law requires that a defendant be present when on trial. It is unconstitutional to then allow this requirement, in effect, to be used against the defendant. This case is, therefore, analogous to the *Griffin* decision and to *Doyle v. Ohio*, 426 U.S. 610 (1976), which ruled that a defendant's silence after receiving Miranda warnings could not be used by the prosecution to attack the defendant's credibility. This case should have been decided accordingly. Cross-examination was the proper time for the prosecutor to question Agard's (D) truthfulness and to demonstrate that he had tailored his testimony. During cross-examination Agard (D) could have defended his version and the prosecutor could have possibly shown the jury that Agard (D) was not being truthful. To allow the prosecutor to question the defendant's testimony during summation

Continued on next page.

when the defense cannot respond, however, does not advance the interests of the truth and invites the jury to convict the defendant on conduct that is as consistent with innocence as it is with guilt.

▶ *ANALYSIS*

The Court draws a distinction between the actions of two prosecutors: (1) urging the jury to do something (take the defendant's refusal to testify as proof of his guilt) that the jury is not allowed to do and (2) allowing the prosecution to point out the obvious to the jury—that the defendant had been present throughout the trial and might, therefore, alter his testimony. While Justice Scalia contends that *Griffin* is not analogous to *Portuondo*, Justice Ginsburg stresses that the prosecutor could have suggested the same fact during cross examination, which would have allowed the defendant to refute the allegation. Ginsburg contends that by allowing these comments on summation, however, the Court allowed the State to suggest that the defendant's testimony, which might be coherent because it was based on the truth, was proof of Agard's guilt.

■■■

Quicknotes

FIFTH AMENDMENT Provides that no person shall be compelled to serve as a witness against himself, or be subject to trial for the same offense twice, or be deprived of life, liberty, or property without due process of law.

FOURTEENTH AMENDMENT Declares that no state shall make or enforce any law that shall abridge the privileges and immunities of citizens of the United States. No state shall deny to any person within its jurisdiction the equal protection of the laws.

SIXTH AMENDMENT Provides the right to a speedy and public trial by impartial jury, the right to be informed of the accusation, the right to confront witnesses, and the right to have the assistance of counsel in all criminal prosecutions.

■■■

Crawford v. Washington

Attempted murder convict (D) v. State (P)

541 U.S. 36 (2004).

NATURE OF CASE: Appeal from an attempted murder conviction.

FACT SUMMARY: When at Michael Crawford's (D) trial, the prosecutor played for the jury a witness's prior out-of-court tape-recorded statement to the police, thus providing Crawford (D) with no opportunity for cross-examination, Crawford (D) argued deprivation of his constitutional rights on the grounds that the Sixth Amendment Confrontation Clause applies not only to in-court testimony.

RULE OF LAW

The Sixth Amendment Confrontation Clause applies not only to in-court testimony.

FACTS: Michael Crawford (D) stabbed a man who allegedly tried to rape his wife, Sylvia. At his trial, the prosecutor played for the jury Sylvia's tape-recorded statement to the police describing the stabbing, even though Crawford (D) had no opportunity for cross-examination. Crawford (D) claimed self-defense. Sylvia did not testify at trial because of the state's marital privilege; in Washington, this privilege does not extend to a spouse's out-of-court statements admissible under a hearsay exception. The Washington Supreme Court upheld Crawford's (D) attempted murder conviction after determining that Sylvia's statement was reliable. Crawford (D) appealed to the U.S. Supreme Court on Confrontation Clause grounds.

ISSUE: Does the Sixth Amendment Confrontation Clause apply only to in-court testimony?

HOLDING AND DECISION: (Scalia, J.) No. The Sixth Amendment Confrontation Clause applies not only to in-court testimony. The history of the Confrontation Clause supports two inferences about its meaning. First, the principal evil at which it was directed was the civil-law mode of criminal procedure, particularly its use of ex parte examinations as evidence against the accused. The Sixth Amendment must be interpreted with this focus in mind. Leaving the regulation of out-of-court statements to the law of evidence would render the Clause powerless to prevent even the most flagrant inquisitional practices. This focus also suggests that not all hearsay implicates the Sixth Amendment's core concerns. An off-hand, overheard remark, for example, might be unreliable evidence and thus a good candidate for exclusion under hearsay rules, but it bears little resemblance to the civil-law abuses the Clause targeted. On the other hand, ex parte examinations might sometimes be admissible under modern hearsay rules, but the Framers certainly would not have condoned them. Statements taken by police officers in the course of investigations, as here, are testimonial evidence under even a narrow standard. Police interrogations bear a striking resemblance to examinations by justices of the police in England; the statements are not *sworn* testimony, but the absence of oath was not dispositive. In sum, police interrogations fall squarely within the class of statements to which the right of confrontation is historically required. Secondly, the Framers would not have allowed admission of testimonial statements of a witness who did not appear at trial unless unavailable and the defendant had had a prior opportunity for cross-examination. The text of the Sixth Amendment "does not suggest any open-ended exceptions" from the confrontation requirement to be developed by the courts. Dispensing with confrontation because testimony is "obviously reliable" is akin to dispensing with jury trial because a defendant is "obviously guilty." Reversed and remanded.

CONCURRENCE: (Rehnquist, C.J.) Although the wife's statement should have been excluded, adoption of a new approach in this area is not backed by sufficiently persuasive reasoning to overrule long-established precedent.

▶ ANALYSIS

In *Crawford*, the Supreme Court makes clear that where testimonial evidence is involved, the Framers did not intend to leave the Sixth Amendment's protections "to the vagaries of the rules of evidence, much less to amorphous notions of 'reliability.'" Admitting statements deemed reliable by a judge is fundamentally at odds with the right of confrontation. The Confrontation Clause commands, not that evidence be reliable, but that reliability be assessed in a particular manner: by testing in the crucible of cross-examination.

■══■

Quicknotes

CONFRONTATION CLAUSE A provision in the Sixth Amendment to the United States Constitution that an accused in a criminal action has the right to confront the witnesses against him, including the right to attend the trial and to cross-examine witnesses called on behalf of the prosecution.

■══■

Gray v. Maryland

Criminal defendant (D) v. State (P)

523 U.S. 185 (1998).

NATURE OF CASE: Appeal of a criminal conviction for murder.

FACT SUMMARY: When a jury convicted Gray (D) of murder following a trial at which a codefendant's redacted confession had been introduced, Gray (D) appealed, claiming that his constitutional rights had been violated.

🏛 RULE OF LAW
Redacted confessions that replace the proper name with an obvious blank, the word "delete," or a symbol that notifies the jury that a name has been deleted, violate a defendant's Sixth Amendment rights if introduced into evidence insulated from cross-examination.

FACTS: Gray (D) and a codefendant were both indicted for murder. Gray's (D) motion for a separate trial was denied, and Gray (D) was convicted after the codefendant's redacted confession incriminating Gray (D) was introduced at the joint trial with a limiting instruction. Gray (D) appealed the verdict, claiming that under *Bruton v. United States*, 391 U.S. 123 (1968), his Sixth Amendment rights had been violated.

ISSUE: Do redacted confessions that replace the proper name with an obvious blank, the word "delete," a symbol or similarly notify the jury that a name has been deleted, violate a defendant's Sixth Amendment rights if introduced into evidence insulated from cross examination?

HOLDING AND DECISION: (Breyer, J.) Yes. Redacted confessions that replace the proper name with an obvious blank, the word "delete," or a symbol that similarly notifies the jury that a name has been deleted, violate a defendant's Sixth Amendment rights if introduced into evidence insulated from cross-examination. Under *Bruton*, the introduction at trial of the powerfully incriminating extrajudicial statements of a codefendant who does not testify and cannot be cross-examined violates a defendant's Sixth Amendment rights. The introduction of the redacted confession of Gray's (D) codefendant with the blank prominent on its face, "facially incriminated" Gray (D). There were no questions of policy to be considered here, since the connection of the defendant to the confession did not depend on the introduction of other evidence later in the trial. This case was not like *Richardson v. Marsh*, 481 U.S. 200 (1987), where the confession of the codefendant had been redacted, eliminating all reference to his codefendant and any indication that anyone else at all was im-

plicated in the crime, and becoming incriminating only when linked to other evidence. The powerfully incriminating effect of an out-of-court accusation creates a special, and vital, need for cross-examination. Redactions that simply replace a name with a blank leave statements that, considered as a class, so closely resemble *Bruton's* unredacted statements that, in our view, the law must require the same result. Reversed.

DISSENT: (Scalia, J.) The Court's extension of *Bruton* to name-related confessions "as a class" will seriously compromise society's compelling interest in finding, convicting, and punishing those who violate the law. The Court's analogizing of "deleted" to a physical description that clearly identifies the defendant does not survive scrutiny. By "facially incriminating," we have meant incriminating independent of other evidence introduced at trial. The issue is not whether the confession incriminated Gray (D), but whether the incrimination was so "powerful" that we must depart from the normal presumption that the jury follows its instructions. It was not, and the line for departing from the ordinary rule at the facial identification of the defendant makes more sense than drawing it anywhere else.

▌ ANALYSIS

Since the redacted confession in this case referred directly to the "existence" of the nonconfessing codefendant, the court found more similarities with *Bruton* than with *Richardson*. In *Bruton*, the confession was held to be "incriminating on its face," while in *Richardson*, the confession became incriminating only by inference, and only when "linked" to other evidence. This "linkage" has proved problematic in other cases where the effect of a confession cannot be predicted until after the introduction of all the evidence.

■ ■ ■

Quicknotes

CROSS EXAMINATION The interrogation of a witness by an adverse party either to further inquire as to the subject matter of the direct examination or to call into question the witness' credibility.

LIMITING INSTRUCTION Directions given to a judge or jury prior to deliberation.

Continued on next page.

REDACTION Alteration of a confession to remove any reference by one joint defendant to any codefendant.

SIXTH AMENDMENT Provides the right to a speedy trial by impartial jury, the right to be informed of the accusation, to confront witnesses and to have the assistance of counsel in all criminal prosecutions.

CHAPTER 13

Sentencing

Quick Reference Rules of Law

Ewing v. California

Convicted thief (D) v. State (P)

538 U.S. 11 (2003).

NATURE OF CASE: Appeal from conviction for theft.

FACT SUMMARY: When Gary Ewing (D) was sentenced, under California's Three Strikes Law, to 25-years-to-life for theft of golf clubs valued at $1,197, he argued that the sentence constituted cruel and unusual punishment prohibited by the Eighth Amendment.

🏛 RULE OF LAW
A Three Strikes Law is not so grossly disproportionate as to constitute cruel and unusual punishment under the Eighth Amendment.

FACTS: Under the California Three Strikes Law, when a defendant is convicted of a felony, and he or she has previously been convicted of one or more prior felonies defined as "serious" or "violent," the defendant must receive an indeterminate prison term of 25-years-to-life. Gary Ewing (D) walked into a pro shop and left with golf clubs valued at $1,197 concealed in his pants leg. He was caught, tried, and convicted of the crime. He had previously committed several felony robberies and burglaries, making him eligible for sentencing under the Three Strikes Law; he was sentenced, accordingly, to a prison term of 25-years-to-life. Ewing (D) appealed, arguing that the sentence was so disproportionate to the $1,197 theft as to constitute prohibited cruel and unusual punishment under the Eighth Amendment. The California Court of Appeal affirmed the sentence, and the Supreme Court of California denied Ewing's (D) petition to hear the case. Ewing (D) appealed to the U.S. Supreme Court.

ISSUE: Is a Three Strikes Law so grossly disproportionate as to constitute cruel and unusual punishment under the Eighth Amendment?

HOLDING AND DECISION: (O'Connor, J.) No. A Three Strikes Law is not so grossly disproportionate as to constitute cruel and unusual punishment under the Eighth Amendment. In weighing the gravity of Ewing's (D) offense, we must place on the scales not only his current felony, but also his long history of felony recidivism. Recidivism has long been recognized as a legitimate basis for increased punishment. Any other approach would fail to accord proper deference to the policy judgments that find expression in the legislature's choice of sanctions. Four years after the passage of California's Three Strikes Law, the recidivism rate of parolees returned to prison for the commission of a new crime dropped by nearly 25 percent. Ewing's (D) sentence is justified by the state's public-safety interest in incapacitating and deterring recidivist felons, and amply supported by his own long, serious criminal record. His prior "strikes" were serious felonies, including robbery and three residential burglaries. To be sure, Ewing's (D) sentence is a long one; however, it reflects a rational legislative judgment, entitled to deference, that offenders who have committed serious or violent felonies and who continue to commit felonies must be incapacitated. Here, therefore, Ewing's (D) situation does not constitute "the rare case" in which a threshold comparison of the crime committed and the sentence imposed leads to an inference of gross disproportionality. The Eighth Amendment does not require strict proportionality between crime and sentence. Rather, it forbids only extreme sentences that are grossly disproportionate to the crime. Affirmed.

CONCURRENCE: (Scalia, J.) Ewing's (D) sentence does not violate the Eighth Amendment's prohibition against cruel and unusual punishments. Ewing's (D) sentence is justified by the state's public-safety interest in incapacitating and deterring recidivist felons.

CONCURRENCE: (Thomas, J.) The Cruel and Unusual Punishments Clause of the Eighth Amendment contains no proportionality principle.

DISSENT: (Stevens, J.) Proportionality review is not only capable of judicial application but also required by the Eighth Amendment. By broadly prohibiting excessive sanctions, the Eighth Amendment directs judges to exercise their wise judgment in assessing the proportionality of all forms of punishment. The absence of a black-letter rule does not disable judges from exercising their discretion in construing the outer limits on sentencing authority that the Eighth Amendment imposes.

DISSENT: (Breyer, J.) This sentence amounts to a real prison term of at least 25 years. Ewing's (D) sentence on its face imposes one of the most severe punishments available—25 years to life—for the theft of golf clubs valued at $1,197. Here, the "sentence-triggering behavior" ranks well toward the bottom of the criminal conduct scale. The case before us is a "rare" case—one in which a court can say with reasonable confidence that the punishment is "grossly disproportionate" to the crime.

Continued on next page.

▶ *ANALYSIS*

As the Supreme Court notes in its Ewing decision, the Eighth Amendment, which forbids cruel and unusual punishments, contains a "narrow proportionality principle" that applies to noncapital sentences. The essential four principles of proportionality review are, according to the Supreme Court, (1) the primacy of the legislature (2) the variety of legitimate penological schemes (3) the nature of the federal system and (4) the requirement that proportionality review be guided by objective factors.

■━━■

Quicknotes

EIGHTH AMENDMENT The Eighth Amendment to the federal constitution prohibits the imposition of excessive bail, fines, and cruel and unusual punishment.

■━━■

Williams v. New York

Convicted murderer (D) v. State (P)

337 U.S. 241 (1949).

NATURE OF CASE: Appeal from conviction of first-degree murder.

FACT SUMMARY: Williams (D) appealed from being sentenced to death for first-degree murder on the ground that the trial judge, in passing sentence, considered facts not introduced into evidence and ignored the jury's recommendation of a sentence of life imprisonment.

> ## 🏛 RULE OF LAW
> In passing sentence on a criminal defendant, a trial judge may consider information obtained outside the courtroom from persons whom the defendant has not been permitted to confront or cross-examine.

FACTS: A New York jury found Williams (D) guilty of first-degree murder and recommended a sentence of life imprisonment. Five weeks later, after a presentence investigation report was submitted to the judge, Williams (D) was sentenced to death. At sentencing, the judge commented that pursuant to New York Criminal Code § 482, the jury had considered evidence from other sources. The information was of a nature inadmissible for consideration by the jury on the issue of guilt. Williams (D) appealed his sentence contending that the sentencing judge should not consider information obtained outside the courtroom from persons whom he had not been permitted to confront or cross-examine. The New York Court of Appeals affirmed, and Williams (D) appealed.

ISSUE: In passing sentence on a criminal defendant, may a judge consider information obtained outside the courtroom from persons whom the defendant has not been permitted to confront or cross-examine?

HOLDING AND DECISION: (Black, J.) Yes. In passing sentence on a criminal defendant, a trial judge may consider information obtained outside the courtroom from persons whom the defendant has not been permitted to confront or cross-examine. Different evidentiary rules pertain to trial as opposed to sentencing procedures. Trial rules confine the issue to evidence strictly relevant to the offense charged. A sentencing judge, however, is not confined to the narrow issue of guilt. Enlightened modern theories of sentencing seek rehabilitation rather than punishment. To deprive sentencing judges of access to probation and sentencing reports would undermine such a carefully considered policy. Such reports draw on information concerning every aspect of the defendant's life. The Due Process Clause should not be treated as a device for freezing the evidential procedure of sentencing in the mold of trial procedure, and no constitutional distinction need be drawn where the death penalty may be imposed. Affirmed.

▶ ANALYSIS

The late J. Lewis B. Schwellenbach in his article on the difficulties confronting a sentencing judge wrote: "The knowledge of the life of a man, his background and his family, is the only proper basis for the determination as to his treatment. There is no substitute for information. The sentencing judge in the federal court has the tools with which to acquire that information. Failure to make full use of those tools cannot be justified." Schwellenbach, Information vs. Intuition in the Imposition of Sentence. 27 J.An. J.Jud. Sol. 52 (1943).

Quicknotes

DUE PROCESS CLAUSE Clauses found in the Fifth and Fourteenth Amendments to the United States Constitution providing that no person shall be deprived of "life, liberty, or property, without due process of law."

McMillan v. Pennsylvania

Convicted felon (D) v. State (P)

477 U.S. 79 (1986).

NATURE OF CASE: Appeal of sentence imposed upon conviction.

FACT SUMMARY: McMillan (D) was sentenced under a Pennsylvania law that required a minimum sentence of five years for certain felonies if the sentencing judge found by a preponderance of the evidence that the offender visible possessed a firearm" during commission of the crime.

🏛 **RULE OF LAW**
Due process does not require a sentencing court to find any facts used in sentencing to be proven beyond a reasonable doubt, by clear and convincing evidence, by a preponderance of the evidence, or by any other burden of proof.

FACTS: McMillan (D) was sentenced under a Pennsylvania law that required a minimum sentence of five years for certain felonies if the sentencing judge found by a preponderance of the evidence that the offender "visibly possessed a firearm" during commission of the crime. McMillan (D) appealed his sentence, arguing that due process requires "visible possession of a firearm" to be proven by at least clear and convincing evidence.

ISSUE: Does due process require a sentencing court to find any facts used in sentencing to be proven by clear and convincing evidence?

HOLDING AND DECISION: (Rehnquist, J.) No. Due process does not require a sentencing court to find any facts used in sentencing to be proven beyond a reasonable doubt, by clear and convincing evidence, by a preponderance of the evidence, or by any other burden of proof. Sentencing courts traditionally have heard evidence and found facts without any burden of proof at all. So long as the fact to be proved is not an element of the offense, as here, no burden of proof need be imposed simply because the fact concerns the crime, as opposed to the background or character of the offender. Thus, McMillan (D) was properly sentenced. Affirmed.

DISSENT: (Marshall, J.) The distinction between aggravating and mitigating facts is formalistic. This Court must remain ready to enforce the guarantee of *Winship* "should the State, by placing upon the defendant the burden of proving certain mitigating facts, effectively lighten the constitutional burden on the prosecution to prove the elements of crime."

DISSENT: (Stevens, J.) Once a state legislature defines a criminal offense and threatens to stigmatize or incarcerate an individual for engaging in the prohibited conduct, it may not dispense with the Due Process Clause by declaring that the prohibited conduct is not an element of the crime. The prosecution must prove each element of a crime beyond a reasonable doubt. If a state provides that a specific component of a prohibited transaction shall give rise to both a special stigma and to a special punishment, that component must be treated as a fact necessary to constitute crime. Furthermore, the Due Process Clause does not invalidate every instance of burdening the defendant with proving an exculpatory or mitigating circumstance if it is not an element of the crime. The difference between aggravating and mitigating circumstances is based in part on the idea that, although states may reach the same destination either by criminalizing conduct and allowing an affirmative defense or by prohibiting lesser conduct and enhancing the penalty, legislation proceeding along these two paths is very different even if it might theoretically achieve the same result. Legislative mitigation of punishment in lieu of the requirement of proof beyond a reasonable doubt cannot exist nor can those individuals convicted of engaging in antisocial conduct be subject to further punishment for aggravating conduct that has not been proved beyond a reasonable doubt.

▶ *ANALYSIS*

The defense in *McMillan* pointed to prior Supreme Court decisions holding that due process required proof by at least clear and convincing evidence in involuntary commitment procedures and procedures to terminate parental rights. However, the Court distinguished sentencing procedures from those types of cases, because where an offender is being sentenced he has already been proven guilty of a crime beyond a reasonable doubt. The Court also held that the aggravating factor of visible possession of a firearm can constitutionally be treated as a sentencing consideration as opposed to an element of the charged offense.

Quicknote

DUE PROCESS CLAUSE Clauses found in the Fifth and Fourteenth Amendments to the United States Constitution providing that no person shall be deprived of "life, liberty, or property, without due process of law."

Blakely v. Washington

Convicted kidnapper (D) v. State (P)

124 S..Ct. 2531 (2004).

NATURE OF CASE: Appeal from a conviction for kidnapping.

FACT SUMMARY: When Blakely (D) was sentenced by a judge to more than three years beyond the statutory maximum for the crime to which he had pleaded guilty (because of a statutory enhancement based on a fact not included within the guilty plea), he argued that a sentencing procedure which deprives a defendant of the right to a jury determination of all facts essential to the sentence violates the Sixth Amendment.

> 🏛 **RULE OF LAW**
> A sentencing procedure which deprives the defendant of the right to a jury determination of all facts essential to the sentence violates the Sixth Amendment.

FACTS: The State (P) charged Blakely (D) with first-degree kidnapping. Upon reaching a plea agreement, however, the State (P) reduced the charge to second-degree kidnapping involving domestic violence and use of a firearm. Blakely (D) entered a guilty plea admitting the elements of the second-degree kidnapping and the domestic violence and firearm allegations, but no other relevant facts. The case proceeded to sentencing. The facts of his plea, standing alone, supported a maximum sentence of 53 months. Pursuant to state law, however, the judge imposed an "exceptional" sentence of 90 months after making a judicial determination that Blakely (D) had acted with "deliberate cruelty." Faced with an unexpected increase of more than three years in his sentence, Blakely (D) argued that since the State's (P) sentencing procedure deprived him of the right to a jury determination of all facts essential to the sentence, his Sixth Amendment rights were violated. The state court of appeals affirmed the conviction, and the Washington Supreme Court denied discretionary review. Blakely (D) appealed to the U.S. Supreme Court.

ISSUE: Does a sentencing procedure which deprives the defendant of the right to a jury determination of all facts essential to the sentence violate the Sixth Amendment?

HOLDING AND DECISION: (Scalia, J.) Yes. A sentencing procedure which deprives the defendant of the right to a jury determination of all facts essential to the sentence violates the Sixth Amendment. Blakely (D) was sentenced to prison for more than three years beyond what the law allowed for the crime to which he confessed, on the basis of a disputed finding that he had acted with "deliberate cruelty."

The Framers would not have thought it too much to demand that, before depriving a person of three more years of liberty, the state should suffer the "modest inconvenience" of submitting its accusation to the unanimous suffrage of twelve of the accused's equals and neighbors, rather than a lone employee of the State. Here, the facts supporting the finding of "deliberate cruelty" were neither admitted by Blakely (D) nor found by a jury. The statutory maximum a judge may constitutionally impose must be based solely on the basis of the facts reflected in the jury verdict or admitted by the defendant. In other words, the relevant statutory maximum is not the maximum sentence a judge may impose after finding additional facts, but the maximum he or she may impose "without any additional findings." Finally, whether the judge's authority to impose an enhanced sentence depends on finding a specified fact, one of several specified facts, or an aggravating fact, it remains the case that the jury's verdict alone does not authorize the sentence. Reversed and remanded.

DISSENT: (O'Connor, J.) The effect of today's decision will be greater judicial discretion and less uniformity in sentencing. It is implausible that the Framers would have considered such a result to be required by the Due Process Clause or the Sixth Amendment. Prior to Washington's sentencing reform legislation, the state's unguided discretion inevitably resulted in severe disparities in sentencing received and served by defendants committing the same offense and having similar criminal histories. Because of today's decision, over 20 years of sentencing reform are all but lost, and tens of thousands of criminal judgments are in jeopardy.

DISSENT: (Kennedy, J.) The majority disregards the fundamental constitutional principle that different branches of government converse with each other on matters of vital common interest. Sentencing guidelines are a prime example of this collaborative process. However, in view of the majority's decision, numerous states with sentencing guidelines similar to those of Washington are now commanded "to scrap everything and start over."

DISSENT: (Breyer, J.) The difference between a traditional sentencing factor and an element of a greater offense often comes down to a legislative choice about which label to affix. However, I cannot jump from there to the conclu-

Continued on next page.

sion that the Sixth Amendment always requires identical treatment of the two scenarios. Such a jump is fraught with consequences which threaten the fairness of our traditional criminal justice system.

▶ *ANALYSIS*

As the Supreme Court stresses in *Blakely*, the need to provide intelligible content to the right of jury trial is no mere procedural formality, but a fundamental reservation of power in our constitutional structure. The *Blakely* case was not about whether determinate sentencing is constitutional, only about how it can be implemented in a way that respects the Sixth Amendment.

■══■

Quicknotes

SIXTH AMENDMENT Provides the right to a speedy and public trial by impartial jury, the right to be informed of the accusation, the right to confront witnesses, and the right to have the assistance of counsel in all criminal prosecutions.

■══■

Double Jeopardy

Quick Reference Rules of Law

Fong Foo v. United States

Criminal defendant (D) v. Federal government (P)

369 U.S. 141 (1962).

NATURE OF CASE: On certiorari from writ of mandamus vacating an acquittal in federal district court.

FACT SUMMARY: A corporation and two of its employees were tried before a jury on an indictment charging con-spiracy and concealment of material facts. After seven days of testimony, the district judge ordered a directed verdict of acquittal as to all the defendants. The record shows that the judge's action was based on supposed improper action by the prosecutor, an assistant United States attorney, and upon a supposed lack of credibility in the testimony of one of the Government's (P) witnesses.

🏛 **RULE OF LAW**
A verdict of acquittal may not be reviewed without putting the defendant twice in jeopardy.

FACTS: A corporation and two of its employees were indicted on charges of conspiracy and concealment of material facts. They were tried before a jury in federal district court. After several witnesses for the prosecution testified, the judge directed a verdict of acquittal as to all defendants. The order was based on the supposed improper conduct of the prosecutor and the supposed lack of credibility in the testimony of one of the witnesses who had testified for the Government (P). On appeal, the court of appeals reversed the acquittal and ordered a new trial.

ISSUE: May an appellate court review a judgment of acquittal?

HOLDING AND DECISION: (Per curiam) No. A verdict of acquittal may not be reviewed without putting the defendant twice in jeopardy. Although the court of appeals thought, not without reason, that the acquittal was based on an egregiously erroneous foundation, the acquittal was final and could not be reviewed without violating the Double Jeopardy Clause of the Constitution. The judgment of the court of appeals is reversed.

CONCURRENCE: (Harlan, J.) A retrial of petitioners is permissible if the acquittal was clearly based solely on the exercise of a power the trial judge unquestionably did not have. However, an examination of the record does not lead to a conclusive decision that the district court judge based his order solely on the exercise of a nonexistent judicial power.

DISSENT: (Clark, J.) The trial judge clearly had no power to direct a verdict of acquittal. The word "acquittal" is no

magic "open sesame"; in this case, the judgment of acquittal was null and void.

▶ **ANALYSIS**

Federal law prohibits an appeal from an acquittal, even to clarify a point of law, because of the "case and controversy" requirement of Article III. In some states, the government may appeal an acquittal to seek clarification of the law; however, the acquittal will stand even if the state prevails on the point of law.

Quicknotes

CONSPIRACY Concerted action by two or more persons to accomplish some unlawful purpose.

DIRECTED VERDICT A verdict ordered by the court in a jury trial.

WRIT OF MANDAMUS A court order issued commanding a public or private entity, or an official thereof, to perform a duty required by law.

Ashe v. Swenson

Criminal defendant (D) v. Government official (P)

397 U.S. 436 (1970).

NATURE OF CASE: Appeal from conviction for robbery.

FACT SUMMARY: Ashe (D) was acquitted of robbing a participant in a poker game but was later convicted of the same offense against a different participant in the same card game.

 RULE OF LAW
Collateral estoppel is part of the Fifth Amendment's guarantee against double jeopardy.

FACTS: Six men playing poker were robbed by three or four armed men. Ashe (D) was tried for robbery of Knight, one of the card players. At trial, persuasive evidence was not given as to Ashe's (D) guilt and he was acquitted. Six weeks later, Ashe (D) was tried for robbery of another participant in the same poker game. Ashe's (D) motion to dismiss based on his previous acquittal was overruled. Witnesses were substantially the same but gave substantially stronger testimony on Ashe's (D) identity. One weak witness from the first trial was not called. Ashe (D) was convicted and sentenced to 35 years' imprisonment. He appealed, urging that, under the guarantee against double jeopardy, the determination that he was not present at the robbery by the first jury collaterally estops a retrial of that issue.

ISSUE: Is the doctrine of collateral estoppel a part of the Fifth Amendment's guarantee against double jeopardy?

HOLDING AND DECISION: (Stewart, J.) Yes. When an issue of ultimate fact has once been determined by a valid and final judgment, the issue cannot again be litigated between the same parties in any future lawsuits. In criminal cases, collateral estoppel is not to be applied hypertechnically. Where there has been a general verdict of acquittal, the court must examine the record of the prior proceeding and conclude whether the jury could have grounded its verdict upon an issue other than that which the defendant seeks to foreclose from consideration. "The single rationally conceivable issue in dispute before the jury was whether the petitioner had been one of the robbers." The jury found he was not. Under double jeopardy, that issue cannot be relitigated. Reversed.

DISSENT: (Burger, C.J.) The collateral-estoppel concept ordinarily applies to parties on each side of the litigation who have the same interest as, or who are identical with, the parties in the initial litigation. Here, the complainant in the second trial is not the same as in the first even though the State is a party in both cases. Courts that have applied the collateral-estoppel concept to criminal actions would certainly not apply it to *both* parties, as is true in civil cases. For example, here, if Ashe (D) had been convicted at the first trial, presumably no court would then hold that he was thereby foreclosed from litigating the identification issue at the second trial.

ANALYSIS

Prior to this case, double jeopardy was generally thought of as applying only to applications of res judicata. In other words, it prevented relitigation of an entire action. The present action represented an expansion of the prohibition against double jeopardy, applying it to collateral estoppel's concerns of a previously litigated issue as opposed to a complete case.

Quicknotes

COLLATERAL ESTOPPEL A doctrine whereby issues litigated and determined in a prior proceeding are binding upon all subsequent litigation between the parties regarding that issue.

DOUBLE JEOPARDY A prohibition against a second prosecution for the same offense after an acquittal or conviction for that offense in a prior proceeding or against multiple punishments for the same offense

FIFTH AMENDMENT Provides that no person shall be compelled to serve as a witness against himself, or be subject to trial for the same offense twice, or be deprived of life, liberty, or property without due process of law.

Oregon v. Kennedy

State (P) v. Criminal defendant (D)

456 U.S. 667 (1982).

NATURE OF CASE: Appeal from dismissal of prosecution for theft.

FACT SUMMARY: Tried for theft, Kennedy (D) moved for a mistrial based on the prosecutor's misconduct during direct examination of the State's (P) expert witness. Kennedy (D) successfully appealed to the Oregon Court of Appeals, which ruled that the prosecutor's misconduct was overreaching.

RULE OF LAW

Where a defendant in a criminal case successfully moves for a mistrial, he may not then raise the bar of double jeopardy against a second trial unless the intent of the government's conduct in the first trial was intended to goad the defendant to make such a motion.

FACTS: Kennedy (D) was charged with the theft of an oriental rug. During the redirect examination of the State's (P) expert witness, the prosecutor asked if the witness had never done business with the defendant because Kennedy (D) was a crook. Kennedy (D) then moved for and was granted a mistrial for prosecutorial misconduct. The same trial court then determined, after a hearing on the matter, that since the prosecutor had not intended to cause a mistrial, double jeopardy principles did not bar a retrial. Kennedy (D) was then retried and convicted. He then appealed to the Oregon Court of Appeals, which sustained his double jeopardy claim due to overreaching by the prosecutor.

ISSUE: Can a defendant who, on his own motion, moves for and is granted a mistrial, be retried for the same crime?

HOLDING AND DECISION: (Rehnquist, J.) Yes. There is a balance between a defendant's right not to be tried twice for the same crime and the state's societal interest in enforcing its criminal laws. The Court's case law indicates that there is a narrow exception, relating to prosecutorial misconduct, in which the Double Jeopardy Clause of the Fifth Amendment is a bar to retrial. If such misconduct leads the defendant to request a mistrial, the prosecutor may be deliberately goading the defendant to make such a request. To evaluate this conduct, there exists a standard for determining the motives of prose-cutorial intent. It calls on the trial court to make a finding of fact, which is a manageable standard for a court to apply and does not subvert the protections under the Double Jeopardy Clause. A defendant may, therefore, only invoke the bar of the Double Jeopardy Clause of the Fifth Amendment in cases where the government's conduct, which led to the granting of a motion for mistrial, was intended to provoke the defendant to move for such a motion. Because the lower courts found the prosecutor did not intend to cause a mistrial, that ends the inquiry.

ANALYSIS

One of the concerns in granting a mistrial is that either the prosecution or the defense may be attempting to cause a mistrial because its members want a new jury selected since they are dissatisfied with the jury that was impaneled. The Kennedy decision attempts to balance this concern with consti-tutional protections by having a judge decide whether the prosecutor's motives that led to the mistrial request were questionable. *Oregon v. Kennedy* limits the Court's previous broader rulings on the Double Jeopardy Clause.

Quicknotes

DOUBLE JEOPARDY A prohibition against a second prosecution for the same offense after an acquittal or conviction for that offense in a prior proceeding or against multiple punishments for the same offense.

United States v. Dixon

Federal government (P) v. Criminal defendant (D)

509 U.S. 688 (1993).

NATURE OF CASE: Consolidated appeals cases from ruling barring subsequent criminal prosecution in one and allowing it in the other.

FACT SUMMARY: Dixon (D) was convicted of criminal contempt in connection with alleged underlying criminal conduct and argued that the Double Jeopardy Clause barred any subsequent criminal prosecution on charges arising out of the same criminal conduct.

RULE OF LAW
The Double Jeopardy Clause does not permit subsequent prosecution of an offense that has already been the basis of criminal contempt proceedings.

FACTS: Dixon (D) had been arrested for second-degree murder. The form by which he was released on bond specified that he was not to commit "any criminal offense" and warned that any violation of the conditions of release would subject him "to revocation of release, an order of detention, and prosecution for contempt of court." While awaiting trial, Dixon (D) was arrested and indicted for possession of cocaine with intent to distribute. He was found guilty of criminal contempt and sentenced to 180 days in jail. The trial court later granted Dixon's (D) motion to dismiss the cocaine indictment on double jeopardy grounds. The Government (P) appealed. The court of appeals ruled that the subsequent prosecution was barred by the Double Jeopardy Clause. The Government (P) appealed.

ISSUE: Does the Double Jeopardy Clause permit subsequent prosecution of an offense that has already been the basis of criminal contempt proceedings?

HOLDING AND DECISION: (Scalia, J.) No. The Double Jeopardy Clause does not permit subsequent prosecution of an offense that has already been the basis of criminal contempt proceedings. This protection applies both to successive punishments and to successive prosecutions for the same criminal offense. This Court has concluded that where the two offenses for which the defendant is punished or tried cannot survive the "same-elements" test, the double jeopardy bar applies. The same-elements test inquires whether each offense contains only elements contained in the other; if so, they are the "same offense" and double jeopardy bars additional punishment and successive prosecution. If not, they are not the same offense, and there is no double jeopardy bar. Dixon's (D) cocaine possession, although an offense under the D.C. code,

was not an offense under the contempt statute until a judge incorporated the statutory drug offense into his release order. Here, where the contempt sanction was imposed for violating the order through commission of the incorporated drug offense, the later attempt to prosecute Dixon (D) for the drug offense resembles the double jeopardy situation. Affirmed.

CONCURRENCE AND DISSENT IN PART: (Rehnquist, C.J.) A defendant who is guilty of possession with intent to distribute cocaine has not necessarily satisfied any statutory element of criminal contempt. Nor can it be said that a defendant who is held in criminal contempt has necessarily satisfied any element of possession with intent to distribute cocaine. The offense for which Dixon (D) was prosecuted in this case cannot be analogized to greater and lesser included offenses; hence, they are separate and distinct for double jeopardy purposes.

CONCURRENCE AND DISSENT IN PART: (White, J.) The Double Jeopardy Clause bars prosecution for an offense if the defendant already has been held in contempt for its commission. Thus, the subsequent prosecutions in both Dixon (D) and Foster (D) were impermissible as to all counts.

CONCURRENCE AND DISSENT: (Souter, J.) The prosecution of Dixon (D) should be barred by the Double Jeopardy Clause.

▶ ANALYSIS

The same-elements test was first enunciated by the Court in *Blockburger v. United States*, 284 U.S. 299 (1932), and is commonly referred to as the "Blockburger" test. In arriving at its ruling in the instant case, the majority overruled its recent decision in *Grady v. Corbin*, 495 U.S. 508 (1990), which held that in addition to passing the Blockburger test, a subsequent prosecution must satisfy a "same-conduct" test to avoid the double jeopardy bar. The *Grady* test provided that if, to establish an essential element of an offense charged in that prosecutiov, the government would prove conduct that constituted an offense for which the defendant had already been prosecuted, a second prosecution may not be had. In the majority's view, *Grady* was not only wrong in principle, but had already proved inconsistent in application.

Continued on next page.

Quicknotes

CONTEMPT An act of omission that interferes with a court's proper administration of justice.

DOUBLE JEOPARDY A prohibition against a second prosecution for the same offense after an acquittal or conviction for that offense in a prior proceeding or against multiple punishments for the same offense.

■▬■

Heath v. Alabama

Convicted murderer (D) v. State (P)

474 U.S. 82 (1985).

NATURE OF CASE: Review of murder conviction.

FACT SUMMARY: After being convicted of murder in Georgia, Heath (D) was convicted of murder in Alabama (P) for the same homicide.

RULE OF LAW
Successive prosecutions by two states for the same conduct are not barred by the Double Jeopardy Clause.

FACTS: Heath (D) was charged in Georgia with murder, arising out of his allegedly hiring certain individuals to kill his wife, who was in fact killed. Part of the crime occurred in Alabama (P). Heath (D) was convicted by a Georgia jury and sentenced to life imprisonment. He was then charged with murder by Alabama (P). He was convicted and sentenced to death. His double jeopardy claims were rejected at the trial level and on appeal as well. The Supreme Court accepted review.

ISSUE: Are successive prosecutions by two states for the same conduct barred by the Double Jeopardy Clause?

HOLDING AND DECISION: (O'Connor, J.) No. Successive prosecutions by two states for the same conduct are not barred by the Double Jeopardy Clause. A crime is an offense against the sovereignty of a government. When an individual breaks the laws of two states, he has committed two distinct offenses. Each sovereign is entitled to have its law adjudicated in its own courts, so it is no answer to the above principle that the trial in Georgia regarded the same sort of offense involved in Alabama (P). Essentially, when two laws derive from two different ultimate sources, two separate offenses occur when the laws of each ultimate source are broken. Here, two separate sovereigns, Alabama (P) and Georgia, are involved, and consequently two different offenses occurred. Affirmed.

DISSENT: (Marshall, J.) When two states are involved in a single transaction, the issues of sovereignty for each state are identical. Vindicating the laws of one state in a prosecution automatically vindicates the laws of the other.

▶ ANALYSIS

The analysis of the Court here does not apply in all cases where the laws of multiple jurisdictions are broken. For instance, if a single act violates similar laws in a county and a state, the violator may not be tried twice. Counties are not sovereigns, but rather subdivisions of a sovereign state.

■▬■

Quicknotes

FULL FAITH AND CREDIT Doctrine that a judgment by a court of one state shall be given the same effect in another state.

■▬■

United States v. Ursery

Federal government (P) v. Convicted drug manufacturer (D)

518 U.S. 267 (1996).

NATURE OF CASE: Appeal from reversal of conviction for drug possession.

FACT SUMMARY: Ursery (D) was caught growing marijuana in his house but claimed his criminal conviction violated double jeopardy because the Government (P) had already conducted forfeiture proceedings on his home.

🏛 RULE OF LAW
The government may pursue both criminal charges and civil forfeitures without violating the Double Jeopardy Clause.

FACTS: Ursery (D) was caught by the Michigan police growing marijuana in his home. The United States (P) instituted civil forfeiture proceedings against the house, alleging that the house had been been used to facilitate the processing and distributing of controlled substances. Ursery (D) paid $13,250 to settle the forfeiture claim in full. Meanwhile, Ursery (D) was indicted for growing marijuana and was later convicted. Ursery (D) appealed his criminal conviction, contending that it violated the Double Jeopardy Clause of the Fifth Amendment. The Sixth Circuit reversed the conviction, and the Government (P) appealed.

ISSUE: May the government pursue both criminal charges and civil forfeitures consistent with the Double Jeopardy Clause?

HOLDING AND DECISION: (Rehnquist, C.J.) Yes. The government may pursue both criminal charges and civil forfeitures without violating the Double Jeopardy Clause. The Double Jeopardy Clause provides that persons are not subject to successive punishments and prosecutions for the same offense. Since the earliest years of this nation, Congress has authorized parallel in rem civil forfeiture actions and criminal prosecutions based upon the same underlying events. This Court has consistently concluded that the Double Jeopardy Clause does not apply to civil forfeitures because they do not impose "punishment." This conclusion is based on the distinction between civil property forfeitures and personal civil penalties. Penalties issued against a defendant may be punitive in nature, but an action against property used in a crime is not intended as punishment. This Court's decision in *United States v. Halper*, 490 U.S. 435 (1989), finding that a civil penalty could be so disproportionate to the actual damages that it amounted to a second punishment is not applicable here. Civil property forfeitures are different in nature than civil penalties. Therefore, there is no basis for overturning Ursery's (D) criminal conviction based on the prior civil forfeiture of his home. Reversed.

CONCURRENCE: (Scalia, J.) The Double Jeopardy Clause prohibits successive prosecution, not successive punishment. Civil forfeiture proceedings are not criminal prosecutions.

CONCURRENCE AND DISSENT IN PART: Stevens, J.) The majority has misread the *Halper* line of cases. There is no absolute distinction between civil forfeitures and civil penalties. The instant case provides an example; homes cannot "facilitate" narcotics offenses, they are not instruments of drug trafficking. Thus, the *Halper* test of looking to see whether the civil action is punitive in nature is proper.

▎*ANALYSIS*

The decision also ruled on Arlt's (D) and Wren's (D) virtually identical cases involving the production of methamphetamines and a deferred forfeiture proceeding. This case marks a change in direction for the Court on the issue of civil penalties for criminal offenses. *Halper* in 1989, *Austin v. United States* in 1993, and *Department of Revenue of Montana v. Kurth Ranch* [no cites given for these cases] in 1994 represented a string of cases suggesting that the Court was cracking down on the use of civil penalties.

■■■

Quicknotes

DOUBLE JEOPARDY A prohibition against a second prosecution for the same offense after an acquittal or conviction for that offense in a prior proceeding or against multiple punishments for the same offense.

FIFTH AMENDMENT Provides that no person shall be compelled to serve as a witness against himself, or be subject to trial for the same offense twice, or be deprived of life, liberty, or property without due process of law.

■■■

Quick Reference Rules of Law

Chapman v. California

Criminal defendant (D) v. State (P)

386 U.S. 18 (1967).

NATURE OF CASE: Appeal from conviction of robbery, kidnapping and murder.

FACT SUMMARY: Chapman (D) and Teale (D) contended that because the prosecutor committed a constitutional error by commenting on their failure to testify on their own behalf, as a matter of law such error was reversible.

🏛 RULE OF LAW
A federal constitutional error may be found to be harmless where such is shown beyond a reasonable doubt.

FACTS: Chapman (D) and Teale (D) were arrested for kidnapping, robbery, and murder. Neither defendant testified at trial. The prosecution commented heavily on their failure to testify, and they were convicted. While the case was on appeal, the U.S. Supreme Court held that it was a deprivation of a defendant's constitutional rights for the prosecution to comment on his failure to testify. Chapman (D) and Teale (D) contended that because the error was constitutional, as a matter of law it was reversible error. The California Supreme Court held the error to be harmless. The U.S. Supreme Court granted review.

ISSUE: May constitutional error be held harmless where such is shown beyond a reasonable doubt?

HOLDING AND DECISION: (Black, J.) Yes. It must be shown beyond a reasonable doubt that constitutional error was harmless or such will be considered reversible. Not all federal constitutional errors are reversible. However, the highest level of proof must be presented to hold such an error harmless. It is not harmless error to effectively deprive a defendant of his right against self-incrimination. By commenting on his failure to testify, the prosecution suggests that such failure is an admission of guilt. Thus this is reversible error. Reversed and remanded.

CONCURRENCE: (Stewart, J.) It should not be assumed that that the same harmless-error rule should apply indiscriminately to all constitutional violations. A harmless-error rule might be appropriate for one type of constitutional error and not for another. Moreover, the adoption of any harmless-error rule commits this Court to a case-by-case examination. It is, therefore, inappropriate to inquire whether the violation of *Griffin v. California*, which occurred in this case, was harmless by any standard.

▶ ANALYSIS

Some commentators suggest this opinion implies that constitutional errors are, by their nature, more important errors than others. The abuse of constitutional as opposed to statutory or state common law standards is considered fundamentally more erosive of the justice system.

■■■

Quicknotes

HARMLESS ERROR An error committed uring trial which is not sufficient in nature or effect of warrant reversal, modification, or retrial.

■■■

Teague v. Lane

Convicted felon (D) v. Government official (P)

489 U.S. 288 (1989).

NATURE OF CASE: Review of denial of habeas corpus.

FACT SUMMARY: Teague (D) argued in a habeas proceeding that a post-conviction judicial decision had rendered his conviction invalid.

> 🏛 **RULE OF LAW**
> Except in special circumstances, case law will not be retroactively applied in collateral review.

FACTS: Teague (D) was charged with various felonies. An all-white jury convicted Teague (D), a black man, of attempted murder, robbery, and battery. The prosecution had used all its peremptory challenges to exclude blacks from the jury. Teague (D) appealed, contending that this denied him due process. On appeal the conviction was upheld. Teague (D) subsequently petitioned for habeas corpus, contending that he had been entitled to a jury consisting of a cross section of the community. The district court denied his petition on the merits, as did the court of appeals. The Supreme Court granted review.

ISSUE: Will case law be retroactively applied in collateral review?

HOLDING AND DECISION: (O'Connor, J.) No. Case law will not be retroactively applied in collateral review. Habeas corpus provides an avenue for upsetting judgments that otherwise would be final. It is not intended to be a substitute for direct review. Both the state and criminal defendants have an interest in leaving concluded litigation in a state of repose. If new rules of constitutional law were to be applied retroactively, any litigation might be reopened if the new rule were to be applicable. Further, the purpose of habeas is that its presence creates an incentive for trial and appellate judges to conduct their proceedings in a manner consistent with established constitutional principles. To apply new principles retroactively would actually subvert this purpose. Therefore, unless the post-conviction rule announced is so fundamental to the concept of ordered liberty that it would be unconscionable not to retroactively apply it or unless it places "certain kinds of primary, individual conduct beyond the power of the criminal law-making authority to proscribe," retroactive application will not be given. A necessary corollary to this rule is that no new rule of constitutional criminal procedure should be announced in a habeas proceeding. Here, to rule as Teague (D) urges would amount to that. Therefore, without ruling on the merits of the claim, the denial of habeas must be affirmed.

CONCURRENCE: (Stevens, J.) When a criminal defendant claims that a procedural error tainted the conviction, an appellate court often decides whether error occurred before deciding whether such error is harmless or requires reversal. A parallel approach should be followed in cases raising novel questions of constitutional law on collateral review. If error has been found to occur, factors relating to retroactivity should be examined before granting relief.

DISSENT: (Brennan, J.) Permitting the federal courts to decide novel habeas claims not substantially related to guilt or innocence has profited our society immensely. In the face of congressional acquiescence to this practice, it is ill-advised for the Court to now fashion such a major change in habeas jurisprudence.

▶ **ANALYSIS**

The opinion in fact announces two rules, the first being that stated above and the second being that new constitutional issues cannot be announced in a habeas proceeding. The latter rule is potentially much more significant than the first. It is important to note, however, that only four justices joined the section announcing that rule, which limits its precedential value.

∎▬∎

Quicknotes

COLLATERAL ESTOPPEL A doctrine whereby issues litigated and determined in a prior proceeding are binding upon all subsequent litigation between the parties regarding that issue.

HABEAS CORPUS A proceeding in which a defendant brings a writ to compel a judicial determination of whether he is lawfully being held in custody.

∎▬∎

Terry Williams v. Taylor

Convicted murderer (D) v. Government official (P)

529 U.S. 362 (2000).

NATURE OF CASE: Habeas corpus petition challenged validity of a death sentence.

FACT SUMMARY: Williams (D) brought a habeas corpus petition challenging his capital punishment sentence on the basis that he was denied effective assistance of counsel.

🏛 RULE OF LAW
The Antiterrorism and Effective Death Penalty Act of 1996 (AEDPA) requires that, for a defendant to be entitled to federal habeas corpus relief, the state court determination must be based on "clearly established federal law" and must be "contrary to, or involve an unreasonable application of" that clearly established law.

FACTS: Williams (D) was convicted of robbery and murder. At his sentencing hearing, the prosecution proved that Williams (D) had been convicted of armed robbery and burglary and grand larceny on two prior occasions. The prosecution also described two auto thefts and two assaults on elderly victims. Williams's (D) counsel asked the jury to give weight to the fact that he had turned himself in on four crimes. The weight of the closing was devoted to explaining that it was difficult to find a reason to spare Williams's (D) life. The jury sentenced Williams (D) to death and the Virginia Supreme Court affirmed. Williams (D) filed for state collateral relief and an evidentiary hearing was held by the same judge who presided over the trial on the claim that trial counsel had been ineffective. The Virginia Supreme Court disagreed that Williams (D) suffered sufficient prejudice to warrant relief. Williams (D) then sought a federal writ of habeas corpus, and a federal judge found that the death sentence was constitutionally infirm. The federal court of appeals reversed. The Supreme Court granted certiorari.

ISSUE: Does the AEDPA require that, for a defendant to be entitled to federal habeas corpus relief, the state court determination must be based on "clearly established federal law" and must be "contrary to, or involve an unreasonable application of" that clearly established law?

HOLDING AND DECISION: (Stevens, J.) Yes. The AEDPA requires that, for a defendant to be entitled to federal habeas corpus relief, the state court determination must be based on "clearly established federal law" and must be "contrary to, or involve an unreasonable application of" that clearly established law. When federal judges exercise their federal

question jurisdiction under the judicial power of Article III, it is their duty to say what the law is. A reading of the AEDPA that would cede such authority to the state courts would be inconsistent with Article III. In interpreting § 2254(d)(1), the requirement that the determinations of state courts be tested only against clearly established federal law and the prohibition on the issuance of the writ unless the state court's decision is contrary to or involved an unreasonable application of the clearly established law. In *Teague v. Lane*, this Court held that petitioner was not entitled to federal habeas corpus relief since he relied on a federal rule of law that had not been announced until after his conviction became final. The AEDPA codifies this holding to the extent that it requires courts to deny federal habeas corpus relief contingent upon a rule of law not clearly established at the time the state decision became final. Teague also provides that a federal habeas court may apply a rule dictated by precedent. A rule that breaks new ground or imposes a new obligation falls outside this scope. The AEDPA has further added to the clearly established law requirement a clause limiting the area of relevant law to that determined by the Supreme Court of the United States. A rule failing to satisfy these criteria is not available as a basis for relief in a habeas case to which the AEDPA applies. With respect to the "contrary to, or an unreasonable application of" requirement, it seems that Congress intended federal judges to invoke the utmost care to state court decisions before concluding issuance of the writ was warranted, but the act does not require them to defer to the opinion of every reasonable state court judge on the content of federal law. If, after carefully weighing the reasons for accepting the state court's judgment, a federal court is convinced that a prisoner's custody is unconstitutional, then that judgment should prevail. Here Williams (D) contended that he was denied his constitutionally guaranteed right to effective assistance of counsel when his lawyers failed to investigate and present substantial mitigating evidence to the sentencing jury. The initial inquiry under the AEDPA is whether Williams (D) seeks to apply a rule of law that was clearly established at the time his state court conviction became final. Williams (D) is entitled to relief if the Virginia Supreme Court's decision was either "contrary to, or involved unreasonable application of" the clearly established law. It was both. Reversed.

CONCURRENCE IN PART: (O'Connor, J.) This case is not governed by the pre-1996 version of the habeas

Continued on next page.

statute, but by the statute as amended by the AEDPA. The Virginia Supreme Court's adjudication of Williams's (D) application for habeas corpus relief did result in "a decision that was contrary to, or involved an unreasonable application of, established Federal law" and, therefore, a federal court may grant a writ of habeas corpus. The majority, however, errs regarding the standard to be applied under the AEDPA in evaluating Williams's (D) claims on habeas. Since the present case is not governed by the federal habeas statute as it was enacted prior to the adoption of the AEDPA in 1996, Williams's (D) petition for habeas relief must not be granted based on the prior standard, which would have concluded whether or not his Sixth Amendment right to effective assistance of counsel had been violated. The AEDPA places a new constraint on the power of a federal habeas court to grant a state prisoner's application for a writ of habeas corpus with respect to claims adjudicated on the merits in state court. Under this act, the writ may only be issued if the state court adjudication satisfies one of the following conditions: (1) The decision was contrary to clearly established federal laws as determined by the Supreme Court of the United States or (2) The decision involved an unreasonable application of clearly established federal law as determined by the Supreme Court of the United States. Contrary to the majority's opinion, the AEDPA does alter the previously settled rule of independent review. The "contrary to" and "unreasonable application" clauses of the act are to be given independent meaning. Under the "contrary to" clause, a federal habeas court may grant a writ if the state court (1) arrives at a conclusion opposite to that reached by this Court on a question of law or (2) decides a case on a set of materially indistinguishable facts differently than the Supreme Court has. The text of AEDPA, therefore, suggests that the state court's decision must be substantially different from the relevant precedent of the Supreme Court. The act does not, as the majority's opinion suggests encompass routine state-court decisions that apply the correct legal rule but reach a different result than the Supreme Court. Under the "unreasonable application" clause, a federal habeas court may grant a writ if the state court identifies the correct governing legal principle from this Court's decisions but unreasonably applies that principle to the facts of the prisoner's case. The majority's opinion that the debate in Wright concerned only the meaning of the Teague non-retroactivity rule is simply incorrect because an "unreasonable application" of federal law is different from an "incorrect application."

CONCURRENCE AND DISSENT IN PART: (Rehnquist, C.J.) The Court's interpretation of the AEDPA is correct, but the majority's decision to grant habeas relief in this case is in error. Counsel's performance fell below an objective standard of reasonableness and the evidence in

the prejudice inquiry overwhelmingly showed that the defendant presented a future danger to society. It was not, therefore, unreasonable to believe that a jury would not have been swayed by evidence demonstrating that the defendant had a terrible childhood and a low IQ. In addition, jury members would probably have viewed the proffered mitigation evidence that he was not dangerous while in detention as unconvincing upon hearing of the defendant's actions while he was in detention.

▶ ANALYSIS

The court concluded that Williams (D) had a fundamental right to provide the jury with mitigating evidence that his trial counsel either failed to discover or failed to offer. The Virginia court erred in requiring a separate inquiry into fundamental fairness even when Williams (D) was able to show that his counsel was ineffective and such ineffectiveness adversely affected the result of the proceeding. The court's decision also fulfilled the contrary to or unreasonable application of requirement with respect to the prejudice determination insofar as it failed to evaluate the totality of the mitigation evidence available and its decision turned on the erroneous view that a difference in outcome is not sufficient in itself to establish ineffective assistance of counsel.

Quicknotes

HABEAS CORPUS A proceeding in which a defendant brings a writ to compel a judicial determination of whether he is lawfully being held in custody.

Wainwright v. Sykes

Government official (D) v. Convicted murderer (P)

433 U.S. 72 (1977).

NATURE OF CASE: Habeas corpus challenge to a murder conviction.

FACT SUMMARY: Sykes (P) sought a review of his murder conviction via a habeas corpus proceeding, but he had failed to comply with state procedural rules in not raising the underlying claim at trial.

🏛 RULE OF LAW
One who did not comply with state procedural rules by not raising his federal claim at trial cannot obtain federal habeas corpus review of his state criminal conviction unless he shows "cause" for noncompliance and shows "prejudice" as a result of the claimed error in the original proceeding.

FACTS: Sykes (P) violated a state procedural rule by not raising, at trial, his claim that the incriminating statements admitted against him were involuntary because he did not understand the Miranda warnings that he had been given. When he was convicted in state court for murder, Sykes (P) then presented a federal habeas corpus challenge to that conviction based on the aforementioned contention. Opposing such action, Wainwright (D) argued that the rule in *Francis v. Henderson*, 425 U.S. 537 (1976), should be extended to cover this case. That rule was that federal habeas corpus review was barred absent a showing of "cause" and "prejudice" where the challenge was to the makeup of a grand jury. Sykes (P) argued that *Fay v. Noia*, 372 U.S. 391 (1963), had laid down an all-inclusive rule rendering state timely objection rules ineffective to bar review of underlying federal claims in federal habeas corpus proceedings absent a showing of "knowing waiver" or a "deliberate bypass" of the right to so object.

ISSUE: In order to obtain federal habeas corpus review of his state criminal conviction, must one who did not comply with state procedural rules in raising his federal claim at trial show "cause" for noncompliance and show "prejudice" resulting from the claimed error in the original proceeding?

HOLDING AND DECISION: (Rehnquist, J.) Yes. If one who suffered a state criminal conviction did not comply with state procedural law by bringing up his federal claim at trial, he cannot obtain federal habeas corpus review of the conviction unless he shows "cause" for noncompliance and shows "prejudice" as a result of the claimed error in the original proceeding. A state's contemporaneous objection rule is designed to ensure that constitutional claims are heard when they are fresh, not years later in a federal habeas corpus proceeding. Furthermore, to apply the "knowing waiver" or "deliberate bypass" standard, the more lenient of those suggested, would encourage "sandbagging" by lawyers who would take their chances on a not guilty verdict at trial with the intent to raise their constitutional claims in a federal habeas corpus court if their initial gamble does not pay off. The "cause" and "prejudice" rule herein adopted attempts to make the state trial on the merits the "main event" rather than a "tryout on the road." In this case, the required showing of cause was not made. Remanded with instructions to dismiss the petition for a writ of habeas corpus.

CONCURRENCE: (Burger, C.J.) The "deliberate bypass" standard does not lend itself to cases where it is the attorney and not the defendant who makes the decision not to raise a claim. It would be impossible for the attorney to stop the trial all the time to make sure his client was giving knowing and intelligent approval to each of the myriad of tactical decisions made during trial.

CONCURRENCE: (Stevens, J.) In applying the "deliberate bypass" standard, courts have found the client impliedly consents where, as here, his attorney decides as a tactical ploy not to raise a constitutional objection at trial. Furthermore, there is no evidence that the trial lacked fundamental fairness. So, there is no reason to allow collateral attack in this case regardless of which rule is chosen.

DISSENT: (Brennan, J.) The Court is not justified in imposing a stricter standard than the "deliberate bypass" test. It is the harshest test possible that still distinguishes between intentional and inadvertent noncompliance by counsel with procedural rules. Most procedural defaults are born of the inadvertence, negligence, inexperience, or incompetence of trial counsel, and it is unfair to make the criminal defendant accountable for the naked errors of his attorney. The mistakes of a trial attorney should be visited on the head of a federal habeas corpus applicant only when this Court is convinced that the lawyer actually exercised his expertise and judgment in his client's service, and with his client's knowing and intelligent participation, where possible.

Continued on next page.

▶ *ANALYSIS*

One possible result of this case may be that defendants are pushed into making more claims based on ineffectiveness of counsel to fulfill the requirement that they show "cause." That is, a particular procedural default will simply be cited as an example of general incompetence of counsel. The effect would be merely to transform the old claims alleging deprivation of constitutional rights to new claims alleging ineffectiveness of counsel, with all the attendant problems which will engender.

■━━■

Quicknotes

HABEAS CORPUS A proceeding in which a defendant brings a writ to compel a judicial determination of whether he is lawfully being held in custody.

■━━■

Stone v. Powell

Accused (D) v. State (P)

428 U.S. 465 (1976).

NATURE OF CASE: Writ for federal habeas corpus.

FACT SUMMARY: A prisoner sought habeas corpus relief on the grounds that he was convicted based on evidence obtained in an illegal search or seizure.

🏛 RULE OF LAW
When the state has provided an opportunity for full and fair litigation of a Fourth Amendment claim, the Constitution does not require that a state prisoner be granted federal habeas corpus relief on the ground that evidence obtained in an unconstitutional search or seizure was introduced at his trial.

FACTS: Stone (D) alleged that his conviction was based on evidence illegally obtained, and requested habeas corpus review. After state habeas corpus proceedings, Stone (D) filed a writ for federal habeas corpus, alleging violation of Fourth Amendment rights guaranteed through the Fourteenth Amendment.

ISSUE: When the state has provided an opportunity for full and fair litigation of a Fourth Amendment claim, does the Constitution require that a state prisoner be granted federal habeas corpus relief on the ground that evidence obtained in an unconstitutional search or seizure was introduced at his trial?

HOLDING AND DECISION: (Powell, J.) No. When the state has provided an opportunity for full and fair litigation of a Fourth Amendment claim, the Constitution does not require that a state prisoner be granted federal habeas corpus relief on the ground that evidence obtained in an unconstitutional search or seizure was introduced at his trial. The primary justification for the exclusionary rule is the deterrence of police conduct that violates Fourth Amendment rights; the Fourth Amendment itself is not a personal constitutional right. Fourth Amendment concerns support the implementation of the exclusionary rule at trial and its enforcement on direct appeal of state court convictions. The additional contribution, if any, of the consideration of search and seizure claims of state prisoners on collateral review is small in relation to the costs. Writ denied.

DISSENT: (Brennan, J.) The Court today is ignoring the settled principle that for purposes of adjudicating constitutional claims Congress, which has the power to do so under Article III of the Constitution, has effectively cast the district courts sitting in habeas in the role of surrogate supreme courts. The procedural safeguards mandated by the Congress are not admonitions to be tolerated only to the extent they serve functional purposes. Every guarantee enshrined in our Constitution is endowed with an independent vitality and value, and the court is not free to curtail those constitutional guarantees even to punish the most obviously guilty.

▶ ANALYSIS

The Court has not extended the holding from this case to bar habeas corpus review of other claims based on violations of the Constitution. The Antiterrorism and Effective Death Penalty Act enacted in 1996 limited successive habeas corpus petitions. This Act did not, however, repeal the authority of the court to entertain original habeas corpus petitions.

■━■

Quicknotes

FOURTH AMENDMENT Provides that persons be secure as to their person and private belongings against unreasonable searches and seizures.

HABEAS CORPUS A proceeding in which a defendant brings a writ to compel a judicial determination of whether he is lawfully being held in custody.

SEARCH An inspection conducted in order to obtain evidence to be utilized for the prosecution of a crime.

SEIZURE The removal of property from one's possession due to unlawful activity or in satisfaction of a judgment entered by the court.

■━■

Brecht v. Abrahamson

Convicted murderer (D) v. Government official (P)

507 U.S. 619 (1993).

NATURE OF CASE: Petition for writ of habeas corpus.

FACT SUMMARY: Brecht (D) was charged with the murder of his brother-in-law. While attempting to flee the area, Brecht (D) was apprehended by the police and brought to trial. His defense was that the shooting had been accidental. The prosecution, on cross-examination, asked why Brecht (D) had not told anyone prior to trial that the death was an accident. The defense objected, saying that references to Brecht's (D) silence violated the doctrine underlying the Miranda warnings, and appealed Brecht's (D) conviction.

RULE OF LAW
Habeas petitioners may obtain plenary review of constitutional claims, but they are only entitled to habeas relief for trial error if they can establish "actual prejudice."

FACTS: Brecht (D) shot and killed his brother-in-law and then fled in his sister's car. He subsequently crashed into a ditch. When a police officer offered Brecht (D) assistance, the defendant refused it. While hitchhiking, Brecht (D) was picked up by the police. He identified himself and was arrested. He was arraigned and at that time given his Miranda warnings. Brecht (D) claimed at trial that the shooting had been an accident. The prosecution, on cross-examination, asked if Brecht (D) had ever told anyone at any time prior to trial that the shooting was an accident. Brecht (D) answered "no." The prosecution then made numerous references to this fact during summation. Defense objected at the time of the cross-examination that the State (P), by referencing Brecht's (D) post-Miranda silence, had violated Brecht's (D) rights and prejudiced the jury. Brecht (D), after appeals in state court, sought a writ of habeas corpus under federal law.

ISSUE: Does the prosecution's use of a defendant's post-Miranda silence, for impeachment purposes, cause "actual prejudice" and thereby entitle the defendant to habeas corpus relief?

HOLDING AND DECISION: (Rehnquist, C.J) No. Brecht (D) is not entitled to habeas relief under the standard set forth in *Kotteakos v. United States*, 328 U.S. 750, 776 (1946). The *Kotteakos* harmless-error standard grants habeas relief only if the error had a substantial and injurious effect on the jury's verdict. Habeas relief is an extraordinary remedy. *Chap-*

man v. California, 386 U.S. 18 (1967), establishes the general standard for deciding whether a conviction must be set aside due to a Constitutional error, which is whether the error was "harmless beyond a reasonable doubt. A defendant's right to due process, where the prosecution has used the defendant's post-Miranda silence for impeachment purposes, is governed by *Doyle v. Ohio*, 426 U.S. 610 (1976). Here, neither *Doyle* nor *Chapman* applies. Instead the *Kotteakos* standard, where habeas relief is granted only where the *Doyle* error "had substantial and injurious effect or influence in determining the jury's verdict," applies. *Doyle* should be applied only in cases where the constitutional violation was the result strictly of trial error, which is not the situation here. The test under *Kotteakos*, then, requires habeas petitioners to demonstrate that "actual prejudice" occurred as a result of trial error. In *Brecht*, the prosecution's references to the defendant's post-Miranda silence comprises only two pages of the 900-page trial transcript and the State's case against him, using other evidence, was weighty. The *Doyle* error that occurred during Brecht's (D) trial did not substantially influence the jury's verdict and Brecht (D) is, therefore, not entitled to habeas relief.

CONCURRENCE: (Stevens, J.) The *Kotteakos* standard applied by the majority does not fit the facts of this case. The *Doyle* error that occurred at trial did not in fact have "a substantial and injurious effect or influence in determining the jury's verdict."

DISSENT: (White, J.) The Court's decision is counter to previous precedent. The *Chapman* standard should have been applied here. This standard requires a reversal of a state conviction where there is a constitutional violation that is not harmless beyond a reasonable doubt. Such a violation occurred, and Brecht (D) is entitled to habeas relief.

DISSENT: (O'Connor, J.) Decisions regarding habeas corpus writs demand restraint. The *Kotteakos* standard was incorrectly applied, and the Court's opinion is not in harmony with the remedial and equitable nature of habeas relief.

▶ ANALYSIS

Much of the discussion centers on whether the various standards set forth in *Chapman*, *Doyle*, and *Kotteakos* apply on collateral review, on direct review, or on habeas review. The Court decided that the *Kotteakos* standard, not the

Continued on next page.

Chapman standard, is best suited for collateral review. This decision limits the relief that a defendant may pursue under a habeas corpus writ.

■══■

Quicknotes

HABEAS CORPUS A proceeding in which a defendant brings a writ to compel a judicial determination of whether he is lawfully being held in custody.

■══■

Quick Reference Rules of Law

United States v. Booker

Federal government (P) v. Convicted drug dealer (D)

125 S.Ct. _____ (2005).

NATURE OF CASE: Appeal from the reversal of a judge's sentencing enhancement.

FACT SUMMARY: When the sentencing judge found additional facts (not found by the jury) which resulted in an enhancement of Booker's (D) sentence under the Federal Sentencing Guidelines, the federal court of appeals reversed the enhancement on the grounds that a sentencing procedure which deprives the defendant of the right to a jury determination of all facts essential to the sentence, violates the Sixth Amendment under *Blakely v. Washington*.

RULE OF LAW

Binding rules set forth in the Federal Sentencing Guidelines limit the severity of the sentence that a judge can lawfully impose on a defendant based on the facts found at trial by the jury.

FACTS: A jury found that Booker (D) possessed with intent to distribute 92.5 grams of crack cocaine, which authorized, under the Federal Sentencing Guidelines, 210 to 262 months in prison. At time of sentencing, the judge found by a preponderance of the evidence that Booker (D) actually possessed an additional 566 grams of crack, raising the Guidelines sentence to 360 months to life in prison. Booker (D) received 360 months. The federal court of appeals reversed on the basis of *Blakely v. Washington*, 124 S.Ct. 2531 (2004), which held a sentencing procedure that deprives the defendant of the right to a jury determination of all facts essential to the sentence, violates the Sixth Amendment. The Government (P) appealed. In a case decided together with Booker's (D) case, Fanfan (D) was convicted by a jury of conspiracy to distribute more than 500 grams of cocaine, which authorized a maximum Guidelines sentence of 78 months. At sentencing, the judge found by a preponderance of the evidence that Fanfan (D) actually controlled a much larger quantity of illegal drugs and that he was a leader of the operation, raising the Guideline maximum to 16 years. The judge, however, relying on *Blakely*, imposed the lower Guideline sentence authorized by the jury's verdict. The Government (P) appealed.

ISSUE: Do the binding rules set forth in the Federal Sentencing Guidelines limit the severity of the sentence that a judge can lawfully impose on a defendant based on the facts found at trial by the jury?

HOLDING AND DECISION: (Stevens, J.) Yes. Binding rules set forth in the Federal Sentencing Guidelines limit the severity of the sentence that a judge can lawfully impose on a defendant based on the facts found at trial by the jury. There is no distinction of constitutional significance between the Federal Sentencing Guidelines and the Washington procedures at issue in *Blakely*. This conclusion rests on the premise, common to both systems, that the relevant sentencing rules are mandatory and impose binding requirements on all sentencing judges. If the Guidelines as currently written could be read as merely advisory provisions that recommended, rather than required, the selection of particular sentences in response to differing sets of facts, their use would not implicate the Sixth Amendment. This Court has never doubted the authority of a judge to exercise broad discretion in imposing a sentence within a statutory range. The Guidelines as written, however, are not advisory; they are mandatory and binding on all judges. The statute specifically directs that the court "*shall* impose a sentence of the kind, and within the range" established by the Guidelines, subject to departures in specific, limited cases. The availability of a departure in specified circumstances does not avoid the constitutional issue. This Court rejects the Government's (P) arguments that *Blakely* should not apply to the Federal Guidelines because they were drafted by a commission, rather than the legislature itself; prior Court decisions had upheld the constitutionality of the Guidelines; and doing so would violate the principle of separation of powers because it would effectively convert the Guidelines into new criminal statutes. Newly developing enhanced sentencing practices have required this Court to address the question how the right of jury trial could be preserved, in a meaningful way guaranteeing that the jury would still stand between the individual and the power of the government under the new sentencing regimes. Affirmed. [Justice Breyer separately delivered part of the Court's opinion, concluding that in view of the Court's holding, the provisions of the Guidelines having the effect of making the Guidelines mandatory, must be invalidated.]

DISSENTING IN PART: (Stevens, J.) [Responding to Justice Breyer's portion of the opinion.] There is no need to invalidate provisions of the Sentencing Guidelines to avoid

Continued on next page.

violations of the Sixth Amendment. The Court's decision to do so constitutes an unnecessary "extraordinary exercise of authority."

DISSENTING IN PART: (Scalia, J.) Appellate review for unreasonableness may simply add another layer of unfettered judicial discretion to the sentencing process. It may become a mere formality, used by appellate judges only to ensure that district judges say all the right things when they explain how they have exercised their newly restored discretion.

DISSENTING IN PART: (Thomas, J.) While portions of the Guidelines should be invalidated as applied to Booker (D) and similar cases involving Guidelines sentences based on judicial factfinding, the Guidelines should be upheld as constitutional in all other cases, including Fanfan (D), where application of the Guidelines would not result in a Sixth Amendment violation.

DISSENTING IN PART: (Breyer, J.) [Responding to Justice Stevens's portion of the opinion.] Nothing in the Sixth Amendment forbids a sentencing judge to determine the *manner* or way in which the offender carried out the crime of which he or she was convicted.

▶ *ANALYSIS*

In *Booker*, the Supreme Court, while recognizing that in some cases jury factfinding may impair the most expedient and efficient sentencing of defendants, nevertheless emphasized that the interest in fairness and reliability protected by the right to a jury trial—a common law right that defendants enjoyed for centuries and that is now enshrined in the Sixth Amendment—has always outweighed the interest in concluding trials swiftly.

■■■■

Quicknotes

SIXTH AMENDMENT Provides the right to a speedy and public trial by impartial jury, the right to be informed of the accusation, the right to confront witnesses, and the right to have the assistance of counsel in all criminal prosecutions.

■■■■

Common Latin Words and Phrases Encountered in the Law

A FORTIORI: Because one fact exists or has been proven, therefore a second fact that is related to the first fact must also exist.

A PRIORI: From the cause to the effect. A term of logic used to denote that when one generally accepted truth is shown to be a cause, another particular effect must necessarily follow.

AB INITIO: From the beginning; a condition which has existed throughout, as in a marriage which was void ab initio.

ACTUS REUS: The wrongful act; in criminal law, such action sufficient to trigger criminal liability.

AD VALOREM: According to value; an ad valorem tax is imposed upon an item located within the taxing jurisdiction calculated by the value of such item.

AMICUS CURIAE: Friend of the court. Its most common usage takes the form of an amicus curiae brief, filed by a person who is not a party to an action but is nonetheless allowed to offer an argument supporting his legal interests.

ARGUENDO: In arguing. A statement, possibly hypothetical, made for the purpose of argument, is one made arguendo.

BILL QUIA TIMET: A bill to quiet title (establish ownership) to real property.

BONA FIDE: True, honest, or genuine. May refer to a person's legal position based on good faith or lacking notice of fraud (such as a bona fide purchaser for value) or to the authenticity of a particular document (such as a bona fide last will and testament).

CAUSA MORTIS: With approaching death in mind. A gift causa mortis is a gift given by a party who feels certain that death is imminent.

CAVEAT EMPTOR: Let the buyer beware. This maxim is reflected in the rule of law that a buyer purchases at his own risk because it is his responsibility to examine, judge, test, and otherwise inspect what he is buying.

CERTIORARI: A writ of review. Petitions for review of a case by the United States Supreme Court are most often done by means of a writ of certiorari.

CONTRA: On the other hand. Opposite. Contrary to.

CORAM NOBIS: Before us; writs of error directed to the court that originally rendered the judgment.

CORAM VOBIS: Before you; writs of error directed by an appellate court to a lower court to correct a factual error.

CORPUS DELICTI: The body of the crime; the requisite elements of a crime amounting to objective proof that a crime has been committed.

CUM TESTAMENTO ANNEXO, ADMINISTRATOR (ADMINISTRATOR C.T.A.): With will annexed; an administrator c.t.a. settles an estate pursuant to a will in which he is not appointed.

DE BONIS NON, ADMINISTRATOR (ADMINISTRATOR D.B.N.): Of goods not administered; an administrator d.b.n. settles a partially settled estate.

DE FACTO: In fact; in reality; actually. Existing in fact but not officially approved or engendered.

DE JURE: By right; lawful. Describes a condition that is legitimate "as a matter of law," in contrast to the term "de facto," which connotes something existing in fact but not legally sanctioned or authorized. For example, de facto segregation refers to segregation brought about by housing patterns, etc., whereas de jure segregation refers to segregation created by law.

DE MINIMUS: Of minimal importance; insignificant; a trifle; not worth bothering about.

DE NOVO: Anew; a second time; afresh. A trial de novo is a new trial held at the appellate level as if the case originated there and the trial at a lower level had not taken place.

DICTA: Generally used as an abbreviated form of obiter dicta, a term describing those portions of a judicial opinion incidental or not necessary to resolution of the specific question before the court. Such nonessential statements and remarks are not considered to be binding precedent.

DUCES TECUM: Refers to a particular type of writ or subpoena requesting a party or organization to produce certain documents in their possession.

EN BANC: Full bench. Where a court sits with all justices present rather than the usual quorum.

EX PARTE: For one side or one party only. An ex parte proceeding is one undertaken for the benefit of only one party, without notice to, or an appearance by, an adverse party.

EX POST FACTO: After the fact. An ex post facto law is a law that retroactively changes the consequences of a prior act.

EX REL.: Abbreviated form of the term ex relatione, meaning, upon relation or information. When the state brings an action in which it has no interest against an individual at the instigation of one who has a private interest in the matter.

FORUM NON CONVENIENS: Inconvenient forum. Although a court may have jurisdiction over the case, the action should be tried in a more conveniently located court, one to which parties and witnesses may more easily travel, for example.

GUARDIAN AD LITEM: A guardian of an infant as to litigation, appointed to represent the infant and pursue his/her rights.

HABEAS CORPUS: You have the body. The modern writ of habeas corpus is a writ directing that a person (body) being detained (such as a prisoner) be brought before the court so that the legality of his detention can be judicially ascertained.

IN CAMERA: In private, in chambers. When a hearing is held before a judge in his chambers or when all spectators are excluded from the courtroom.

IN FORMA PAUPERIS: In the manner of a pauper. A party who proceeds in forma pauperis because of his poverty is one who is allowed to bring suit without liability for costs.

INFRA: Below, under. A word referring the reader to a later part of a book. (The opposite of supra.)

IN LOCO PARENTIS: In the place of a parent.

IN PARI DELICTO: Equally wrong; a court of equity will not grant requested relief to an applicant who is in pari delicto, or as much at fault in the transactions giving rise to the controversy as is the opponent of the applicant.

IN PARI MATERIA: On like subject matter or upon the same matter. Statutes relating to the same person or things are said to be in pari materia. It is a general rule of statutory construction that such statutes should be construed together, i.e., looked at as if they together constituted one law.

IN PERSONAM: Against the person. Jurisdiction over the person of an individual.

IN RE: In the matter of. Used to designate a proceeding involving an estate or other property.

IN REM: A term that signifies an action against the res, or thing. An action in rem is basically one that is taken directly against property, as distinguished from an action in personam, i.e., against the person.

INTER ALIA: Among other things. Used to show that the whole of a statement, pleading, list, statute, etc., has not been set forth in its entirety.

INTER PARTES: Between the parties. May refer to contracts, conveyances or other transactions having legal significance.

INTER VIVOS: Between the living. An inter vivos gift is a gift made by a living grantor, as distinguished from bequests contained in a will, which pass upon the death of the testator.

IPSO FACTO: By the mere fact itself.

JUS: Law or the entire body of law.

LEX LOCI: The law of the place; the notion that the rights of parties to a legal proceeding are governed by the law of the place where those rights arose.

MALUM IN SE: Evil or wrong in and of itself; inherently wrong. This term describes an act that is wrong by its very nature, as opposed to one which would not be wrong but for the fact that there is a specific legal prohibition against it (malum prohibitum).

MALUM PROHIBITUM: Wrong because prohibited, but not inherently evil. Used to describe something that is wrong because it is expressly forbidden by law but that is not in and of itself evil, e.g., speeding.

MANDAMUS: We command. A writ directing an official to take a certain action.

MENS REA: A guilty mind; a criminal intent. A term used to signify the mental state that accompanies a crime or other prohibited act. Some crimes require only a general mens rea (general intent to do the prohibited act), but others, like assault with intent to murder, require the existence of a specific mens rea.

MODUS OPERANDI: Method of operating; generally refers to the manner or style of a criminal in committing crimes, admissible in appropriate cases as evidence of the identity of a defendant.

NEXUS: A connection to.

NISI PRIUS: A court of first impression. A nisi prius court is one where issues of fact are tried before a judge or jury.

N.O.V. (NON OBSTANTE VEREDICTO): Not withstanding the verdict. A judgment n.o.v. is a judgment given in favor of one party despite the fact that a verdict was returned in favor of the other party, the justification being that the verdict either had no reasonable support in fact or was contrary to law.

NUNC PRO TUNC: Now for then. This phrase refers to actions that may be taken and will then have full retroactive effect.

PENDENTE LITE: Pending the suit; pending litigation underway.

PER CAPITA: By head; beneficiaries of an estate, if they take in equal shares, take per capita.

PER CURIAM: By the court; signifies an opinion ostensibly written "by the whole court" and with no identified author.

PER SE: By itself, in itself; inherently.

PER STIRPES: By representation. Used primarily in the law of wills to describe the method of distribution where a person, generally because of death, is unable to take that which is left to him by the will of another, and therefore his heirs divide such property between them rather than take under the will individually.

PRIMA FACIE: On its face, at first sight. A prima facie case is one that is sufficient on its face, meaning that the evidence supporting it is adequate to establish the case until contradicted or overcome by other evidence.

PRO TANTO: For so much; as far as it goes. Often used in eminent domain cases when a property owner receives partial payment for his land without prejudice to his right to bring suit for the full amount he claims his land to be worth.

QUANTUM MERUIT: As much as he deserves. Refers to recovery based on the doctrine of unjust enrichment in those cases in which a party has rendered valuable services or furnished materials that were accepted and enjoyed by another under circumstances that would reasonably notify the recipient that the rendering party expected to be paid. In essence, the law implies a contract to pay the reasonable value of the services or materials furnished.

QUASI: Almost like; as if; nearly. This term is essentially used to signify that one subject or thing is almost analogous to another but that material differences between them do exist. For example, a quasi-criminal proceeding is one that is not strictly criminal but shares enough of the same characteristics to require some of the same safeguards (e.g., procedural due process must be followed in a parole hearing).

QUID PRO QUO: Something for something. In contract law, the consideration, something of value, passed between the parties to render the contract binding.

RES GESTAE: Things done. In evidence law, this principle justifies the admission of a statement that would otherwise be hearsay when it is made so closely to the event in question as to be said to be a part of it, or with such spontaneity as not to have the possibility of falsehood.

RES IPSA LOQUITUR: The thing speaks for itself. This doctrine gives rise to a rebuttable presumption of negligence when the instrumentality causing the injury was within the exclusive control of the defendant, and the injury was one that does not normally occur unless a person has been negligent.

RES JUDICATA: A matter adjudged. Doctrine which provides that once a court of competent jurisdiction has rendered a final judgment or decree on the merits, that judgment or decree is conclusive upon the parties to the case and prevents them from engaging in any other litigation on the points and issues determined therein.

RESPONDEAT SUPERIOR: Let the master reply. This doctrine holds the master liable for the wrongful acts of his servant (or the principal for his agent) in those cases in which the servant (or agent) was acting within the scope of his authority at the time of the injury.

STARE DECISIS: To stand by or adhere to that which has been decided. The common law doctrine of stare decisis attempts to give security and certainty to the law by following the policy that once a principle of law as applicable to a certain set of facts has been set forth in a decision, it forms a precedent that will subsequently be followed, even though a different decision might be made were it the first time the question had arisen. Of course, stare decisis is not an inviolable principle and is departed from in instances where there is good cause (e.g., considerations of public policy led the Supreme Court to disregard prior decisions sanctioning segregation).

SUPRA: Above. A word referring a reader to an earlier part of a book.

ULTRA VIRES: Beyond the power. This phrase is most commonly used to refer to actions taken by a corporation that are beyond the power or legal authority of the corporation.

Addendum of French Derivatives

IN PAIS: Not pursuant to legal proceedings.

CHATTEL: Tangible personal property.

CY PRES: Doctrine permitting courts to apply trust funds to purposes not expressed in the trust but necessary to carry out the settlor's intent.

PER AUTRE VIE: For another's life; during another's life. In property law, an estate may be granted that will terminate upon the death of someone other than the grantee.

PROFIT A PRENDRE: A license to remove minerals or other produce from land.

VOIR DIRE: Process of questioning jurors as to their predispositions about the case or parties to a proceeding in order to identify those jurors displaying bias or prejudice.

Casenote Legal Briefs